COMICS AND COLUMBINE

AN OUTCAST LOOK AT
COMICS, BIGOTR
SCHOOL SHOO1

GW00642266

TOM CAMPBELL

Sparsile Books Ltd
Po Box 2861
Glasgow
G61 9ED

SPARSILE BOOKS

For Steven and all the others

Contents

INTRODUCTION

On April 20 1999, two American boys, Eric Harris and Dylan Klebold, slaughtered twelve of their fellow students and one teacher at Columbine High School in Littleton, Denver before turning their guns on themselves. They were in the last year of their schooling and had decided to make an example of their place of education. I don't agree with what these two young men did but I would be a liar if I said I shed any tears that day.

Twenty years earlier, 1979, I was in my last year of schooling at Whitehill Secondary School, in Glasgow, Scotland. At Whitehill the senior students had a common room to meet during breaks and between lessons. This was a place where they could hang out and discuss the kind of topics that interested these educated semi-adults. At the left hand side of the door leading into this common room, was a notice board. On this particular day, a cartoon had been posted there. It had been produced by the students for their own entertainment.

The subject of the cartoon was me. It was a caricature that mocked me, my clothes, my hair and anything else that could be attacked. It was not the first cartoon of this kind to adorn the board either. I stood and looked over the vicious lines and mocking text of the image as I heard the snickers of the entire common room behind me. I am sure the rest of the students – none of whom would have been labelled bullies - would have argued this was just harmless prank. However, I am also sure that at least some of them knew, or at least thought they knew, how much pain that they were causing me. In reality, they didn't have the slightest understanding of the truth: that their handiwork was almost the last straw in a lifetime of unendurable abuse stretching from my earliest school years to the point where I now stood facing this latest assault.

Had I been black, my treatment at the hands of these ordinary, well educated young people would have been called racism. But I wasn't; I was simply different. This 'difference' could have been anything. In my case, it was Asperger syndrome, a form of autism. Nowadays, autistics are accepted as an emergent minority. This was not the case back then. There was no recognition of the learning or socialization difficulties associated with this condition. In those days, anyone unable to conform to the norm was simply a *weirdo*, and as such, a 'bad' person. I've had to wait twenty seven years for a diagnosis to free me from this stigma, I'm still waiting for a name to confront the prejudice that inflicted it upon me in the first place, a prejudice that motivates even the educated and morally aware to alienate and devalue those who do not conform to their ideas of normalcy.

Had I a gun, I would have sprayed that common room with bullets and felt no guilt. I would have taken pleasure in the act, slaughtering every person there regardless of whether they had been guilty or innocent, secure in the belief that killing was the *right* thing to do.

By the age of seventeen, as an outcast and object of constant mockery, I had realized the truth: my fellow students were simply 'The Enemy', nothing more. They were criminals who had carried out an unending catalogue of crimes against me. Killing them would not have been murder, it would have been self defence. Had I actually carried this out, I would probably have been called a monster and a coward (coward would certainly have been accurate). Far from being insulted, I would have taken pride in such labels as even they would have been infinitely preferable to the worthless nothing I had been branded up till that moment.

Perhaps some of the blame for my actions would have been placed on the steady diet of comics that I lived on. I have no doubt that the 'insane' and 'violent' fantasies of this dubious art form would have been seen as a factor that perverted a young man into such a twisted maniac. Nothing could have been further from the truth. Comics were my one avenue of escape from a world that had never stopped attacking me. Comics opened a door to a better place, one that kept me sane. This resulted in a love affair with the medium that has lasted to this day.

The moment, in the school common room, when I stood before that cartoon was monstrous. I would like to say that I have passed beyond it now but that would not be true. Due to my condition, I have an involuntary ability to record certain memories in perfect, appalling detail and to experience them almost as clearly as if they were still happening. Unfortunately, this process is almost totally focused on my school experiences. The pain they inflicted on me is as fresh now as the moment it occurred. Part of me is still stuck in front of that sick cartoon, still listening to the laughter and still twisting with fear and rage.

I often look upon this area of my thinking as being a form of emotional cancer. Unfortunately, even a cursory glance at modern youth culture and its reflective literature will show I am not the only one to have this particular mental malformation forced upon me. When the phenomena of school shootings began to surface, I watched these tragedies unfold with a clear understanding of their inevitability. Listening in to the opinions of many of today's youth, I realized this understanding wasn't just limited to me.

By virtue of shared experiences, I have found myself, time and time again, drawn to the perspectives of school shooters. These, disturbingly, made greater sense to me the longer I focused on them, despite attempts to dismiss them through rationalization. What has challenged this train of thought in recent years is the lessening of my outcast status. I have friends now, genuine friends, many of whom have children of their own. It is through watching them grow, that I have come to understand the value of young life and question my loathing of it. It is this new perspective that compels me to write.

This book is about hatred. There is a plethora of literature on the development of all other emotions but an odd dearth when it comes to this one. The story in these pages concerns the teaching of hatred in our schools on a daily basis. It is a step-by-step guide that includes observations of the various 'blameless' institutions and attitudes found in our places of learning; attitudes which nurture this twisted state of mind on a daily basis. Using myself as an example, I give a picture of how a young person can be taught hatred, how hatred can rule their thoughts and what exactly those thoughts are.

Personally, I have found most literature on the subject of school violence to be overly clinical and unconvincing in its attempts to understand the subject. This is perhaps due to a subtle reluctance on the part of most authors to identify the true source of this evil. I intend to avoid such an approach in this book. I will have no hesitation when it comes to pointing the finger of blame; and what I say, I will say in plain language.

Airing my beliefs on this phenomenon may not be to everyone's tastes. There is a possibility that some will be offended or even angered by what they will read here. Some of the opinions I express may be considered extreme and even repugnant. Many may call them sick. Regardless of people's opinions, I think that these are important viewpoints that need to be aired, if only to achieve a greater understanding of this problem and to arrive at realistic methods of dealing with it.

By now, people have realized that school shootings are not going away. Worse still, they have become accepted and even romanticized by many of our young. Many outcasts have made heroes of these killers and openly expressed admiration and support for their 'achievements' online. I don't advocate killing at all; the taking of even one life is not acceptable to me. More than anything, I would like to see an end to these atrocities. Unfortunately this will not happen until we confront the forces that provoke them in the first place.

Recent profiles of the school shooter have begun to drift away from the classic bullied outcast. Many believe there are additional forces that shape these killers. This may be the case with a few, but I know from experience that all it needs to drive a young soul to the point of carrying out mass slaughter is an ordinary school and the ordinary attitudes found there. Indeed, the mechanics of these tragedies are so obvious I am often surprised by the inability of others to see them. The only conclusion I can draw from this is that a society-wide culture of deliberate ignorance and avoidance, a kind of moral blindspot is at work here, particularly within the ranks of those who consider themselves experts in this field. For this reason, I think it important to take a look into this 'blindspot' as well.

~~~

I don't pretend to have all the answers but I suspect I have more than most, and I may be able to add a new angle, an outsider's or perhaps even an *insider's* perspective to this problem. Whether or not people are open minded enough to accept what I have to say and perhaps learn by looking at things from this angle is up to them.

On the occasions on which I have communicated these perspectives, some have reacted with distaste and hostility, but there have been others who have said that it has opened their eyes to a world that they were not aware of. It is they who advised me to write this book.

This is an outcast's look at the socially acceptable evils that drive young minds to carry out these atrocities. Using my life as an example I intend to give you a step-by-step account of the development of the school shooter's mentality. It will not be a comfortable read, as it will condemn many of the things we take for granted and respect not only within education but within society itself.

It has been pointed out that those on the autistic spectrum tend to see things from unusual angles, are renowned for asking wrong and tactless questions, and have a habit of putting their foot in things. This book will be filled with all the wrong questions and observations and will persistently put its foot in things for the simple reason that tact, in this area, kills as effectively as a loaded gun.

OTHER WORLDS

YOUR MOTHER WAS MAD

'Your mother was mad! She was mad! Say she's mad! SAY SHE'S MAD!'

'She's mad Daddy!'

I speak carefully as my mouth is filled with blood and spilling blood is as big a crime as being insane.

'You're mad too! Say you're mad! SAY YOU'RE MAD... SAY YOU'RE MAD YOU'REMADDSAYYOU'REMADDD!!'

'I'm mad Daddy!'

I don't speak quickly enough and *The Arm* lashes out. Poor Dad; poor stupid, cowardly, self-obsessed, self-pitying, wife beating, child beating, scum, half-wit, idiot, animal, $#@*head, cripple, Dad. The fool has no idea that he has lost the battle, that he cannot defeat me. I have protection now; I have SUPERMAN on my side. I have discovered COMICS.

~~~

Dad —The Halfman— only has one arm. He lost the other falling under the wheels of a train when he was nineteen and it's all my fault; it's everyone's fault. The Campbell family will spend every minute of every day of their lives paying for its loss. His remaining limb, The Arm, is massive, overdeveloped and used without mercy. The Halfman is always angry, never normal; at best surly with the threat of instantaneous, explosive rage. He is also a Communist, a great man, the best, a genius. For such a giant amongst men to have a mentally ill son is a terrible disgrace. It is my shame that I have spent time in a children's psychiatric ward. No-one is able to figure out what is wrong with me because no-one recognises Asperger syndrome. Before my spell in 'the madhoose', I have spent much of my childhood in and out of ordinary hospitals, having my nose cauterised on a regular basis. The doctors never figured out why it bled as copiously and as often as it does. This is probably because none of them have seen The Arm in action.

I must remain upright during my punishment. Movement, like crying or any other display of emotion, is totally forbidden and I have so many other crimes to answer for. In addition to missing a limb, The Halfman also lacks a thyroid gland; a medical blunder killed it. The thyroxin the doctors prescribe will keep him awake into the early hours of the morning; me too.

Night after night, without fail, The Halfman will tell me about his life as a vagrant, riding the trains in Canada during the Great Depression, and before that, of his childhood in the Catholic boys' home, and of the notorious De La Salle brothers who tortured him there. He remembers their names and crimes in perfect detail. With his awesome memory he will list and curse every person who has crossed him in all the years of his long life; what was said, where and when their crimes were carried out. He quotes, without deviation, entire exchanges of hostile dialogue from decades past. I must remember the names and cruel words of these long-vanished people as they are more important than the events of my own life (and I may be quizzed later about what I have been told).

In between bouts of cursing, The Halfman will tell me the truth about life itself: that God is not real; all religion is rubbish invented to oppress and exploit man; when you are dead you are dead and that is all there is to it. He will spend a great deal of time attempting to communicate the concept of non-existence; that void of total blackness which awaits me when my heart stops.

Next, he will explain that burning is the worst way to die, and that he would rather throw me to my death than allow me to burn. As a demonstration of how good a father he is, he occasionally forces me out of our top floor window to show me the exact spot on the ground below where he will throw me to my death as an alternative to my being 'burnt black'. Once this is finished, he will drag me back in and talk about communism. He will explain

Campbell family dynamics

that all the evil in the world springs from opposing this perfect system. As an accompaniment to his lecture, I will be made to listen to his recordings. Since he is partially deaf, he plays these, as loudly as possible, on his big reel-to-reel machines throughout the night. Most are music, some are chunks of speeches. Once he has finished, he will rewind, just like one of his precious tapes, and begin ranting about my insanity once again; then The Arm will come back into play.

The Halfman seldom works. Despite this, he is actually very skilled. His motto is 'Construct, not destruct'. Much of the furniture and decorations in our house have been made by him. He made the table and the cabinet. He made our bedroom out of a cupboard and a recess. He made his own custom enlarger for when he took photographs. On the dining room walls, hang a series of stylized paintings of brightly dressed women rendered on glass. These are his 'crinoline ladies'. As the years have gone by he has painted the image of this woman over and over without deviation. Each lady stands in a lush garden stretching her delicate arm out towards a dove. Were you to look closely you would see her wrists and fingers are a melding of tiny, perfectly tapered strokes.

He made a beautiful glass cabinet filled with a tea set that is never used. Not far from it, sits a tea trolley on wheels; this also is one of his creations and, like the tea set, it seems to be waiting for a life that will never happen. The trolley is a two level affair that could pass for the work of any professional craftsman. The front ends of both levels are perfectly curved without any bumps or irregularities. They are topped by glass sheets whose edges have been cut to perfection. Sandwiched between the glass and the wooden supports are two high-quality art prints. The print on the bottom is of a little girl crying into a wall as a dog - a collie - sits looking at her. The print on top depicts two fishermen in blue waterproofs walking by an upturned boat that has been converted into a house. Atop this lovely trolley, The Halfman will place a wicked looking knife used to threaten his children. 'Construct, not destruct' is indeed his motto, but it only applies to furniture.

~~~

My birthday is September the eleventh, a grim date by the standards of many (by morbid coincidence also that of Dylan Klebold). I was a silent baby, apparently needing to be woken in order to be fed and, according to Mum, spent most of my childhood 'off in a world of my own'. I wasn't the only one.

Our house, 109 Firpark Street, was a self-contained little universe caught in the gravity of The Halfman's rage and self-importance. There could be no other opinions, logic or thoughts in his lair. All rhyme and reason was distorted to fit his beliefs without the slightest compromise. There were no conversations; he never spoke to us, only at us, and we were never invited to reply with thoughts of our own, only to listen and agree. The entire family - me, my mother, two brothers and two sisters - simply had to accept his judgments like bad weather.

Firpark Street was situated on the edge of the Glasgow Necropolis, one of the largest cemeteries in Scotland. Built during the Victorian era, this cemetery is situated near Glasgow Cathedral and covers 37 acres. Overlooking 3,500 tombs with some 50,000 residents, the view out of our kitchen/dining room window was a picture postcard of mortality that stretched from one side of the horizon to the other. This view was caught in the opening shots of Bertrand Tavernier's Glasgow-filmed Science Fiction tragedy DEATH-WATCH/LA MORT EN DIRECT (1980). One of the film's first images —that of a little girl playing with her skipping ropes in front of a tomb— was shot in the Necropolis, not a hundred yards from our kitchen window. Had Tavernier's camera swung a few degrees to the right, Firpark Street would have been immortalized on film forever.

~~~

For those who are interested, there is plenty of literature available on Aspergers these days. My childhood pretty much followed the usual pattern. My interests would be tightly focused to an extent uncommon in other children. I had a desperate need for routine, ritual and precision. My mind required 'anchoring points', rigid facts or rules to operate around and draw perspective from. These were utterly inflexible; if something was not 'right' - a bed sheet incorrectly tucked in for example - I could respond with agitation or hysteria. Were this to happen, I would eventually soothe myself by rocking back and forth or biting my hands and arms (or alternatively, The Halfman would beat me insensate). For reasons I still cannot explain, I found myself threatened by the curve in hairpins and compulsively straightened them whenever possible; but only after eating the protective plastic bud from both ends.

I collected and arranged things with a passion. I loved to watch things spin and loved to spin myself. Certain textures, both visual and physical, absorbed me, particularly the dotted halftone textures found in old newspaper photos. I related to objects far more easily than people as I had problems accepting anything which functioned independently of my will (my first memory of betrayal occurred upon discovering my mother had moved from the position I had 'left' her in). I could not accept the MONKEES being both singers and actors as this breached the unspoken law of singular function I assumed the universe to be based on.

As I grew older, I found my head filled with empty areas or 'holes' where my thinking didn't go. This was both intellectual and emotional. Certain responses or feelings other people seemed to possess were entirely absent in me. My ability to process information was vastly slower and more literal than normal. When I eventually learned to read (something that took far longer than usual), I would memorise the statistics of dozens of different dinosaurs, their diets, what groups they belonged to and quote entire chapters from palaeontology books while still unable to count past seven, tie my shoe laces, clothe myself or even make basic eye contact. My learning curve was so uneven that, on occasion, I would be called retarded (an acceptable term back in those un-PC days), while on others, my higher-than-average achievements would result in accusations of wilful ignorance for past failure. The various behavioural differences caused by my condition would result in my being dragged from the classroom and hauled over the coals by senior teachers for my entire stay in education.

My childhood vice was eating inanimate objects and material, particularly paper. I mentally catalogued the different textures and flavours of this lovely substance and often used it to rid my mouth of the repugnant taste of 'real' food. I was something of a rodent back then; compulsively gnawing holes in blankets and clothes, masticating small pieces of wood and plastic into a pulp and swallowing them. Plastic, in particular, yielded a double treat in that, if it was chewed for long enough, it would leave a tangy sensation on the side of my tongue. In my teenage years I took to chewing drawing pins and the ring pulls from drinks cans into balls of compressed metal (chewing, like rocking, tended to soothe my persistent state of nervous tension). My senses have always been a little off-key. I never feel cold but cannot stand the warmth most people consider comfortable. My reaction to smell and textures is also quite extreme. Some smells are impossible for me to detect, some are very soothing, while still others are repulsive. The high-pitched scent of freshly cut grass can make me vomit, while a variety of chemical odours and even the granular texture of fine dust found at the top of wardrobes can cause me to salivate uncontrollably.

In early years, I was completely withdrawn; communicating only when spoken to and often, not even then. The overload of the world was usually more than I was able to deal with. The more it tried to communicate with me, the more my brain shut off from the invading information. If a new group of facts were in any way to differ from or challenge what I already knew, this unresolved conflict would cause my brain to shut down or 'crash' regularly. Under these circumstances, learning was a problem.

All was not lost. I was about to encounter a language tailor-made for the autistic brain. This would allow me to break through these barriers and focus on the world. It was a language that needed no confusing words, only a series of little pictures placed one after the other.

UP, UP AND AWAY

The first comics I was given tasted delicious. A neighbour, who I suspect took pity on us, handed a bundle in to Mum. These were a selection of British children's comics typical of the period: THE DANDY, THE BEANO, THE SPARKY, THE LION and a colourful sports orientated comic called THE TIGER. I remember liking the Sparky because its paper tasted slightly of wood. The Tiger, on the other hand, had a sweet and oily flavour which put me off. For the most part, it remained uneaten.

At some point, I started to look at the pages I was eating. This led to something truly extraordinary: I examined a piece of paper without actually wanting to consume it. In time, I became totally absorbed by the images I found there and desired to know what they meant. Since The Halfman was only interested in discussing communism or my current range of crimes, I directed my questions at Mum. These conversations occurred before her collapse into sleeping pill addiction and alcoholism. I consider them a brief, wonderful period during which I was able to communicate with the woman who bore me before The Halfman destroyed her.

In comics, I found the perfect means of assimilating information. Even after learning to read I still had difficulties with text. This had nothing to do with dyslexia; I was fully capable of recognising different letterforms. My problem lay with the feeling of fear and intense revulsion I would experience when seeing a sequence of impenetrable letters, or worse still, words. I loathe the unknown and hate waiting for anything, particularly information. If I am given a book, I will read the last pages first, and always need to know how a film ends before I watch it. My brain desires to get to the heart of the matter as quickly as possible; any delay will cause agitation. Back then, even a small paragraph was as thick as lead and vast as the Atlantic Ocean. Facing such a cliff-face of information would produce a feeling of physical nausea I call 'learning vertigo'. Given these limitations, I needed another method of absorbing knowledge; in comics I found it (although encounters with certain old-style British comics that stood their panels atop blocks of dense text nearly put me off as these slowed my eyes down like a roadblock). A comic page presented a maximum of easily absorbed information with a minimum of vile text. The sequence of events depicted in a comic page could be taken in a single, long glance. This initial scan bypassed the vertigo stage by making the information 'known territory' as quickly as possible; a more detailed study could be made - without fear - thereafter.

My exposure to American super-hero comics commenced with a pile of 'Eighty-Page Giants' handed in by the same neighbour. Eighty-Page Giants were comic anthologies produced by DC Comics at the time. The main character found in these was a brightly dressed hero called SUPERMAN. With his great strength, Superman fought people (and things) who were breaking the law. The law was a set of adult anchoring points that revolved around something called right and wrong. 'Right' was acceptable to others, 'Wrong' was not. If you did right, you were accepted, if you did wrong you were punished. The idea of a being able to impose order on all that was wrong, or in my case, painful and chaotic, was very attractive indeed. From this, my addiction to super-hero comics was born.

There was a safety in these stories and their simplistic renderings. Everything was constant and properly contained within the panels. The art was attractive with light open shapes and thin lines repeating themselves beautifully. Then there was the content: Superman had the ability to stabilize his, usually antagonistic, environment via his super strength. The best I could do to deal with mine was rock back and forth. However, the Man of Steel did possess an ability which confused me: his power of flight. Unlike a bird or the enormous television robot GIGANTOR (real name: TETSUJIN 28) Superman had neither wings nor a jet pack to break the bonds of gravity. These days it's common knowledge that Superman flies through a combination of his body being saturated with solar energy and the Earth's gravity being far less than that of his home planet Krypton. Mum was unaware of this when I asked her to explain the mechanics of the Man of Steel's flight. To me, this was a logical enough question. To a working class, Glaswegian housewife of the 1960's, it must have presented a problem. Her solution was fairly imaginative, however. She made a faint gesture, almost like a bird flapping its wings.

'Well, he's got wee fingers in his cape that he can move and flap about.'

I accepted this slightly grotesque explanation because it was at least mechanically sound, and continued reading the comic. This led to many more questions. After mastering the written word, my appreciation of Superman's exploits increased dramatically over the years. I had little time for 'real' world people; conversely I found myself poring over the interaction of their paper counterparts as they were a more ordered breed. Unless they were villains, comic characters tended to engage in conversation without hitting each other. I found this to be novel and pleasing. The 'constant' nature of these characters was also very comforting. These people had specific roles they tended to stick to. In time, I developed a rudimentary understanding of the bizarre behaviour of 'normal' people by seeing its simplified representation on these paper pages. Thought balloons, in particular yielded, insight into this. Comic characters - who were representations of real life people - had thoughts. The revelation, when it hit me, was astonishing: *people had thoughts*, thoughts that were independent from mine.

Although my teachers considered me stupid when I started school, I was anything but. Unfortunately, I only learned under certain, very specific, circumstances. This involved grabbing my attention visually while using a minimum of written information. I discovered the correct spelling of the word 'what' from a British cartoon strip in which the protagonist was about to be shot by a firing squad. When the execution is called off, the fat guard holding the sabre loudly exclaims 'What!' I memorized the presence of the letters 'h' and 'a' in the word and used them when all others in my class still spelled it as 'wot'.

FLINTSTONES and PLASTIC MAN comics yielded some memorable biology lessons. In one story, Fred Flintstone's cold was studied by his little alien friend, the Great Gazoo, who revealed that the bug behind the common cold was a virus and that viruses were far smaller and more difficult to deal with than bacteria. In the Plastic Man story, a character's death from 'the bends' drew my attention to the presence of gasses in the blood. These drawings, the text, and finally the facts themselves, like many others, were all recorded for

My first comic

immediate recall. I was picking up, and storing information effortlessly using this system. I would even begin to grasp abstraction in conversation from the sassy 60's and 70's-style dialogue in the MARVEL comics of my teens.

Comics led to my taking up art. I had no interest in any form of expression until discovering them. Even when ordered to draw a flower or a cup by my teacher, I would simply produce an intricate pattern which I found attractive but made no sense to anyone else. It was after assimilating the alphabet of form found in my comics that these doodles metamorphosed into the tighter abstraction of cartooning. Lacking any imagination, I simply copied. My main template was the Superman artist WAYNE BORING. Boring's work had featured prominently in my Eighty-Page Giants. I found his stiff, simplistic renderings easier to memorise than the more realistic efforts of artists like MURPHY ANDERSON.

For a primary school child, rendering the full intricacy of the human form is virtually impossible. In this area comics offer a tidy alternative, a visual shorthand that breaks the human form down into a series of simplistic shapes as easy to remember as letterforms. In the real world, the human mouth is composed of a multitude of complex and, in my case, threatening surfaces. Its comics equivalent can be as easy and elegant as two lines drawn one above the other. This kind of simplification is perfect for introducing the fledgling artist to the wonders of three-dimensional form. In time, I memorised as many different shorthand forms as possible. With enough of these in place, I started producing images of my own. However, despite this skill, I was still incapable of creating an image that was truly original; but that was soon to change.

My first attempts to create an original character were sketched in the margins of a huge atlas. This particular volume was in no danger of being eaten due to its repulsive, waxy tasting paper. The subject of my drawings was The Halfman. My first rendering was his raging face; the drawing was an interesting failure due to my inability to get his mouth right. I repeatedly rubbed out the offending orifice until giving up, whereupon I discovered that the twisted face, sans mouth, was a striking image by itself. I was to repeat this drawing - which I came to call NO SCREAM - for years to come. The next piece was far more successful; it was a full figure rendering of The Halfman as an asymmetrical troll wearing an old vest and pair of underpants – his occasional mode of dress in the morning. The figure was misshapen, almost hunchbacked, with a massive right arm. This drawing led to my first actual comic strip.

Admittedly a comic with only two panels can hardly be considered an epic, but I managed to pack a considerable amount of storytelling into those little frames. The first was another rendering of The Halfman in his normal state of fury as he brandishes the knife from the tea trolley. His mood was depicted by a halo of 'anger lines' - an abstract graphic used in humorous comics to indicate a character is in a state of rage - surrounding his head. The effect was not entirely successful as the lines were radiating upwards not outwards and, as a result, looked more like 'smell lines' - another comic graphic used to suggest a bad odour. The second panel depicts a child, my brother, sobbing as The Halfman's claw-like hand enters the frame and hovers over his face.

The miserable expression and sobbing (a single tear drawn at the outer corner of the left eye) were effects I had lifted from British children's comics. In real life, I was unable to read expressions. However, thanks to the visual shorthand of comics, I had begun to grasp that the differing positions of facial features indicated different moods. If a comic character's mouth was turned down, like the letter 'n', and the outer edges of their eyebrows were also slanting downwards, then they were unhappy, like my brother. If, instead, the *inner* edges of their eyebrows were slanting down, then this meant that they were angry, like The Halfman. Despite some inaccuracies (the second frame depicts a left hand, The Halfman does not have one of those), the strip was surprisingly sophisticated for a child as it communicates the concept of impending violence and suffering.

I suppose my reasons for producing it were an attempt to deal with all that was happening around me. It's fortunate that comics gave me a means of doing so. It's equally fortunate that The Halfman never saw any of these strips, as the penalty for such subversion would have been too terrible to even contemplate.

ENEMIES OF THE STATE

The knock would come in the early hours of the morning as the Campbell children always knew it would. We waited in dread for the sound, knowing it would herald the beginning of the terror. This would start with sleep deprivation. We would be kept awake for hours on end and marched across the floor should we display any signs of tiredness. Occasionally, we would be sent back to our room for some much needed sleep only to be dragged out again a few minutes later. During this period, the questioning would begin. We would be encouraged to report on each other's activities during the day. Accusations and denouncements were the norm. Once a general air of guilt had been established a list of specific crimes would be drawn up. The nature and repercussions of these would be examined and re-examined in excruciating detail and depth throughout the night and into the early hours of the morning. An early confession could lessen the severity of the outcome, but often we were denied this, as part of the process was the torturous lead-up to the punishment itself. The penalty for subversion was brutal and often carried out to the sound of Petula Clark singing 'I couldn't live without your love'.

~~~

In addition to being a dedicated child abuser, The Halfman was also a rabid communist. His return from his local pub - the Saracen Head - was a guaranteed highpoint in our evening's entertainment. Firpark Street was his now. His brutality had driven Mum out; the last straw being his second attempt on her life. Using his weapon of choice, the window, he tried to throw her out to her death. Mum fought, slicing her arm open on the glass, before fleeing. I remember the police photographer taking pictures of the shattered window from the football pitch directly opposite our house. This made me angry because I was not allowed into my room to read my comics. These meant more to me than the sight of my beaten mother cradling the mass of black stitching which was her left arm. Mum had been deteriorating for some time prior to this latest attack. Over the years, she had developed an addiction to sleeping pills. The resulting 'illness' had robbed me of someone to discuss comics with, a fact that annoyed me no end. Despite being arrested (and incarcerated in a psychiatric ward himself), The Halfman returned within a couple of days, as Mum refused to press charges. He beat her senseless upon return and she responded with another overdose.

After this, The Halfman informed us that Mum was mad and that she would not be coming back. She made one appearance outside our door in an attempt to get us to come with her. We could not, as The Halfman's regime was all we had ever known. We clung to his familiar oppression; more terrified of change than anything else. We even asked Mum to come back and live with us, not understanding that doing so would have meant a death sentence.

The sight of her children siding with the man who had systematically destroyed her must have been the worst moment of her life. She left to spend the next decade a hopeless alcoholic. We watched her walk down the stairs to The Halfman's mocking cry of 'Good riddance to bad rubbish!' Mum was gone now. There were no witnesses as something very much like an iron curtain closed around us.

~~~

The Halfman simply lived in the wrong country. In Scotland he was an asymmetrical grotesque, who punctuated his speech with politics and poison. In the USSR, his totalitarianism and viciousness would have earned him a job as an interrogator for the KGB and probably a senior post at that. In his own 'Little Russia' of Firpark Street, he crafted a reign of terror that would have made Joe Stalin proud. Our father, the greatest man who had ever lived, our creator (he eventually wrote Mum out of the equation), our master and owner, who art in Little Russia, *was* the state; and the state was enraged and unforgiving.

There were no such things as mistakes or accidents in Little Russia, only crimes: small mishaps and errors magnified into colossal acts of subversion. There was no such thing as the passage of time either; 'crimes' committed months, even years past —even as toddlers— were considered as fresh as those committed mere moments ago and were dredged up for infinite re-examination during our denouncements. At the age of eight, I had been sent to buy a bag of porridge oats from a local grain store. I returned with a bag of oatmeal (whose preparation involved the added chore of being soaked overnight). Rather than sending me back to change it, The Halfman beat me almost unconscious. It didn't end there: he continued to invoke the shadow of this terrible crime as an excuse for further violence throughout the rest of my childhood and adolescence. Didn't I see that I had jeopardised - perhaps deliberately - the breakfasts of all the family? Well, perhaps I should be *made* to see...

'...YOU DID THAT, YOU BASTARD, YOU DID THAT!! I COULD HAVE KILLED YOU WITH A PUNCH, KILLED-YOU-WITH-A-PUNCH!!'

My stay in the children's psychiatric ward at Yorkhill hospital was a major focus for his bile. I'd been transferred to Yorkhill from Glasgow's Royal Infirmary, where I'd been hospitalised for my never-ending nosebleeds. The doctors at the Royal had noticed certain oddities to my behaviour, and not just the autistic sort. I'd been experiencing a new emotion – a strange, empty emotion - since just after my seventh birthday. I first noticed it as I watched the closing credits for 'I dream of Jeannie.' (It was the episode in which Tony and Jeannie encounter the Blue Djinn who was even more powerful than Jeannie herself). As the credits rolled and I readied myself for sleep I thought it would be nice if I didn't wake up in the morning, in fact it would be nice if I didn't wake up ever. This was depression. It was the beginning of my lifelong struggle with the condition.

Looking back now, I can see that my 'madness' had drawn attention to The Halfman; and that was something he couldn't allow. Didn't I understand that I had endangered the whole family? That, because of what I had 'done' we could all be sent away into 'homes' where we would never see each other again? Didn't I see how evil and selfish I was in my madness? Well, perhaps I should be *made* to see...

Guilt was our natural state. Campbell children were born guilty, guilty until proved innocent, and innocence was never proven. We failed him, betrayed him; we were the worst kids who had ever lived, ungrateful bastards who deserved neither his love nor his caring. It was as simple as that.

Communism was a simple thing to explain. It was a perfect system of government that freed all men from the shackles of the corrupt capitalists who were exploiting the workers of the world. Communism opposed religion because religion was all about making people feel guilty and controlling them through that guilt. Communism was inevitable. Soon, all countries would embrace it. They had good reason: the unified forces of communism had gifted us with the free world we took for granted. The communists had won the Second World War, smashing back the Nazi war machine where all others (British, Americans, Canadians, French, etc.) had failed. Indeed, Hitler's biggest mistake was assuming his second-rate armies could stand, even for a second, against the unstoppable and righteous communist forces.

The communists lived far behind a magic wall in a place called RUSSIA or the SOVIET UNION. This was the most advanced country in the world, where all men walked free. The 'State' (the government) gave its citizens everything they wanted, no matter what it was. There were no kings or queens, no lords or ladies, no rich people there to rub poverty in your face. All men were equal and no-one had to call anyone 'sir'. Life behind that wonderful wall sounded truly magical. Perhaps the communists might not even care about the Campbell family's bad clothes. A land in which we wouldn't be called 'tramps' (Glaswegian slang for a person at the lowest end of the financial/social spectrum), it defied imagination.

There was more: in addition to being the bravest, most powerful, most civilised people in the world, the communists were also technologically more advanced than everyone else. They had put the first satellite and the first man into space, much to the shock and horror of the corrupt, backward west. When the Americans finally reached the moon in 1969 that wasn't really a problem because the communists had a MACHINE waiting there for them (presumably one of their probes, The Halfman never explained exactly what this MACHINE was supposed to do when the Americans arrived). Yet all this paled beside their greatest achievement: the communists could bring the dead back to life.

As told, Soviet doctors had developed a special drug during the Second World War. When this was injected in the hearts of dead soldiers they returned to life. Wasn't I amazed? Didn't I understand, THE COMMUNISTS HAD BEATEN DEATH? His words roared in my ears: '...An' these men were DEAD, and this stuff was INJECTED into their HEARTS, and they CAME BACK TO LIFE, and they could be DIRECTING TRAFFIC NOW, and the thing that killed them was STILL in their hearts, but this stuff was keeping them ALIVE despite the fact that they HAD BEEN DEAD, do you HEAR me, YOU BASTARD? I SAID THEY WERE DIRECTING TRAFFIC NOW, BUT INSIDE THEY WERE DEAD, DEAD AND THEY WERE DIRECTING TRAFFIC, DIRECTING TRAFFIC!!'

He was clearly talking about an adrenalin shot. I know such a thing can actually restart a heart after it has ceased beating but I'm not so sure it was invented by the Soviets and I'm fairly sure that, once a heart has been restarted, the person is no longer clinically dead, whether directing traffic or not. The truth was irrelevant. He believed it and that made it so. THE COMMUNISTS HAD CONQUERED DEATH, and that was all there was to it.

Finally, there was the robot arm. Communist doctors had perfected an artificial limb worked by tiny motors. These picked up impulses directly from the brain and converted them into movement. One day (when the wall expanded to engulf everything in the west), this fantastic device would become available to all loyal party members. The Halfman would be restored and we would all become part of the great communist spirit. Amen.

The Halfman's other passion lay in recording. He had two large reel to reel machines used to play his collected music. This was the soundtrack of our unhappy childhood, odd assemblies of the same piece of music or narration continually looped. Playing one tape could mean listening to a continual repeat of Garry Cooper's conversation with Lon Chaney Junior from HIGH NOON (over which can be heard the classic ballad 'Do not forsake me, oh my darling'). This particular section of the classic western was looped no less than six different times, finally focusing on Cooper's line 'You've been a lawman all your life.' This individual line was then repeated a total of four more times. Perhaps he was listening to the music, perhaps it was the significance of the line itself, I will never know. A retrospective diagnosis on The Halfman has indicated that he too, was on the autistic spectrum; although the thing he became had less to do with autism and more with the emotional mutilation that occurs with difficult family backgrounds.

There was a definite pattern to the way he listened to his recordings. If singers like RICHARD TAUBER, FRANK IFIELD or songs from recorded musicals like OKLAHOMA or CARMEN JONES were played as a starter to the evening, then things would run relatively smoothly with only medium-level threats and violence to be expected. I began to understand that these pieces were somehow neutral, that they did not involve explosive emotional content. On the other hand, were the dulcet tones of Petula Clark played early on, this would be the opening theme for The Arm.

Petula's songs were on a reel of transparent plastic as opposed to the grey reels that housed all other recordings. As we sat listening to her, The Halfman's mood would blacken and he would begin to growl about Mum:

our mother, our vile mother, the devil woman, the monster, who had betrayed him, deserted him, betrayed the entire family, a woman of hereditary madness whose own father had been a 'Slabbering MADMAN in a MADHOOSE!'; a woman whose monstrous children were as guilty of her crimes as she was. This led to the inevitable. At the time I didn't know that Petula Clark was one of Mum's favourite singers and that the music and the impossibly twisted emotions were really about her. Petula has a great voice but, for some reason, I've never really taken to her.

His obsession with making his own recordings increased. I found myself being forced to recite Robert Burn's famous dinner grace 'Some hae' meat and cannae' eat' into the microphone on several occasions. Strangest out of all these sessions, involved a constant repetition of the limerick 'Doctor Foster went to Gloucester.' At his insistence, I had to repeat this limerick over and over again, into the microphone; and each time with greater speed. Were I to make a mistake with any recital, I would be thumped. Eventually, I broke down under the pressure and he recorded that as well. It was the only time he ever allowed me to cry. As it transpired, I wasn't the only one whose tears he recorded.

In many ways we, his children, became The Halfman's ultimate recording medium. He was terrified of death and incapable of believing in the afterlife. His magnificence, his divinity could not be allowed to cease, such a thing was unthinkable. Immortality through recording; imprinting every aspect of himself onto us was his ultimate solution. All the events of his life: his enemies, his greatness, his travels, his spikes of hatred and despair, his vicious triumphs, all encoded into his offspring. I suspect this was one of the reasons behind his denouncements and his regime of guilt. In order to properly record onto something, you must first erase what was originally there.

~~~

Free will in his children must have genuinely frightened The Halfman. One incident of my childhood particularly highlighted this. I only really took an objective look at it after I was discharged from the psychiatric hospital in the middle 80's. At that point I found myself in a halfway house for ex-psychiatric patients situated in Glasgow's West End. Regular counselling was part of the program at the place. During one session my counsellor reacted with astonishment when I told her how The Halfman had bugged our bedroom with a microphone.

Back then, my brothers and I were squeezed into one big bed in The Halfman's old workroom; two at the top and one at the bottom. The top of the bed had a large, veneered headboard, with a symmetrical pattern, that looked like the opening titles for DOCTOR WHO. It was behind this headboard that he placed the microphone. He never hid the fact that he was putting it there. He told us that it was an experiment, a joke. It was the only time in our entire lives that he ever seemed to justify himself. The microphone was actually a speaker he had removed from one of the televisions he repaired. He had rigged the thing so that it would function both as microphone and speaker. We were forbidden to talk in bed, but that had never stopped us in the past; all that was soon to change. Shortly after the placing of the mike, my brother and I were both marched out of bed to be confronted by a recording of our own whispering voices. Thankfully, the content of our conversation was not in any way subversive (i.e. about him) but this did put an end to any conversation thereafter.

He never took the thing away; it sat there, behind our heads, for the remaining years we lived in the house and slept in that bed. We were barred from ever touching it. On one occasion in which my younger brother did, The Halfman exploded instantly. I have wondered about the 'bug'. Was it just a grotesque example of his sense of humour, or was he so paranoid he actually had to spy on his own children? I think the truth lay somewhere in the middle. Had he genuinely wanted to spy on us, then I don't think he would have told us what he was doing. I believe the true purpose of the thing was to serve as threat to deter possible troublemaking, not detect it. In reality, the microphone was probably just another reminder that Big Brother was watching us.

~~~

'WHAT did your mother SAY?'
'Nothing.'
'NOBODY f***in' says NOTHING. Now WHAT did SHE talk about?'
'I can't remember.'
Wrong answer, The Arm was let loose once more.

~~~

Mum had gotten herself a house in a nearby area. She was in the early stages of her drinking and relatively sober most of the time. It was agreed that she would have custody of both my younger sister and brother over each weekend. My job was to escort them to her. This brings me to an important part of this book: the only happy memory I have from childhood. It runs like this:

...All three of us leave the house. The door clicks behind us and The Halfman is no longer real. We head downstairs and into the street. We turn left and walk up towards the cement factory that sits at the top of the hill. As we reach the main gates the hill begins to drop and veer to the right. After about twenty seconds, the view down the hill becomes visible. On the left hand side is the Stationery depot (a source of comics); on the right is a small wall at the base of the cement factory fence. Mum is sitting on this, waiting for us. This 'checkpoint' is as close as she can come to Little Russia.

Up till this moment Mum has meant little to me since she has been out of sight, and if you are out of sight to me, then you are out of mind. When I see her sitting in the near distance, bag at her left hand side, she becomes real again and I remember what she means. Upon seeing her, my siblings run ahead to embrace her. For some reason, probably because I don't like crowds, I hang back. This distance is just right for me. Then we are all together, at the bottom of the hill. Mum asks me how I am. My reply is, 'Fine.' She asks me how my older brother is and I reply, 'Fine.'

The wall that Mum has been sitting on is made of red brick with curved edges. The surface of this brick is heavily textured and embedded with tiny, smooth stones. I have often run my fingertips across this as I find its surface pleasant: long patches of rough pumice that drag at the skin; these are broken by the smooth highlights of the little polished stones. This is the texture of happiness. Years from now the wall will be torn down but that won't matter as I have a perfect recording of it on my fingertips. Mum is saying something but I don't hear, I never do; she is there, the texture of the wall feels right and that is all that matters. To be honest, I am not really listening to Mum as, on this particular day, something is niggling at the back of my head, a little unresolved problem. After a while, everyone leaves for Mum's house. Sometimes I walk along with them for a distance; other times, I cannot, as The Halfman often orders me to return immediately. As always I look back at the three figures while they walk away, holding each other. It is a good image, one I will record. Then they are gone. Turned a corner; out of sight and out of mind, off to a better place. Whatever emotions I was feeling vanish with them and I am back to being me. I return to Little Russia for my interrogation.

~~~

'WHAT did she say, ya' bastard yae... TELL me TELLMEYABASTARD-TELLMETELLME!!'

The interrogation was not going well. The Halfman's need to know what subversions 'the other side' was peddling behind his back was all-consuming. No scrap of information was too small to warrant his attention. Unfortunately, his need far outstripped my capacity to remember. I never listened to anything Mum talked about unless the topic was comics. This lack of information was not acceptable, and The Arm swung into action.

I was dizzy with pain but I didn't care. The fool didn't know the truth: that he no longer had all of me to hurt. Despite appearances, I wasn't really in the room at that point. Though nodding in apparent acquiescence, my mind was somewhere else, thinking, not about my crimes, but about the little problem that had been niggling at me when I saw Mum earlier: HYPERMAN.

Hyperman was an alternative version of Superman who appeared in Action Comics # 265, 'The Superman from outer space' (June 1960). I was introduced to him through my Eighty-Page Giants. Hyperman was the hero of a distant planet with an origin strikingly similar to that of the Man of Steel. Just as Superman had been rocketed from Krypton to Earth, moments before the planet exploded, so Hyperman was dispatched from his native world of Zoron to an Earth-like world called Oceania. Due to exactly the same circumstances which occurred on Earth, Hyperman - or CHESTER KING as he was known in his secret identity - acquired 'hyper-powers' identical to those of Superman. The similarities did not end there. Both heroes worked as reporters for a top newspaper; and both were being pestered by a nosey love-interest determined to uncover their true identity.

During the course of the story, Hyperman enlists Superman's help to deal with this familiar problem. As it transpires, the robots Hyperman has built in an effort to conceal his true identity persistently malfunction due to an element in Oceania's atmosphere. Because he is Hyperman's double (though their costumes are very different) Superman is asked to impersonate Oceania's mightiest hero in order to get LYDIA LONG – Hyperman's love interest - off his back. What starts off as a mildly amusing romp deepens into tragedy when Superman discovers that Hyperman - unknown to himself - is actually dying. The hero has been poisoned by exposure to 'Blue Zoronite', a Kryptonite-like chunk of his home planet that he has unwittingly stored in his underwater Fortress of Secrecy. In order to give his counterpart a final year of normal life, Superman exposes Hyperman's identity to Oceania just before the lethal radiation strips him of his powers. At the story's emotional conclusion, Superman and his cousin Supergirl use their telescopic vision to watch Hyperman's final moments as the stricken hero eventually dies in the arms of his beloved.

The story made an impression on me as it was the first time I saw Superman, or rather, someone like him, die. The note of tragedy it ended on was a departure from the norm that perplexed and slightly disturbed me. But there is a silver lining to every cloud as I was to discover. The tragedy of Hyperman took my mind away from the immediate problem of The Arm; something that, up till this point, I had used textures to deal with.

The world of texture and details was often my escape from pain. If accu-

Keeping tabs on the subversives

sations and interrogations were carried out in our living room, I could study the structures of The Halfman's artificial arm. Unlike its Soviet counterpart, this prosthetic was not moved by sophisticated sensors and motors but by an assortment of leather straps or tendons running through tiny metal hoops adorning its surface. These were attached to a harness stretching across his back. By flexing this harness in different directions he brought limited movement to the limb. (My interest in drawing robots sprang from my studies of this fascinating mechanism.) As the blows fell, my eyes would journey across the length and intricacy of the thing, following the 'tendons' as though they were railway lines, stopping off here and there to study a recessed screw or an interesting piece of stitching.

Were the denouncement to occur in the kitchen, I would instead focus on the plastic edging of the dinner table. This was a translucent amber strip laced with light and dark flecks of gold. Focusing in on the flecks then moving back and forth within the strip to find, and list, similar-sized pieces was an effective anaesthetic. The problem lay in never wanting to leave the strip.

Abused children have a tendency to retreat into themselves; this is even more of a problem for ASD youngsters for whom withdrawal is often second nature. As a child, I found myself at a crossroads between two worlds. One was filled with the ever changing, nonsensical and frighteningly violent things called people. This place, often referred to as 'real life', was a source of pain and fear. The other world was far better. It was filled with details, lovely textures and clean chemical tastes. There were no people there, it belonged to me, and me alone. I think I would have drifted down this route forever had comics not offered me an alternative. Through this fantastic medium I began to develop an interest in the world around me that, up till this point, had never existed beyond the immediate and sensory. Thanks to comics, I started to return from the addictive world of minutiae I had been hiding in. Life was still violent and frightening, but I now had the opportunity to occasionally escape 'next door' to a far better place that, despite being a refuge, still allowed me to keep in touch with the real world. Comics made me follow stories and ask questions of the world around me. They drew my attention to cause and effect. In time, they would help me express myself as well.

I wandered through the panels of Hyperman's story as The Arm went about its business. I no longer needed to hide within the amber strip at the edge of the table. For every accusation there would be giant robots, floating cities, wizards, sea monsters, alien invaders and a hero to deal with them. For every sweep of The Arm there would be lost lands, dinosaurs or something equally magic to dull the pain. The Halfman had no hope of ever reaching this new haven. I have heard that great dreams are often born under the shadow of oppression. For some of us, denied imagination in our formative years, they have to be constructed from second-hand pieces gifted by others. The Halfman never realized that, through these pre-packaged, over-the-counter fantasies, I was no longer within his total grasp; that at least some of me had discovered a way of escaping the tyranny of his Little Russia and out into other, better worlds.

STICKS AND STONES

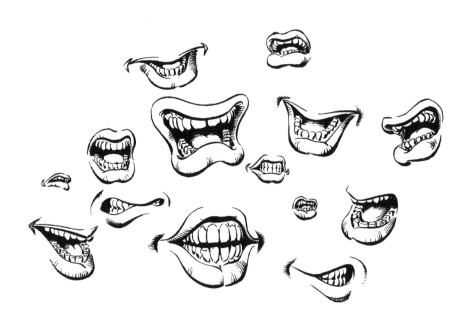

'C ampbell...'
  'Campbell...'
  'Campbell!!'

  They are calling me names. They never stop calling me names. They never stop laughing. They are kicking me on the legs. One of them kicks me in the stomach. They punch me in the face. They kick me down the stairs. They hit me with stones and then with bricks. They tear at my clothes. They tear my hair out. They throw me into the urinal. They spit on me. They force earth down my throat. They surround me and rush me, all as one. They are a wall of hatred around and inside me.

  For the Aspergers child, school is often the place of nightmares. Golfhill Primary School was no different. The overload of the place was terrible. Too hot, too much noise and too many unnecessary bodies swirling all around me. I would twitch and rock and occasionally 'crash' to the frustration and confusion of my teachers. The lessons were impossible. 1960's education had little understanding of learning difficulties. You were either functional or you were retarded. I was semi-functional and therein lay the problem. Information was being imparted at a speed far too rapid for me to process. The teachers jumped from subject to subject faster than I could follow. Attempting to do so at such a dizzying pace was impossible. Worst of all, there were gaps in the lessons, gaps I was expected to fill in by myself, but could not. Unlike the other pupils, I was incapable of certain intuitive leaps; attempting such things brought me back in contact with my inbuilt mental holes: blank areas lacking in thoughts or responses. The teacher's response was to humiliate me for my 'stupidity' in front of giggling classrooms or threaten me with the belt: a leather strap struck across the hand as a painful punishment for misbehaviour. My misbehaviour consisted of being unable to look teachers in the eye or properly converse with them no matter how much I was threatened. I was to become very familiar with that strip of leather during my time in school.

The belt was nothing by comparison with the terror of the playground. My memories of that place are the building blocks that make up my childhood. The other kids detected me quickly enough: bad clothes, smaller and weaker and, best of all, strange. The sign above my head read 'Attack' and they did, all of them. This was worse than The Halfman; at least his attacks came from one direction; these came from everywhere and all at once. I discovered that seeking help from the teachers was pointless as there was no way they could, or seemed even inclined to, protect me. The response of an older teacher on one occasion was to actually walk away from me while I asked her for help. After reporting a particularly violent group assault, I was quizzed by another teacher as to what I had done to make the other children attack me.

What had I done to make them attack me?

This became a familiar question during my years in education. In its own insidious way it threw the blame for my persecution back onto me. On the two instances that my attackers were confronted by staff, they stopped for all of ten minutes. Returning to the playground, the bullies commenced more attacks. I made the mistake of telling The Halfman about it. He beat me for 'allowing' myself to be bullied (this was not limited to me; he thumped anyone in the family who was 'weak' enough to allow themselves to be put upon in this fashion). Mum told me that the bullies would eventually leave me alone. They never did. I asked her why they attacked me. She could not answer.

~~~

HOUSE OF MYSTERY and HOUSE OF SECRETS were two DC supernatural comics I had been given in hospital. Each title was an anthology
introduced by a particular host. In House of Mystery, the host was a tall, thin,
bespectacled character called Cain. His House of Secrets counterpart, logically enough, was his rather portly and ineffectual looking brother, Abel. House
of Mystery # 195 (Oct 71) featured the story BAT OUT OF HELL. Written by
JACK OLECK and beautifully drawn by NESTOR REDONDO, this was the
tale of a brutal, drunken father who terrorizes his family (there was a certain
irony in this that was lost on me at the time), eventually murdering his wife
as his children look on. As the story progresses, the man is plagued by a huge
bat which he believes to be his wife reborn as a vampire. Eventually, the creature terrifies the father into plunging to his death from the upper floors of an
abandoned castle. It is then the reader discovers that the 'monster' is just an
ordinary bat (albeit a rather large one) who has been protecting its offspring,
as its nest lies hidden nearby.

Redondo's art utterly engrossed me. He was the master of a technique
called 'feathering', an optical illusion using the subtle thickening of parallel
lines; this fools the eye into seeing areas of grey or deepening shade where
there is only sharp black and white. I found this effect even more attractive
than the old halftones from the newspapers. If I felt okay, I would read the
story. If I felt bad, stressed more than usual, I would study the feathering.

I had memorized the comic in perfect detail and, on this particular occasion, was re-reading it in my head as I stood at the bottom right hand corner
of the boys' playground in Golfhill. I was facing onto the nearby Ark Lane,
with my back turned to the rest of the world, hoping the horrible, hate-filled
place would go away. (In later years, pampered, insulated fools will tell me
this is 'escapism', and that the lifelong pursuit of such is a bad thing.) I was
focussing on the feathering of the bat's left wing in the story's opening panel,
immersing myself in the beautiful world of its ribbed texture. I hoped 'they'
would not come for me. As usual, I hoped in vain; 'they' arrived, calling out
the familiar chant.

'Campbell!'

'Campbell!'

'Campbell!'

'Campbell!!'

'Campbell!!'

There are so many of them. There are always so many of them. In later
years, this will be called 'mobbing'. They ridicule my clothes; they kick me
and punch me. I am ordered to jump from the roof of the toilets that sit at

Football

the other end of the playground. The roof is about twelve feet high. It is fairly easy to climb up there; I have done so in the past. I am dragged up to the toilets and told to get climbing. I really don't think that jumping from this is a good idea and so decline the offer. I try to run into the main building but they catch me near one of the entrances. They knock me to the ground and start to kick me. I curl up as more of them join in. This is their favourite game: football, with me as the ball. I double up and think about the bat's wings…

~~~

The damage inflicted by the playground is more than just physical. One of the most irresponsible of all school myths was printed on a poster adorning one of the classroom walls in Golfhill. This read: STICKS AND STONES MAY BREAK MY BONES, BUT NAMES WILL NEVER HURT ME. I have no idea who first coined that particular phrase, but I would sincerely like to break a few of their bones as it is one of the most naïve and destructive of all lies.

Ceaseless name calling had begun to hurt. This was due to association with the beatings which came with it. There was no contact, no communication with my peers other than abuse. This was not a 'little bit of rough and tumble'- as I have so often heard this process described - this was a collective assault that never ended. In time, I would find myself the prey of entire classrooms. When insulted, I had no way of answering back. There were no sarcastic replies inside my head, only the same, empty space that stopped me engaging in normal conversation. In addition, I was beginning to entertain the possibility that 'they' were right: that I was not as 'good' as them, that I was somehow 'bad'. Through this process, I started to grasp the concept of worth; it was something I did not possess. Golfhill was pain and fear and more: it was the beginning of shame.

The shame started with some of the books I was forced to read: these occasionally referred to something called 'friends'. Apparently a friend was a type of child who did not attack you. The idea was wholly alien. I had observed other kids playing together and realized that they must be friends for each other. I knew this was not for me. I cannot say that being without friends really meant anything to me, at least not back then. Other children were simply moving objects I wanted to move away from me. Nonetheless, I had a strong desire to follow the rules, in any shape or form.

The Rules: the ultimate anchoring points; the most important things in the whole world; the underlying sanity that held everything together. Obey The Rules and everything will be alright, The Rules will protect you. I had difficulty grasping what constituted right and wrong in any situation. Things like that were never obvious to me. Being left to my own initiative was like being abandoned at an unfamiliar train station. I needed clear-cut, specific, definitions of what was required. I needed The Rules. If I was able to learn one, then I stuck to it like a castaway clinging to a log. I looked for them even when there were none. If these books were anything to go by, making friends seemed to be an expected behaviour, an important rule. This new failure on my part lodged in me like a barb. It would not begin to fester for several years, but when it did, the anguish and self-hatred tore me apart.

~~~

Eventually, I parted company from my first school. There was a leaving ceremony, held at a local church. I had attended this place occasionally with the school to sing hymns (actually, the other kids did the singing; I sat in silence and ate the blank pages I found at the back of the hymn book). Every pupil leaving that year was given a gift of a book; most of these were brightly coloured picture books for older children. For some strange reason, I was given a paperback novel THE REVENGE OF THE SCARLET PIMPERNEL by Baroness De Orczy. The book had impossibly small type, and its language was ornate and as thick as mud. Later in the week, I ate a couple of its pages while reading my comics; I cannot say they tasted particularly memorable.

I had finished my final year of primary education. During the time I spent in the corridors and playgrounds of Golfhill I had been taught much. I learned that I was stupid and that I did not possess the worth of a normal person. I learned that, no matter what happened to me, I would not be protected. More than this, I was not *deserving* of protection. Through this, I learned fear, pain, and helplessness.

Without trying to sound melodramatic, I call these the 'Dark Lessons'. They are the most real, most primal, and long lasting of all lessons imparted in our schools because the mediums in which they are carried are fear, pain and power. They pollute the lives of all who learn them, victims and bullies alike. They are taught to countless innocents every day by an organisation our culture has placed beyond both question and accountability.

I would carry these poisonous lessons over to my next place of education where I would discover that Golfhill was simply a dry run. I did not know it yet, but I was going to a place that was about to teach me something far worse than either pain or fear.

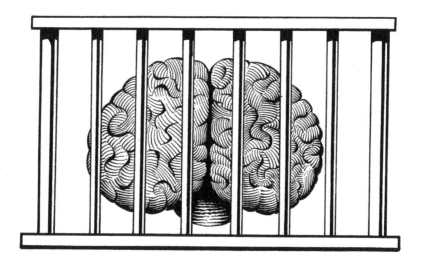

THE LEARNING CAGE

HULK WILL SMASH

'This is BUSHMAN, he's our star attraction of the PLASTI-CINE BRIGADE,' Mr Wood tells his visitor as we queue in the corridors outside the History classes. 'Bushman' is Mr Wood's pet name for me. At thirteen, I am an unkempt mess since abstract concepts like personal grooming are still far beyond me. Plasticine is oil-based clay commonly used by children. 'The Plasticine Brigade' is Mr Wood's term for academic underachievers. In my case, he uses it to suggest idiocy or retardation. I cannot look up at him and instead find myself staring at the interesting texture of the stone floor. I will come to identify different areas of this new building from the distinctive patterns at my feet.

'We haven't taught you to bite the head off chickens yet have we, Bushman?' he chuckles. This makes no sense to me as decapitating fowls is definitely not part of our History lessons. I am ignorant of 'Geeks', those chicken eating side-show grotesques of legend, so Mr Wood's little joke will be lost on me for a decade or so. Mr Wood has a belt called Beelzebub. He brags about just how much pain he is able to inflict with it. 'I'm keeping it well-oiled for the likes of you, Bushman,' he chuckles. I suppose I should consider myself lucky that Mr Wood is not actually my teacher; he just pops into the corridor every now and then for some sport. He finds fault with everything about me. He ridicules my clothes, the way I talk, walk and my difficulty standing still or making eye contact. He notices I sweat constantly and affects a bad smell in my direction. Since he is a teacher, The Rules say he cannot be in the wrong, therefore I am. In Golfhill, I was 'bad'; at this new place, I seem to be even worse. Mr Wood, on the other hand, is a good teacher. He makes the other students laugh. He makes them laugh at me.

Welcome to Whitehill Secondary School.

~~~

'Is there something wrong with you boy?'

'No, there is nothing wrong with me.'

'Then why are you acting as if there is?'

'I'm not.'

'But you are.'

'I'm not.'

'I'm WARNING you...'

As my communication and learning difficulties drew attention to themselves, this became a familiar line of questioning at my new school. My 'stupidity', i.e. problems grasping long verbal instructions resulted in regular punishments, both verbal and physical, usually handed out in front of my snickering peers. Trial by classroom was one of Whitehill's many weapons of torment. I deserved it, of course, for being stupid. Stupid people were inferior, 70's education said so.

My teachers had no idea that my prolonged silences were small 'crashes' during which I was shutting off from the overload around me. Academically, I was at the absolute bottom of the heap. In primary school, lessons tended to be taught in a single classroom. The specialised nature of secondary education meant changing subjects and moving from room to room every hour or so. This was impossible to deal with as the constantly changing lessons whizzed past me with the speed of racing cars. Secondary teaching also involved an even greater amount of 'joining the dots' than in primary. In these more advanced lessons the young mind was expected to assemble given facts into a rudimentary pattern. This approach works fine with a neurotypical youngster. For a mind that simply shuts off if not given precise instructions at every step, it is worse than useless.

The inside of my head was like a mountain of tiny cubicles, each occupied by a tiny man holding onto a single fact. Not one of these little fellows communicated with each other because no-one had told them to. The only subject in which I displayed any real aptitude was Science. For achieving high marks in this, I found myself yelled at once more as I was clearly dragging my heels in other areas. No-one made the connection that Science was the one subject taught using largely pictorial methods like diagrams and charts with a minimum of written language. 'Saturation criticism' of the type employed by Whitehill only served to push me away from the whole educational experience. Although I had learned to keep my body in the class, my mind would still drift away no matter how often it was threatened.

~~~

'What is this Campbell?'
'You said write it down and-'
'No, NO! What is this meant to be? What do you call this?'
The teacher held my page up to the rest of the classroom.
'This scrawl you're doing here is not even the work of a child. This is the work of a SPASTIC!'
Due to undiagnosed Dysgraphia, my handwriting was an indecipherable mess of huge, barely formed, print that meandered across the page from left to right (if you were lucky). When it was discovered that I could neither read nor write in script, it was decided I should attend special handwriting classes. The lady who took these was a French teacher. I think that she had problems understanding me and even got angry once in awhile, but she never shouted, something that was a pleasant departure from the norm. In addition to a futile attempt to improve my handwriting, she asked me some questions about myself. She noticed that I was unable to make eye contact and sweated all the time. When she asked me if I was nervous, I found I couldn't reply. Was I nervous? I had no objectivity about my constant state of agitation. Not getting an answer she made the mistake of asking me what kind of things I liked and paid the price with an extended lecture about THE INCREDIBLE HULK.

~~~

I had discovered The Hulk and MARVEL COMICS towards the end of my stay at Golfhill. The revelation that there was a second American comics company in the world annoyed and unnerved me once again. If DC has been the childhood of my comics obsession, then Marvel became its adolescence. To anyone who had been reared on a diet of 'safe' 60's-style, DC comics, an encounter with their Marvel counterparts came as something of a culture shock. I hated Marvel Comics the moment I opened them up. It was a loathing born of mistrust and fear. Marvel artwork lacked the clean and airy look of DC. There was something inherently wrong with its style: it was too compressed, too dark; it had too many clashing details crushed into each panel; the positions adopted by the characters were far too twisted and extreme.

Particularly unappealing was the revolting intensity of the characters. The Marvel heroes were an odd-looking, sinister bunch who disagreed with each other as often as with the grotesque villains they fought. Even in casual conversation, they looked as though they were about to punch each other's lights out. In DC there were no sharp emotions; heroes, and usually even villains talked to each other in a fairly placid, sensible fashion. Conversations, even at the height of drama, would relay the correct amount of information and nothing more.

Marvel was the opposite: their so-called heroes' speeches were usually peppered with observations and asides that indicated a repulsive and illogical phenomena called 'characterization'. Equally vile, they actually clenched their teeth - something even DC bad guys never did - and on occasion, even sported a gummy strand between their upper and lower mouth that I realised, with disbelief and horror, was saliva (a thread of spittle is comics shorthand for rage or insanity).

All this paled before Marvel's sacrilegious depiction of communists, or 'Reds' and 'Commies', as they called them. Far from being The Halfman's noble guardians of civilisation, Marvel communists were brutish thugs; cowardly, backstabbing and constantly engaged in despicable attempts at world domination. They usually wore heavy overcoats, dull green and dated looking military uniforms or formal suits that looked slightly 'wrong'. Their flat, humourless features were bisected by wide mouths filled with jagged lower teeth. They sported beards, moustaches and thick eyebrows and often looked out through lidded, vaguely reptilian eyes. Far from sharing in the great communist spirit, they seemed to despise and fear each other and, left to their own devices, were more inclined to betray their own people than show loyalty. Some even jumped at the chance to abandon their beliefs and live in the west. Even the lowest communist lackey was depicted as a far more despicable creature than the worst American villain. According to Marvel, communism was not the ultimate political system but a tyrannical regime that served only to crush the spirit of man. The USSR was not the most advanced country on Earth; it was a backward nation living under monstrous oppression, whose technology was mostly stolen (with no mention at all of their ability to conquer death).

Unlike its largely apolitical counterpart, Marvel wore its politics on its

Big trouble

sleeve. Early issues pitted its heroes against the lackeys of the red menace; vile characters sporting names like THE GARGOYLE, GENERAL FANG, THE RED GHOST AND HIS SUPER-APES, THE RADIOACTIVE MAN, and THE CRIMSON DYNAMO. Communists were the bad guys. It was the final straw. I would have quickly given up on this new company had it not filled its pages with another little gimmick that DC had failed to properly dramatize: power. Power. Raw power!

When mild mannered nuclear physicist BRUCE BANNER was exposed to the mysterious gamma rays from his experimental bomb, the timid academic was transformed into comics' greatest incarnation of strength and rage: THE INCREDIBLE HULK. The Hulk, at best, was a surly fellow with a hair-trigger temper, something I was very familiar with (although the Hulk didn't need to lose an arm to end up permanently pissed off). His solution to any problem was equally familiar: he would simply smash it. This was done with a level of realism missing from the medium up till this point. If Superman were to demolish a large robot, he would do so with a minimum of violence and in quite a tidy fashion (usually the robot's head would be cleanly popped off like a cork). If the Hulk was faced with the same problem, the unfortunate autom-ata would find pieces of its body flying off to opposite ends of the horizon.

I grew used to the comforting formula of the Jade Giant's adventures. Each month he would face some new threat; perhaps a glowing alien invader or ranting subterranean warrior from a lost civilization. The first half of the story would introduce this latest aggressor, who would flex their muscles while boasting of their invincible power. The Hulk's response would be to tell the bad guy to shut up as their speeches only made his head hurt. The rest of the story would depict 'ol' Greenskin' flattening this latest menace and their dreams of world conquest. This would be achieved with maximum damage to the surrounding landscape. The bad guy would have a couple of panels in which to marvel at the limitless power of the eponymous character before they were either scrapped or buried under the nearest mountain.

The ability to smash anything that caused pain excited me to an extent nothing on paper had ever managed before. Power was the solution to every-thing; power and more power. It was an appeal which increased as Marvel produced even more extreme embodiments of this principle: ODIN, Thor's father who could shift the entire human race off the Earth with a simple gesture; THE WATCHER, a glowing-eyed space Buddha whose power awed and terrified even the most heinous of villains. Finally, there was GALAC-TUS, a cosmic wanderer who survived of a diet of whole planets. Here were characters so immense they could stub Superman out like a cigarette butt. Absolute power! Not even The Arm or Whitehill stood a chance against such beings. I had been powerless all my life, a fact I was even more acutely aware of in this new place. Marvel comics gave me a taste of the very thing I had never experienced; a safe way of placating that void. This was the reason I had never become a BATMAN fan, despite having read many of his stories in my Eighty-Page Giants. Stripped of his bat-gizmos, the Caped Crusader was just a man, and that was never enough, not against the horrible world around me.

~~~

I almost fall out of my seat as the punches land. I have no way of preparing myself since the ink they have rubbed into my eyes has almost blinded me. I am kicked in the legs and ridiculed. I hear them suggest that I should be made to drink from the bottle of ink. I am told to open my mouth; at that point, I decide to run...

During my second year at Whitehill, A 'core group' of bullies began to fix its attentions on me. The ringleader was one of the most sadistic individuals I'd ever encountered. Initially, he was aided by two others. However, in the space of a few weeks, he added another couple of trainee thugs to his entourage: a smaller, equally vicious boy and a taller, extremely ugly lad with long fair hair and a permanently curled upper lip, whose expression reminded me of the MORLOCKS featured in GEORGE PAL'S film adaptation of THE TIME MACHINE. They were not the only group to target me, but they were the leaders and honed the abuse to a fine art. The only memories I have of this period are of total fear, absolute, saturation fear.

All I could do in the presence of this group was to keep quiet and hope they would not notice me. I dreaded the moment my name would be spoken aloud as this was the signal for yet another round of abuse. The ringleader used his own phrase to call to me. 'Campbell, heel!' he would yell to raucous laughter. I was his personal dog; everyone knew it, including me, particularly me.

This latest attack took place during what was called a 'free period'. This was an occasional break between lessons, usually lasting about forty minutes during which the teacher wandered off for a cup of tea, leaving the class to its own cruelties. During this time, I became the sole focus of their attention. I would sit quietly and be verbally flayed by a dozen students or more for the better part of an hour. Not one single piece of me was left unscarred. I had to take it all because I was alone, totally alone. (Years later I was shocked to learn that religious cults use similar methods to break down initiates.)

Had I given even the slightest hint of a retort then that would have resulted in an immediate escalation to physical violence. The violence came anyway; the best I could do was delay it by keeping silent. These 'group degradation' sessions only served to confirm, beyond question, what I had suspected at Golfhill: firstly that the world hated me, and secondly, that I was not a 'real' person, perhaps not even a human being. I certainly did not have the worth of one.

I thought about the Hulk or any other powerful creature as the diatribes and eventually the fists and boots lashed down on me. It was during one of these ordeals that one of the group found the large bottle of black ink in a cupboard.

After fleeing the classroom, I was discovered trying to wash the ink out of my eyes. Subsequently, the core group were hauled up in front of a senior teacher and told to leave me alone. This bought me a reprieve of two days. I was attacked by the ringleader and another group of boys in a nearby lane outside the school. What I remember of this attack is pretty fragmented as one of the boys repeatedly kicked me on the head while I lay on the ground. I didn't recognise any of these newcomers as none of them attended Whitehill. I was told they were friends of the ringleader and, should I report him again, I would be stabbed. No knife was produced, but I believed them. From that point on, I kept my mouth shut, stopped hoping, and accepted whatever was done to me.

~~~

The Hulk was in big trouble. His latest adversary was like nothing he had ever faced before. It was a swamp monster called THE GLOB (issue #121 November 1969. 'Within the swamp, there stirs The Glob'). I had recently acquired the comic and had been devouring it for a whole week. The Glob possessed unbelievable power; it actually seemed to be stronger than the Hulk. The creature was also completely silent - a reversal of the usual, boastful super villain scenario - and resistant to any damage the Hulk tried to inflict on it. The Hulk, prone to calling his opponents by childish nick names, referred to the Glob, in an unusually respectful tone, as 'the other' and actually asked the creature why it would not talk. The Glob was an utterly primal design. It had no real face, just a curtain of dripping weeds hanging under a pair of near-empty eye sockets. Best of all, its massive, dripping body was rendered almost entirely by feathering. This was the first time I'd ever seen a figure completely defined by the effect. Every panel it appeared in drew my eyes like magnets. My mind would wander back and forth between this visual treat and the profundity of a creature stronger than the Hulk as the real violence around me escalated.

~~~

My shirt is yanked up and wrapped around my head. Through the material, I am punched in the face and stomach. I am kicked in the crotch and double up in agony. Before I hit the ground, they kick me in the stomach. The pain is immense and blots all other things out. I cannot breath. The front of my shirt is bloodied. My comics are yanked out of my hands, torn up and scattered over the street in front of me. I cling to one of the railings for support as the ringleader and his pack wander off, laughing. I am punch drunk, physically and emotionally. The world is whirling around me, a place of limitless hostility. Everything is attacking me. I need something to focus on. I pick up some of the pages and look for panels featuring the Glob so I can have something to take home: an example of how strong he is or at least some of the feathering effects.

SIEGE MENTALITY

C ampbell.. it's Campbell.. yeah…uh!.. (Chuckle) huh! H.. huh!…
Campbell… Looklook.. Look it's CampbellCampbellCampbell..
That's…sssss.. I know… We… nnnttGetttt.. Campbell get him!
(Chuckle).'

~~~

My name, spoken in whispers which fade as I approach: always a bad sign.
Why am I so stupid that I allow this to happen to me every day? Why am I so
weak?

If I am lucky, they will just humiliate me or kick me on the legs once or
twice. My luck is not in. The core group attack me on the stairs to the Modern
Studies department in the new building. They are joined by a younger boy
who has been hanging around with them recently. I am struck in the face. As

I reel from the blow, the younger boy grabs my left hand and yanks my thumb and forefinger in opposite directions. The pain is so great that everything whites out and I pitch down the stairs to the laughter of the others. After they have left, I lie at the bottom of the stairs for a moment or two, unable to get up. When I do, I discover that my nose is bleeding heavily and the front of my shirt is wet with blood.

I was afraid and disorientated after this latest attack. I remember being unwilling to leave the landing. Why was I walking this path into abuse that never stopped? Simple, The Rules said I had to, and The Rules were never wrong. The Rules could not be questioned, they had to be obeyed. As soon as the lesson was over and I left Modern Studies, I was struck in the face and the bleeding started again.

Welcome to Whitehill Mark 2.

~~~

The new Whitehill Secondary was situated a few streets away from the old one. When the original closed for the last time, a small tree eventually grew around the metal of the gate, sealing it shut forever. It is a real shame that no one caught this lovely, sad image in a photograph as it would have made the perfect cover for this book.

Whitehill Secondary Mark 2 was a modern, less impressive building which looked like a cut-rate imitation of 'Moonbase Alpha' from ITC's SPACE 1999. It smelled of glue and a bitter disinfectant that made me salivate. It was supposedly Scotland's first open-plan school, boasting large open areas separated not by rigid walls but movable partitions. The effect vaguely reminded me of the offices of modern police stations in American TV shows. It was apparently filled with bright new ideas and considered a step ahead for education. Decades later, websites would praise it as a 'pupil-friendly environment'. Nothing could be further from the truth. Whitehill Mark 2 was utterly hostile and completely intolerant of anything that did not fit its narrow definitions of normalcy. Open-plan it may have been, open-minded it was anything but.

~~~

'Look at me boy, *I* said look at me. *I'M* TELLING YOU TO LOOK AT ME!!' shrieked The Animal. 'The Animal', as I will call him here, was an official at Whitehill. Like my old nemesis, Mr Wood, he was something of a Dickens-style grotesque who could have been lifted directly from any cheap Victorian novel. His attitude towards students he disliked was totally confrontational, often hostile and occasionally near-hysterical. His demands for eye-contact were lost on me. I could not look up at him no matter how loudly he yelled. Unwilling to be thwarted, he moved his beetroot red face back and forth in a vain attempt to catch mine. Instantly, I looked away towards another section of the floor. Most people had eight pints of blood in their bodies; The Animal appeared to keep eight pints in his face alone. His breath stank and his pronunciation of 'I' was so loaded with egotistical emphasis that it was absolutely repulsive to hear.

To the rest of the pupils in the dinner school, our little head-dance must have looked like some kind of oddball double-act. The Animal had finally noticed me and did not like what he saw. My unkempt appearance enraged him, a fact he made no effort to hide. From now on he would subject me to regular diatribes in public. The Animal could do so with impunity. Considering his position, he had all the authority he needed to openly abuse any young person he took a dislike to. It was clear he took pride in the new school and considered me something of a fly in a brand new jar of ointment.

The Animal was of the opinion that someone who looked the way I did had no place in the dinner school and ordered me out. Up till this point, the dinner school had been one source of food for me. I was reluctant to part with regular eating, but as The Animal represented The Rules…

As I was leaving, he turned on another boy. This lad had stubble on his chin. The Animal would not tolerate such ill-grooming; he snarled this point home to the boy, stabbing him in the chest with his finger to the sound of 'I' this and 'I' that. In the 70's, regulations regarding physical contact between pupils and teachers were far less defined than now, so the boy simply took the abuse along with the finger. There was no reasoning with The Animal. If any of Whitehill's staff were even less tolerant than Mr Wood, and less popular than me, it was this creature.

Everyone watched the freak show with nervous excitement. To his credit, the Animal never made any attempt to hide his true nature. His near hysteria and hostility were a matter of public record and would go on to become legend in the history of Whitehill.

~~~

In the rear playground, the one facing onto the football field, I am punched in the stomach until I double over. As I lie on the ground, covered in spittle and phlegm, someone stamps on my back. They ridicule my clothes, my family and me. They break my glasses. They will not stop…

~~~

'Black paint? What do you want black paint for Campbell?' asked my Art teacher.

I wanted it for the space background behind my latest rendering of 'No Scream', although by this point I had re-titled it 'I have no mouth and I must scream' after reading HARLAN ELLISON's award winning short story of the same name. Marvel had recently published a Science Fiction anthology title: UNKNOWN WORLDS OF SCIENCE FICTION. It was through these comic adaptations of SF stories that I had become interested enough in Fantasy writing to actually start reading SF prose. Having studied many book covers of the period, I had decided to give the distorted face an outer space style background.

'Black is not a real colour. You do not use it in paintings,' he said.

This was untrue. Many artists used it for certain types of mixing and glazing. If there was no need for black paint then it would not exist. Unfortunately I did not have access to such fine logic at that point and could only reply that I needed it for my picture.

'You mix colours to get black, Campbell. Black paint kills a picture. True black does not exist in nature. Name me one subject that you would render with absolute black.'

'Outer space.'

'What?'

'Outer space is absolute black. It is the total absence of light. Mixing colours would be inaccurate and a waste of paint.'

'Don't you get smart with me boy!'

'I'm not, I just mean-'

'I'm warning you, I'll stiffen you!'

'Stiffen' was a general purpose threat he would occasionally bandy about. I had a vague idea what it meant. Still more of a drawing than a painting, 'No Scream' had never met the approval of any Art teacher in all the years I had rendered it. Its lines were so familiar that running the pencil back and forth along them was like walking home. Over time, the expression of agony had become more stretched and extreme. This was a major bone of contention with my Art teachers as such distortion was straying dangerously close to the blasphemy of cartooning and comics (a subject they expressed open contempt for; indeed, I had been banned outright from producing anything comic related in the Art classes). It seemed to infuriate many of them that I persisted in rendering such images.

'Not this again. Your problem is that you see things in terms of lines. You have to blend the paint.'

'How do you do that?'

'You sit and you mix it, son!'

'How?'

I was being told what to do without actually being told how to do it and this upset me deeply. Painting had always threatened me as all attempts to master the art met with no success. Denied the imagination to properly explore and experiment with technique, I pushed paint around as I would the tip of a pencil. All this did was move the mess from one part of the paper to another. It was clear that I was simply banging my head against the wall using this method. I needed precise instructions as how to achieve this legendary 'blending'. Confronting the problem head-on seemed the best approach. The teacher wanted me to paint. I also wanted to do this, but only under certain terms. I needed to produce 'real' paintings with tightly controlled tonal gradations such as those seen on book covers or in art galleries. He was an Art teacher therefore he should have been able teach me how to do this. On the nearby wall hung a fine art print of THE WATER-SELLER OF SEVILLE by the Spanish artist VELAZQUEZ. Although tightly rendered, the picture had a flat, pastel quality that, at least in a technical sense, I did not find threatening. I asked the teacher the obvious question.

'How do you paint like that?'

'Campbell, that has to be the most stupid question that I have ever been asked. Do you expect me to wave a magic wand that will give you some kind of instant knowledge?'

That was not what I had requested. What I desired were some basic instructions that would give me a start, an anchoring point to get to grips with the work.

'Well there are no shortcuts here, laddie. This is something that you'll have to find out for yourself.'

I did not see the logic behind this. If he was an Art teacher, then he had to be an artist. If he was an artist then he had to have been able to paint. If he knew how to paint then he could teach such a thing. Teachers were meant to teach, as least so far as I was aware. Despite this, the man showed no inclination to do anything other than insult and threaten me. Wanting to avoid further delay, the next question was obvious.

'Can you paint like that?'

On reflection, this was the worst thing I could have asked him in public. There was no malice or sarcasm behind the question however, it was simply the most direct and sensible way of obtaining information. I suppose I should have expected the response. He exploded.

'Are you *RETARDED* Campbell. What right have you to ask me that?!!'

'I just wanted to –'

'You think you're smart or something? Well take it from me boy, you're nothing of the sort.' He gestured at my drawing 'Get it through your head that this stuff is rubbish. It has no value. What you do has no value at all. You think you know everything, don't you Campbell eh? Well take it from me, you know nothing and you'll amount to nothing!'

He stomped off, throwing back a little threat as he left.

'You came this close to being kicked out of Art.'

~~~

Pity I wasn't. I never did get my black paint and I never learned to paint there either. The lessons I learned in the Whitehill Art classes were about big-otry amongst the educated and those who really should know better. Art may indeed be something you have to 'learn for yourself' but technique is simply an advanced form of bricklaying; it can be taught, assuming the teacher actually knows it in the first place. English teachers don't start off by teaching poetry. They introduce their students to the building blocks of communication: language, punctuation, structure and then meaning.

Art is relative, teaching is not. The whole point of the profession is to help the young mind. The only way to do that is first to respect it, regardless of how 'strange' you consider it to be. My Art teacher and his ilk did not see a young person with a genuine interest in a specific field of art; someone with a need to express himself and a desire to learn. They saw someone who was 'weird', who had something 'wrong' with them. Someone they could label stupid or even 'retarded'.

Art was all I had. Thanks to Whitehill I had developed a greater under-standing of humanity's contempt for me. There was more to the process than simple physical assault. The world seemed determined to question me at every turn; logically I needed an answer. More than this, I needed credentials. At Golfhill, I drew to impose order on the world around me, at Whitehill I drew to justify myself to it and carried those credentials around in a plastic bag that never left my side. Had I had anything like a motto back then, it would have been: 'I draw monsters, superheroes and robots, therefore I am.' It was in the Whitehill Art classes that even those desperate qualifications were torn from me.

Was it the comics? I mean everyone knows that comics are for kids (or even 'retards'). It is no secret that comics are an inferior art form, if indeed they can be considered an art form at all. A drawing by itself is not a bad thing, but should another drawing be placed after it to suggest a progression of events then it becomes a comic and immediately loses all value. Try as I might, I have never been able to grasp the logic behind this all-pervasive attitude. Our first non-verbal languages - cave paintings - were comic strips. Egyptian hieroglyphics and the Bayeux tapestry were all comic strips. The comic strip predates the abstraction of written language. Though simpler in some aspects, it is able to convey certain types of information more efficiently than any combination of words. For some, it is the perfect medium of communication.

At some point in our history, however, something went wrong, and this language fell out of favour. Perhaps my Art teachers - those open-minded souls - felt insulted that I dared bring a medium so lacking in cultural status into their classroom.

As a medium, comics have fought to regain their status in the face of bigotry and dismissal (a struggle those on the spectrum are themselves quite familiar with). All art is equally valid in the eyes of those who admire it. No-one has the right to say that theirs is the only voice in the world of creativity. Anyone quick to dismiss an art form or human being simply because they do not conform to their limited values is using the part of the brain that, in less subtle individuals, is also used to make a distinction between white and black skin.

~~~

In the Metalwork class, I am stabbed in the buttocks with a large pair of dividers. The points are driven into my flesh and draw blood. Later, the teacher is showing the boys how the belt system works on the lathe. I hang back from the crowd. He turns to me to see if I understood what he has been saying. I cannot grasp the working of the machine even when he explains it to me slowly. I have already had an accident with one of them. I am terrified of its vibration, it makes me feel sick. He shouts at me to get closer. I am also terrified of standing near my attackers. Last week they struck me in the leg with a hammer; my leg was in agony for days after that. This goes on forever. I cannot imagine a time when it will not happen. They never stop and they are getting worse...

~~~

I was not a 'real' person, I knew that. Now I was being taught I was not a man either. PE, that most dreaded of subjects, was upon me once more. The violence always intensified in the changing room or in any of the sports areas. Attempts were made to drown me in Swimming. Balls were hurled into my face or stomach. My legs were kicked so frequently they ended up a permanent shade of yellow-purple. As the years went by, these attacks had been increasing in severity.

Beyond overt physical abuse, PE had made it clear to me, and everyone else, that my body was nothing to be proud of. I was considerably smaller and scrawnier than any of the other boys in my class, had bone-white skin, and possessed terrible muscle co-ordination. The back covers of my superhero comics often featured adverts for Charles Atlas and his 'dynamic tension' method of building up the body. These sported two pictures: the 'before', usually a miserable, weedy-looking guy, and the 'after', a proud, Herculean figure with muscle layered on muscle. The 'before' looked like the Hulk by comparison with me.

My undernourished body was singled out by my peers as being the most laughable in the class. Finally, like many on the spectrum, I was a late developer in puberty. My pitiful frame would not develop any body hair (particularly pubic) until my late teens.

Terrified of this ghastly fact being made public, I asked the PE teacher to excuse me from Whitehill's compulsory showers. As I made my plea I found myself experiencing a new type of shame in the presence of an adult. I knew that the man had little respect for me as he had a habit of shouting at me and my poor physical performance in the sports arena. Despite this, I never got any impression of real malevolence. I reasoned he was probably just a callous sort with no time for weaklings like me. Unfortunately, I had no idea just how callous. He asked me to explain my reasons. I could not as shame froze me. After a torturous thirty seconds or so he suddenly pointed at his crotch and said 'Is it about that? Och, away!' No insult from any student had ever cut so deep. Despite being shocked by the crudity of his gesture, I did not give up. I told him about the humiliation and the beatings. I was clearly terrified for my safety, a fact he had to have been blind not to see. It meant nothing, he simply brushed my pleas aside with a dismissive 'Away, out!' And that was it, I was sent off to the showers. As you can imagine, things went downhill from there on.

~~~

Shortly after this, The Event occurred. The Event was the culmination of the past year's escalating brutality. Afterwards I never looked at the human race with the same eyes. I often wonder if all the previous attacks had been a simple testing of the waters for a new level of assault. It happened on an ordinary day, at the end of a normal PE lesson.

I'd been ridiculed, kicked in the legs and had a football smashed into the side of my head. I was undergoing my usual round of extreme physical humiliation in the changing room when it happened. As I pulled my shirt over my head, I realised the other boys had stopped mocking and were now staring at me in silence. The moment was awful and I knew that it was the prelude for something far worse. It was obvious I had to get out as quickly as possible. I had always made a point of sitting next to the door, so all I needed to do was open it. As I did, the entire room attacked me.

I remember this moment with absolute clarity: I was rising to my feet and reaching to the door at my left. I saw a sudden rush of bodies surging towards me like a wall just instants before someone flicked the light off, pitching the changing room into total darkness. I found the handle a moment before they slammed me into the door, driving the air from my lungs and causing the wood to creak. I was punched from all sides and driven to my knees by kicks to the backs of my legs. Some hands grabbed my hair and dragged me down towards the floor where they started to stamp on me. Falling backwards, I pulled the door towards me, opening a sliver of light into the room; at this, the mass of bodies suddenly drew back and I was able to pull myself up and out into the corridor, colliding with the wall opposite. With the changing room door closed and the room quiet, everything looked perfectly normal. Anyone passing would have no idea what had just happened. I knew I could not go back in there, so I staggered off to the nearby Swimming department. I was bleeding heavily, had double vision and difficulty standing up. I hid in one of the swimming cubicles for a while, glad that no-one found me. I was more afraid of facing the teacher and his 'adult' contempt than another attack.

~~~

It took me years to see just how lucky I was that day. With the room in darkness, the opening of the door must have looked like someone entering from the outside. Had the light not been extinguished as I grabbed the handle, the other boys would have seen it was just me and pulled me away from it. If they had succeeded in dragging me down onto the floor they would have continued or even escalated their attack, stamping on my head as well as my body. Caught up in the violence of the moment, they might not have realised what they were doing until it was too late. They could have left me badly injured or worse.

I'd been mobbed before, but never with such ferocity. There was not even a token pretence at play, no jeers or insults, just a savage, criminal assault carried out in almost total silence by a pack of animals genuinely out to inflict injury. I don't know why the attack was so co-ordinated. Perhaps the boys had planned it or perhaps the moment was just inspired by a perfect storm of predator/prey signals that PE changing rooms are saturated with. The worst thing about the assault was it had not been instigated by any one person. The

The entire room attacked me

ringleader was not there that day; the core group was not even at the front of the attack. What slammed me into that door was a mass of ordinary adolescents who would not even be considered bullies by the standards of this society. One of the boys leading the attack had been relatively civil with me up till that point; actually talking to me on one or two occasions.

I have never left that room. Of all my Whitehill memories, The Event is the most indelibly etched. I am still at that door, trying to open it as they move in on me. I can still feel the pain, the fear and, most cutting, the shame. My teacher's reaction to my earlier plea made it clear that I had no hope for protection, worse still, that I was contemptible for seeking it.

In theory, PE teaches the benefits of healthy physical activity and, through game sports, encourages team behaviour. This is indeed what it would teach in an ideal world, one in which human beings did not attack their disadvantaged. Sadly such a world does not exist and never has. In *this* world, PE teaches pack behaviour by setting young people up in aggressive, competitive situations in which they are able to witness the physical underperformance and deficiencies of their weaker own. In fact, there is considerable research that suggests bullies are able to detect, at an animal level, hesitance borne of vulnerability in the body language and physical performance of their peers. PE is the one subject perfectly designed to focus such awareness.

Adolescents are not children; they are young people with an adult level of bodily awareness and an adult capacity for shame. The brutal reality is that ordinary teenagers, left to their own devices, will mercilessly degrade any anatomy they find wanting, often with appalling consequences. Outcasts and class runts tend to have little physical pride; the ritualised humiliation of PE is the one thing that can be relied upon to mercilessly tear even that from them. Every PE lesson arms bullies with the most terrible ammunition, ammunition which can be used can destroy a young girl's self image or emasculate a young man. By the time PE was finished with me I couldn't look at my own body in the mirror.

I am finding it hard to write this at the moment because of the rage - the outrage - these memories awaken in me. I found myself experiencing similar feelings as a young adult, when I discovered a leaflet extolling the 'benefits' of PE in the waiting room of my local health centre (awaiting medication for mental health problems Physical Education had contributed to). To me, the article read like a piece of Nazi literature. I got halfway through the second page before I tore the thing to pieces. Much of the propaganda centred on the 'boosting of self-esteem and social inclusion in young people'; this was possibly true, Physical Education may indeed promote such things for the average, well-adjusted physical specimen. What I had realized, by that point, is that for those less fortunate it does the exact opposite.

It is truly sickening to listen to praises sung about this vile subject in the face of the damage it inflicts on so many young people. (Regardless of health issues, I have never seen any indication that the amount of pointless activity enforced during PE makes any real difference to the health of the less mobile in our ranks. Nor have I met any of these non-physical sorts who suddenly changed their lifestyles because they discovered the 'joys of physical activity' after years of being conditioned to despise it. Everyone I know abandoned it the moment they left school.)

We've had the benefits of this wonderful practice shoved down our throats for the last century, now let's hear the other side of the story. In outcast culture, PE is the most feared subject of all, a brutal leftover from an earlier era that represents the officially sanctioned face of school cruelty. It destroys self-confidence and inhibits the social inclusion of physically and emotionally disadvantaged youngsters. It is guilty of something no-one within education has ever had the courage to admit; a truth faced by every outcast and under-dog from the very beginnings of the school experience. Physical Education is, and always has been, the one subject which *actually promotes bullying.*

Sadly, the unspoken rule within education is that a young person's suf-fering does not hold the same level of seriousness as that of an adult. This attitude is at its most pronounced in PE, where adolescents (at least at an emotional level) are not looked upon as full human beings, possessed of full emotional depth. Such individuals, according to this robust thinking, are incapable of sustaining lasting emotional damage, regardless of any level of fear, pain or shame inflicted on them. This process of marginalising certain types of person and, in doing so, diminishing both their feelings and their worth, is called dehumanisation; it is an extension of a much larger problem I call the 'Conceit of the Adult' (which I'll address in later chapters). Anyone who wants to argue otherwise should consider this example: our educational system doesn't think twice about subjecting vulnerable young people to the trauma of enforced stripping; a violation of physical privacy which, were it inflicted on an adult, would fall under Rape Crisis Scotland's definition of sexual violence.

This notion that young people can be infinitely tormented without snap-ping poisons the relationship between these youngsters and the system. The lesson it teaches them runs something like this: 'It does not matter what you feel. We say that our methods cannot cause you pain, and if they do then it is your fault. We can do anything we want to you. You are not important. We only care about the normal ones, the strong ones, the better ones, the popular ones, not your kind'. The educational system will always deny teaching this lesson but that is unimportant because I assure you it is the only one my kind have ever received.

~~~

School's capacity to damage may be more profound and serious than even this. Recent studies of children from backgrounds of domestic violence has revealed that abused youngsters' brains often undergo physical changes similar to those of war veterans. Brain scans show that the part of the brain which regulates the flight-or-fight response, the hypothalamic-pituitary-adrenal axis, can be reprogrammed to a hair-trigger, resulting in bursts of aggression with little or no cause. Strangely, I haven't heard of such studies being applied to the neural consequences of school abuse, specifically where this is carried out at a collective level. I only point this out because of certain responses my experiences instilled in me.

The Halfman left me with some serious mental baggage. I've seen a couple of one-armed men since his death and each time my gut has clenched into ice; however this reaction is nothing by comparison with the legacy of White-hill. Aggression, even slight aggression, in individuals is something I find deeply disturbing and can often overreact to. Small threats can all-too often become huge threats in my eyes, and even non-threats can occasionally be misinterpreted as such. However, my response to groups of young males (and not even aggressive ones) is much more extreme. I don't know how much of this is neural or psychological; I suspect a bit of both.

To this day, seeing gatherings of youngsters engaged in even mock aggression produces violent, instantaneous revulsion that far outstrips any other response I am capable of. No matter how often I see or hear this, I never get used to the sharp jolt of panic and involuntary loathing such a sight triggers. This response does not occur with single individuals, no matter how violent (and I've met a few), only with groups, and even with groups who are not aware of my existence.

Thinking logically, I know that these are simply youngsters enjoying their own company. Yet with a certainty as concrete as the ground beneath my feet, every instinct tells me that I am *not* looking at people like me. I am looking at *The Enemy*, a type of animal whose life has no worth; a pack that is dangerous to me, that hates me, wants to hurt me and therefore *has* to be hated and *has* to be hurt in return.

THE WANDERER

I discovered the wonders of truancy by the simple act of turning right and walking down a side street instead of continuing along towards Whitehill. It was almost impossible for me to do this as truancy was in direct violation of The Rules. My reasons for carrying out this monstrous act were simple: I couldn't take any more abuse. After The Event and after the PE teacher's reaction to my plea, I understood the truth: I was prey for all. They could do anything they wanted to me. I could expect no mercy from my peers and no help from authority. Every day I walked the road to school paralyzed with fear at the prospect of being thrown into that arena once more. The only alternative was 'dogging' school (dogging = dodging = truancy).

Some of my truancy was spent at Mum's house, although this wasn't always an option as she was often too drunk to open the door. I was not without shelter however. During the urban overhaul of the 60's and 70's, Glasgow boasted a fine selection of abandoned buildings to lurk in. Rejected by other children and desperate to escape The Halfman's rages, I had made these ruins my playground and sanctuary from earliest childhood.

One voyage of exploration, carried out when I was nine (a month before The Halfman's second attempt on Mum's life) yielded an indescribable treasure: a discarded copy of CREEPY # 28 (August, 1969). This black and white Horror anthology boasted a chillingly surrealistic cover by artist VIC PREZO, depicting a huge, skull-headed bat creature swooping down on a helpless victim. The interior stories were a well-illustrated mixture of Horror, Fantasy and SF with endings far more morbid and downbeat than anything I had read up till that point. The magazine's adverts were as engrossing as its stories. A world of Horror toys and books the like of which I had never dreamed of, and a back issue selection featuring the stunning artwork of FRANK FRAZETTA, his classic covers depicting marauding Neanderthals and 'The Swamp God', a surviving T-Rex lurching out of primordial fog and ooze.

Returning to these empty havens in my adolescence was as natural as breathing (so far as I was concerned, buildings were usually at their best with the unnecessary people removed). I enjoyed an unfamiliar calm as I read and drew there. One of their many benefits was a fine selection of wallpapers to be eaten while rendering the latest image of the Hulk or Iron Man.

The 70's were the most violent period of my life; strangely this seemed to be reflected in the media around me. Television had become progressively harder in its depiction of real-life conflict with swearing and blood where there had only been clenched teeth and raised voices before. Comics also seemed to slip into an unusual viciousness during this period. A British boys' publication called ACTION offered mutilation, decapitation and the sight of the elderly being kicked to death in stories like HOOK JAW and KIDS RULE O.K. (which debuted on my fourteenth birthday: Sept 11 1976). On the other side of the Atlantic, DC and Marvel were venturing into this territory with titles like THE SPECTRE and DEATHLOK THE DEMOLISHER.

The Spectre, easily the most powerful of all DC's characters, was the ghost of a murdered policeman who dispatched killers with methods ranging from the imaginative to the downright ghastly. It's a real shame Hollywood hasn't recognised this character's potential as he incorporates elements ranging from the gothic style of Tim Burton all the way to the graphic viciousness of the SAW movies. Deathlok, on the other hand, was a bad-tempered, partially decomposed cyborg/zombie trying to survive in a post-apocalypse America. Unlike his more glamorous counterparts The Six Million Dollar Man and the Bionic Woman, Deathlok was more inclined to blow an opponent's head off with his trusty laser gun than actually bring them to justice.

The Spectre's and Deathlok's worst excesses paled next to those of WAL-

LESTEIN, a black and white 'adult' Horror digest from Italy that I chanced across while raiding a bin. Wallestein was the same size as the COMMANDO digests I was familiar with. Since I equated this format with war comics I couldn't understand why the volume didn't feature this particular subject. In fact, the contents turned out to be as far from familiar territory as anything I had ever encountered. The hero of the piece, Lord James, or 'Jimmy' Wallestein was a typical playboy adventurer with a beautiful girlfriend and endless amounts of money. Like other adventurers he had a habit of sticking his nose into dangerous situations in the name of justice. At this point, the story departed from the usual formula as Jimmy, in moments of strife, whipped off his rubber mask to reveal he was in fact the fearsome WALLESTEIN MONSTER; a hulking bullet-proof avenger with a face like a bowl of evil porridge.

In this particular issue the violence was unprecedented. Some bad guys had their heads kicked off their shoulders; a number of naked women were murdered; a man was stabbed through the eye with a dagger while another was swung headfirst into tree, smashing his brains out in a spectacular gummy spray. I was appalled. What I was holding was clearly not a 'normal' comic at all. (The idea of comics for adults and not kids was as absurd as men landing on the sun.) It was clearly a 'bad' comic, possibly even an 'evil' comic for people who had something wrong with them. After reading it I threw it away, suspecting I could get into trouble for simply having it in my possession. To be honest, violent fare of this type never inspired similar thoughts in me. It was the brutality of real life, of ordinary people that was responsible for the awful feelings festering inside me, not these pallid imitations I saw on paper.

Truancy was the highpoint of my adolescence. Along with my comics, it helped me survive that terrible time. I sought, and found a magical place where I could be free from pain and persecution; free to read comics without being told how stupid I was; free to draw whatever I wanted without being ridiculed as talentless. I could be myself without fear of being attacked. I could sit on the floor or an old sofa, eat paper and draw monsters and heroes. Several versions of 'No Scream' were produced during my time in these places. I did much of my best drawing as a truant, and even laughed occasionally simply because I was free enough to do so. It was wonderful.

Unfortunately it was also illegal. The authorities eventually caught up with me, dropping in to discuss my attendance record with The Halfman. I was visiting Mum at the time and was told, by phone, to get back to the house. He was waiting for me in the living room when I arrived. He took his time. I couldn't get up off the floor once he was finished. This was a definite no-win situation. He'd shattered an oak walking stick across my back and then lashed me with a leather belt a couple of months earlier for the crime of 'allowing' myself to be bullied, now he was beating me senseless for the crime of trying to avoid it. He had made his mind up anyway: my truancy was due to my being 'MAD like my MOTHER was'.

I lay with my face pressed against the threadbare living room carpet, my mind jumping from subject to subject, a rapid montage of comic images and concepts: alien collectors who stole entire villages, who fed on radio waves and could be poisoned by certain frequencies; a black and white strip from one of my British reprint annuals which ended with the bad guy being eaten by a giant moray eel; another story from an American SF/supernatural anthology comic featuring buried robots with absurd hinges on their necks... who buries robots, and why did they have hinges on their necks in the first place?

~~~

It speaks volumes about the values of education that attendance should be prioritized over protection. Should a young person be attacked mercilessly, they can expect little help; should they try to walk away from this abuse, then they will find the authorities coming down on them like a ton of bricks.

For a long time I was ashamed of my truancy. Being a person who respected and was perhaps even obsessed by The Rules, I considered this shame wholly deserved. With the passage of years, I became stripped of any illusions concerning education and finally understood that truancy was my right and was, in fact, the most sensible thing I ever did in school. These days, I am proud of being a truant. I recommend it to anyone who is being bullied and is thinking of harming themselves; I particularly recommend it to anyone who is considering taking a gun into school.

Reporting your plight may not get you any attention but truancy will. There is a power in that, a power to be used. My last word on the subject is this: you are a human being; school does not own you. If your school is allowing you to be attacked then it is your right to either demand protection or walk away from the source of the abuse. As a citizen of any civilized society, your first right is to protection.

Unfortunately, as so many young people have come to realize, this is the first right education violates with its hopelessly outdated approach to such things. Returning to Whitehill, I was given an attendance card (or 'doggers' card, as it was known). This had to be signed by a senior teacher every day. The teacher in question was an intimidating sort although, after a while, he turned out to be fairly reasonable, if blunt. He asked me why I had been playing truant. For once someone was listening, even if it was simply because he wanted to know my reasons for breaking the law. It was hard not to say something as I was gripped by a terrible sense of shame for this heinous crime and

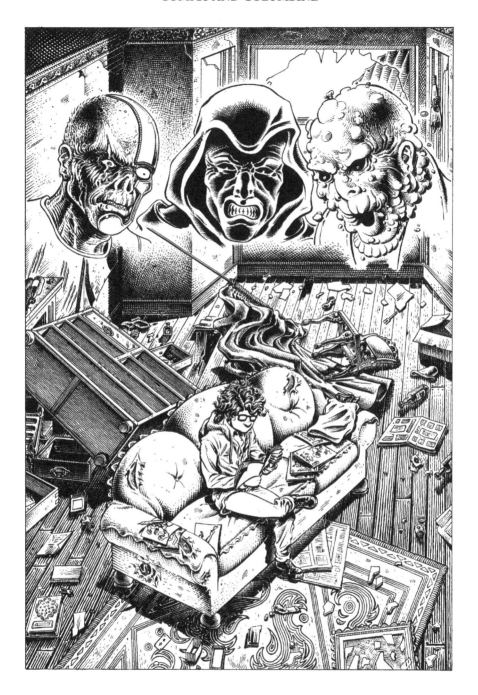

The truant

desperately wanted to explain my reasons. Yet my experience with the PE teacher was so awful that I was afraid of a second contemptuous dismissal. Finally I gave in. Telling the truth hadn't worked with the PE teacher, perhaps it would work with this man. For the first time in my life I told an adult what was happening to me… for all the good it did. After listening, the teacher's response was to ask me the now-familiar question: what was I doing to make the others attack me? He also asked for the names of the boys involved.

At that point, I realized there was some level of confusion going on. The teacher thought I was talking about a specific group. I had made the mistake of focusing on such a thing when I sought help in the old Whitehill, and got nowhere for my efforts. This time, I told the man that it was everyone who picked on me; everyone who constantly humiliated me, even boys, and girls, whose names I didn't know. I told him about The Event in the changing room and all the other group attacks I'd been subjected to, including the assault by the boys from outside the school. I explained that this had been going on from the very first day I had entered education. In my own limited fashion, I tried to communicate what it was like for a person to grow up with an entire species at their throat. This was not easy since there seemed to be no language to properly communicate the scale of the concept. During my explanation, I found myself once more stumbling across a series of 'holes' where there should have been words to explain my plight. I did my best, however. The teacher's response was unnerving: he simply stared at me in silence. After a moment, he signed the card and told me that he wanted see me tomorrow at the same time. And that was it … or so I thought.

A week later, I was removed from class and sent for an interview in a nearby primary school. I think the lady interviewing me was some kind of educational psychologist as many of her questions concerned facts relating to specific lessons. I was able to answer at least some of these. I presumed they were to determine how far I was lagging behind in my learning. Other questions were more abstract and these confused me. I found myself unable to grasp many of them, even after the woman explained what they meant. My responses to those I could answer seemed to confuse her in turn. The overall direction of the questions made no sense to me. I had assumed the purpose of the interview was to help me with the bullying, and wondered why the woman was not asking me about this. Perhaps she looked down on me for being a lousy truant? I was still feeling shame over this and decided that the most sensible thing was to cut to the chase, and tell her what I had told the teacher.

Her reaction was pretty much a replay of his. It was as though I had started speaking in Latin. She stared at me for a moment or two in what may have been disbelief, then asked me if I had reported what was happening. I replied that I had. 'Good, that's the right thing to do,' was her response, and she resumed the test as if nothing had happened. I remember her next question perfectly: what was the height of the average man? Six feet was my reply (I actually had no idea. Six feet just seemed to be a good all-round figure). This reply seemed to interest her far more than my plight. The questioning continued and my situation was not discussed again.

This was my first encounter with the 'blindspot' I referred to in the introduction; the society-wide denial of the scope and intensity of this type of abuse. A blinkered, ignorant viewpoint adopted by every professional I was to deal with in the coming years. Looking back now, it's pretty obvious what I had told these two had pushed the conversation into areas outside their intellectual programming. The idea that a human being could actually grow up outside society was not something either of these 'free thinkers' had been conditioned to grasp.

Once the questions were over, nothing more was done and I was sent back to Whitehill for more of what was deemed good for me. I had explained to a senior teacher and a psychologist the full extent of what was happening yet neither seemed able to accept what I told them. If these two could do nothing for me then what chance had I anywhere else? At this point I finally realised that the bullies could do anything they wanted to me and nothing was going to be done to stop it. I was alone, terrifyingly alone.

~~~

The ringleader has smashed a football into my face again as his cohorts gather around me, wondering what to do next. My glasses - held together by tape - are broken for the umpteenth time and my mouth is filled with all-too familiar taste of copper. Their laughter never stops. Every day I am surrounded by people who find the sight of my blood amusing or even exciting. The next six months, until the end of fourth year, will kill something inside me.

~~~

Then the year was over. We were all approaching sixteen and those who wished to leave school readied themselves for the adult world. And what had they learned? Apart from the academic fluff most would forget thirty seconds after stepping out of the building, they had been taught one lesson above all others: targeting vulnerability for abuse is good; everyone does it and you can get away with it. This 'freedom to hurt' is another of those Dark Lessons I mentioned earlier, the one taught to the bullies. If school was without rules that would be bad enough; the current situation is far worse.

The comparison I would draw to explain this involves the misuse of antibiotics. According to what I have read (and this may be an oversimplification), many of the problems we are experiencing with antibiotic-resistant diseases, stem from the practice of patients not finishing the full course of their medication. Apparently, this has allowed certain germs to survive, adapt and develop immunity to the drug that was used on them; in effect, a form of reverse-immunisation.

I think this is what is happening in our schools, a 'reverse immunisation' that our current system is inadvertently subjecting bullies to. Take a developing mind, a child, and make them aware of the importance of the rules; tell them these must be respected and obeyed. Once you have done this, allow them to break these rules without any real punishment. The lesson taught by this half-hearted exposure to authority at such an early age is simple: the rules are something that can do little to stop or punish you, therefore they are something to disrespect and ignore.

Bullying is the greatest pro-active lesson of all because the medium it is carried in is the pleasure of power. Through bullying, a child has their first real experience of pushing out at the walls of the human world around them, seeing just how far it can be bent out of shape by the power of their will. I'm no psychologist, like that overwhelmingly clever lady who interviewed me, but I'm fairly sure that allowing a young mind power over another, coupled with the guilty pleasure of getting away with something known to be wrong, can generate a thrill unmatched in intensity by any other experience available at an early age. Such a thing must be exciting, rewarding and perhaps even addictive. We know that neural changes can occur in abused children; perhaps similar alterations are possible in children who are abusers themselves.

Even if there are no physical changes, I suspect some profound emotional ones take place. If you allow a child or young person to experience this 'hit' on a daily basis, then the thrill of 'wrong' may become incorporated into their character. In effect, through the excitement of bullying, they become 'immunised' against respect for authority and the rights of others (just as their victims become immunised against self-worth and hope). Assuming this is the case, do you really think that bullies will just abandon this little pleasure after they leave school? This lesson will be carried around for the rest of their lives; it will override all lessons of right and wrong they will encounter in years to come. (Incidentally, the latest research from Harvard School of Public Health shows that men who admit bullying in childhood appear to run an increased risk of 'intimate partner violence' [IPV]. It's actually ridiculous that such an evident truth needed years of research to be recognised.)

Another example of dehumanisation is also taught here. This lack of punishment allows bullies to become accustomed to inflicting pain. In time, this familiarity leads them to see their victim as an object whose function is to soak up abuse (unless of course the object kills itself, in which case it's just a matter of moving on and finding another one). It is fairly grotesque that, through its unwillingness to face certain human facts, the one place intended to teach young people to function as members of our society actually teaches so many of them prejudiced and criminal behaviour.

I have a low opinion of criminals, particularly violent ones, so I am loath to admit that many may themselves be just as much victims of this educational incompetence as their targets. The boys who persecuted me were taught that violence is enjoyable and something they could get away with. Several of them fell foul of the law after leaving school. The ringleader in particular went on to a couple of high-profile criminal assaults. Bullied kids are really just human practice dummies in these unofficial lessons in criminal behaviour. I suppose in my own way I was the key component in the ringleader's learning experience, his training ground, his dry run for adulthood.

CARRIE WHITE BURNS IN HELL

C arrie White was burning in hell long before she died and no-one saw it, at least no-one saw it for what it was. CARRIE, the eponymous heroine of Stephen King's debut novel of the same name, is an isolated girl living with an abusive, religiously fanatical mother. To make matters worse, Carrie also occupies the bottom rung of her school's pecking order and has spent her entire life as the target of every mean joke thrown. What no-one suspects is that Carrie is also telekinetic, that she possesses the ability to influence matter through the power of thought alone.

At the climax of the story, the girl lets loose with her unearthly talent, laying waste most of her school and her town. The line 'Carrie White burns in hell' does not actually feature in the book; it is a piece of graffiti seen at the climax of Brian de Palma's 1976 film adaptation (and the recent remake). The message is clear: despite the appalling and obvious catalogue of abuse that triggered the devastation, the survivors are no closer to grasping the reasons behind the catastrophe.

CARRIE is a strikingly honest and very important book because, so far as I am aware, it is the first piece of popular fiction exploring the life and suffering of an outcast within the school system. In no uncertain terms, the book takes us on a trip through the horrendous cruelty and pressures that constitute the everyday life of a young pariah. Fleshing out his scenario, King also gives us a brief glimpse of the professional incompetence that allows a developing human being to be marginalised and tortured in plain sight. Finally, the book asks the all important question: if this, very real, intolerance is there for the underdog can they be blamed if it is all they have to judge the human race on? Apparently not, as it suggests in the final chapters, Carrie's retaliation is a horrible inevitability.

CARRIE is a book which deserves to be studied in all schools, not just because it is a first-class Horror novel; more importantly it is also an eye opening piece of life-based fiction that manages to communicate the plight of the pariah in popular form. In many ways the story can be seen as a chilling prophecy for the atrocities we are witnessing in schools now, with telekinesis filling in for automatic weaponry.

I first became aware of the book around the time the DePalma film hit the headlines. The subject of telekinesis immediately grabbed my interest as such a thing qualified as a superpower. Indeed one of Marvel Comics' X-MEN characters, MARVEL GIRL - soon to become the awesome PHOENIX - possessed this particular ability. Superpowers were a primarily visual art form; I hadn't seen them depicted in prose and was understandably intrigued enough to seek the book out.

I have to say that much of the novel's subtleties were lost on me, as was the eventual orgy of destruction. Since revenge was not part of my personality back then, the wrecking of the town simply came across as a waste of energy. One element that did stick with me was the opening scene with Carrie's awful experience in the showers during PE. This, above all, triggered some gut-wrenching memories.

What I did find curious were a number of reviews in magazines of the time. Many critics expressed disbelief at the cruelty inflicted on the hapless Carrie by her classmates. These reviewers had no problem accepting the idea of a girl annihilating her school via the power of her superhuman mind, they just could not grasp that the school could provoke such a reaction in the first place. I have to admit these opinions confused me as I knew from years of experience that such viciousness was an accurate depiction of the school experience; it was *exactly* the way teenagers reacted to outcasts.

Telekinesis may be the stuff of fiction but there was no fantasy in the treatment of Carrie herself. In his book ON WRITING and the introduction in the 2007 reissue of the novel, King revealed that his eponymous heroine was an amalgam of two youngsters who attended the same high school as himself. Both girls were outsiders from day one and both became the focus for a catalogue of abuse that maimed their lives. After leaving school, both girls died in tragic circumstances; one by her own hand. King postulates that the girl's high school experiences may have influenced her actions in this area.

Decades of tragic statistics prove this type of damage is commonplace in our society. I think it speaks volumes that, despite such facts being readily available, those worldly-wise reviewers of King's novel still refused to accept that school could inflict suffering of this magnitude. There is clearly a colossal gulf between the ideals of such people and the reality for young outcasts.

~~~

In many ways school culture is a caricature of adult society. Our everyday prejudices pale by comparison with their juvenile counterparts. These bigotries are at their most concentrated in schools where they shape virtually every aspect of adolescent interaction. Social divisions in our schools are far more pronounced due to the extreme nature of adolescent emotions. Left to their own devices, large groups of young people separate out into pecking orders more often than not maintained by intolerance and outright viciousness. In these, you are either accepted or you aren't; you are either 'cool' or 'uncool'; one of 'us' or one of 'them'; the pack or the prey.

In school, our adult intolerances are played out in fast forward with the usual tact and social correctness stripped away, resulting in pressures that would drive an adult to despair being magnified many times over. In all aspects of our lives we seldom, if ever, encounter anything as ferociously judgmental as this particular arena. School - certainly in the later years - is a place where definitions of failure and shame are wielded with the precision of a scalpel.

There is the added complication that we are reluctant to recognise criminal behaviour in juveniles. Except in the most extreme circumstances, our authorities do not attach the same importance to anti-social behaviour carried out within the machine of education. The average bully or group of bullies are able to get away with abuse that, were it inflicted in an adult situation, would result in immediate criminal proceedings.

A perfect example can be found in a recent study by the Woman and Equalities Committee which stated that one in three girls aged sixteen to eighteen has been sexually assaulted in British schools. According to the report, 'Groping, name calling and bullying are part of everyday life – but teachers dismiss the abuse as just banter.' The chairman for the committee expressed the following: 'It is difficult to explain why any school would allow girls to be subjected to sexual harassment that's been outlawed in the adult workplace.'

The example I am referring to is not actually found in the study itself but rather in the limitations of the people who made it. It is both sad and frustrating that the committee didn't have the same problems with the non-sexual, but just as criminal and just as damaging, abuse experienced by both boys and girls as part of the everyday school experience. The lesson here is clear: attach an 'adult' angle like sex to the problem and it will be taken seriously, otherwise it is still 'just banter' to be swept under the carpet.

This means that, for the kids at the bottom of those aforementioned pecking orders, the average school is little more than a torture zone in which these innocents have the foundations of their adult personalities, and lives, ripped from them on a daily basis by abusers who are for the most part beyond the reach of the law because their actions are not recognised as truly criminal.

That damage of this magnitude is regularly inflicted on children and young people in an institution intended to assist in their development is as astonishing as it is sickening. In the face of this, the only possible way for education to carry on with the illusion of righteousness is by doing what any organised body does when confronted with facts that pose a threat to its self image: that is to ignore them.

Sociologists have a term for this process: *Disqualification Heuristic.* This is the act of filtering out information that threatens or contradicts any group's worldview, in other words a closed mind operating at a collective and official level. *Organisational Deviance* is another term whipped up by this group to explain, amongst other things, just how education can inflict such damage in the first place. Roughly, this describes the process by which events in the real world can stray from their intended path, resulting in damage for an organisation or those involved with it. Another way of explaining this is that what is written on paper, what is intended to occur, is not always what will happen in reality. The random nature of real life will result in some level of (often cumulative) deviation from the original objective and it is this deviation which can hurt people.

This may sound like some form of dilute chaos theory, but I know it to be the truth. Education places children and young people in a position where they are able to attack their weaker own on a regular basis; this is Organisational Deviance. Another example of this deviance is evident in education's response. School employs a range of disciplinary methods to crack down on such behaviour; chief amongst these is the word 'Bullying'. As usual, this all works perfectly well on paper. Sadly, as these methods are based on an unrealistic, perhaps idealised, interpretation of human behaviour, they tend to fare badly in practice. There is an entire spectrum of abuse inflicted on school victims that cannot be seen by our society's moral awareness in the same way infrared light cannot be seen by our eyes. In most cases, the two-dimensional nature of these disciplinary methods impedes only the thinnest sliver of this. In real life, the word 'bullying' usually fails to stop bullying, more often than not, it doesn't even slow it down.

Should the young person report this failure and find that the school authorities are unable to accept what is happening, this is a Disqualification Heuristic at work. Carried to its ultimate level, this heuristic will allow the school to ignore any amount of abuse up to and including severe physical assault; a story we are all sadly familiar with.

Organisational Deviance, Disqualification Heuristic, wonderful terms; complex, serious and so understanding, yet, ultimately clinical, two-dimensional and communicating not the slightest iota of the unbelievable anguish and life-warping torment they allow. I'll try to rectify this mistake by adding a few of my own here.

SCHOOL ABUSE/COLLECTIVE ABUSE: these terms are intended to replace the useless word 'bullying' as it carries little seriousness in adult language.

HUMAN EROSION: the emotional and intellectual wearing down of a human being's sense of self by persistent abuse at the hands of their peers.

PROGRAMMED WORTHLESSNESS: this term is intended to replace the rather ineffectual phrase 'low self esteem' as it more effectively describes the type of damage inflicted by a lifetime of 'human erosion'.

SCHOOL POISONING: The process by which a young mind is clogged and warped by the negativity of their peers.

EDUCATIONAL MUTILATION: this is an all-round term to describe the, often irreparable, damage caused by overexposure to all of the aforementioned processes.

I offer these terms to anyone who has issues with their schooling. They might protect you or your children. Remember, the more they are used, and the more who use them, the more real they will become, and the greater protection they may offer.

~~~

I think of those tragic girls in King's books. Had they been raped, then their experiences would have been recognised as profoundly damaging; there would have been understanding and help for them. Sadly this is seldom the case with this type of violation. For these young women, there was no recognition. I think the worst thing for them must have been knowing they were alone; that no-one stood with them, no-one was there to tell them what had happened had not been their fault. I don't doubt that, had they sought help, they would have been told to 'come to terms' with their experiences. To this day, Educational Mutilation is amongst the most devastating and least recognized forms of damage inflicted within our society. Its capacity to cripple is seldom recognised even at the psychiatric level (although, as of this writing, recent studies at Warwick University now show that School Abuse is capable of inflicting greater and longer lasting damage than that inflicted by adults).

It is accepted that within relationships a person (husband, wife or otherwise) is capable of emotionally crippling their partner through a combination of sustained mental and physical abuse, much as The Halfman did it with Mum. The term for this is 'Learned Helplessness'. Although learned helplessness usually occurs within abusive relationships, it is actually at its most effective within abusive societies. A collective version of this Human Erosion, inflicted by groups of children onto their weaker own, will have a far more devastating effect than in any adult situation.

When you are exposed to such negativity during your formative years, it becomes something you carry around with you for the rest of your life; you are never truly free of it, you have no choice in the matter. Again I'm drawing on my own experiences but I don't think the girl in King's school took her own life because of what happened to her. I have a feeling she died because of what was *still happening* to her.

Incredibly, this level of mutilation is considered little more than 'rough and tumble' by much of our society. This is best demonstrated in online forums covering the subject. Many contributors to these sites dismiss school abuse as 'a fact of life', an inevitability that has to be accepted. Others express the opinion that it 'prepares youngsters for the realities of adult life'. The worst by far are those who suggest it is 'character building' and therefore actually beneficial. One thread that often crops up is the assertion by many that, had they been subjected to similar abuse, then they would have just 'stood up for themselves' or simply 'shrugged it off'.

These people have no idea what they are talking about. Theirs is the argument of someone fortunate enough to have experienced a little 'rough and tumble' and nothing more. It is not the argument of a person who has known the true helplessness of Educational Mutilation. The appreciation of abuse is relative and always worse for the abused. 'Character building' experiences of this sort are responsible for suicides and shootings alike. If we take this thug logic to its obvious conclusion then these individuals should have no problem with school shootings as such events simply prepare children for life in a gun-orientated society.

To any half-wit who still considers bullying character building, I recommend BULLYCIDE: DEATH AT PLAYTIME By Niel Marr and Tim Field. This book - an exposé of child suicide caused by bullying - is as harrowing a read as you will find. Its opening chapter- Strawberry Fields Forever - tells the story of Steven Shepherd, Britain's first recorded bullycide in 1967.

Beaten and degraded from his earliest school memories, eleven-year-old Steven's one day of happiness came from picking strawberries in a field near the village of Newburgh for three bob (fifteen pence). Stanley Holland, Steven's one childhood friend, remembers that Steven never stopped talking about the adventure. Steven returned to the field and lay down to die of exposure in a drainage ditch after a particularly vicious group assault by his classmates. He had trekked ten miles through a bitterly cold Northern rainstorm, discarding his shoes and spectacles on the way as he no longer had any need of them. His last words to Stanley after the beating were: 'I have said a prayer to God. Why do I have to live like this? If I do, I must kill myself.' His pitiful remains were found after fifty-one days.

At first, no-one was prepared to accept the reasons behind his death. Police pored over details of his life and quizzed residents of both his village and that near to where he was found. The word Bullycide, the very concept, did not exist back then. People preferred to believe that Steven was the victim of a child-murderer. No-one considered that he had done the job himself. Eventually, after an exhaustive investigation, during which details of the boy's tragic life came to light, the Coroner's verdict was: death by exposure. His closing statement was: 'This was the tragedy of an unhappy child who recollected one particular place where he had spent perhaps the happiest day of his life and in his unhappiness decided to go back to that spot.'

Steven's story is not is not the only one you will find in the book. There is Britain's youngest bullycide - Marie Bentham - who had just turned eight when she hanged herself with skipping ropes rather than face the torment heaped on her by her classmates; Denise Baillie who killed herself with an overdose after a barrage of terrifying threats; Vijay Singh who hanged himself; Maria McGovern, more pills... All the young souls snuffed out. Not even the tip of the iceberg; less than the smallest scraping of this hidden butchery, innocence driven to self-destruction by an evil many blithely accept as a fact of life. In the face of such facts, suggestions that school abuse is character building become little more than attempts to justify child-murder, pure and simple.

~~~

I had firsthand experience of this type of professionally-accepted brow-

Steven Shepherd and his strawberry field

beating during my counselling sessions at Huntley Lodge (a halfway-house I was living in after discharge from psychiatric hospital). My first counsellor was a very considerate woman who, despite problems grasping the ideas I brought to our meetings, was open minded enough to form a middle ground to help me communicate them. Sadly she left to be replaced by another person, one totally unsuited to the profession. In sharp contrast to her predecessor, this new counsellor seemed prone to interpreting things from a rigid and subjective point of view; this included a now-familiar attitude towards my schoolyard woes. During our sessions, she diminished the effects of my experiences by splitting them into single easy-to-deal-with (i.e. dismiss) events. No matter how hard I tried to describe exposure to persistent brutality, she insisted on focussing only on isolated incidents. This approach completely missed the point, that the most damaging aspect of this abuse is its *cumulative* nature. Like water, it has weight, enough of it will crush you.

I don't think my new counsellor employed this method consciously. Over the years I've encountered its use by many. Most people have neither the honesty nor the breadth of vision to see the cumulative effects of this problem. The impression I'm given is of a defence mechanism, a deliberate blindness akin to that used by my guidance teacher. I now know this is the result of another Disqualification Heuristic; a particularly entrenched one.

I liken our schools to Victorian factories. Both institutions churned out a specific product - textiles or educated young people - and both also produced toxic by-products. In the case of the factories it was poisonous chemicals dumped into the rivers with little care for their long-term effect (usually a lot of dead fish). In the case of our schools it is a form of human pollution - the collective negativity of their peers - that is dumped onto the kids at the bottom of the pecking orders; poisoning them to produce a sub-class of damaged young people. It took decades for the consequences of environmental pollution to be addressed and dealt with. It is appalling that we are still not honest enough to recognise the consequences of school poisoning in the human environment.

At this point, a comparison might be drawn between the creation of a classroom avenger and that of a cancer cell. In nature the runt dies, in human nature they often self-destruct or undergo horrific emotional malformation. Bombard a cell with toxins long enough and it will either die or become cancerous. Bombard a child with emotional toxins and they may self-destruct like little Steven, alternatively you may create a form of human tumour that will grow with little or no concern for the tissue around it. I think you can follow the analogy from here on.

As a culture we don't accept the truth about this crime because we have the luxury of ignoring it. We use terms like 'bullying' and 'teasing' to diminish its effect. But what if this insulating dishonesty were stripped away and this abuse inflicted on a group with the capacity to demand recognition within our society? Interestingly enough, such a thing did occur, at an American University called Stanford.

STANFORD

In 1971, psychologist, Phillip Zimbardo carried out the now-legendary Stanford Prison Experiment in the basement of Stanford University in California. Funded by the US Office of Naval Research, the study was intended to determine the causes of conflict between military guards and prisoners. It involved the creation of a mock-prison staffed by 24 student volunteers divided into guards and inmates, with Zimbardo as the superintendent. The objective was to study the degree to which even civilised individuals could abandon their own moral codes and slip into predetermined roles should circumstances demand. The results were not at all what anyone was expecting. Although intended to last two weeks, the experiment was terminated after six days due to the actions of the 'guards' who had begun to display increasingly sadistic tendencies towards the prisoners. This involved violent abuse with a focus on emasculation and dehumanisation.

Prisoners were regularly insulted and threatened; an atmosphere of powerlessness and subservience was enforced with sexual humiliation often used as a 'disciplinary method'. This regime was so effective that, even before the termination of the experiment, five of the prisoners had to be removed due to severe emotional trauma: depression, rage, acute anxiety and, in the case of one, signs of actual insanity. Curiously, although more than fifty people were aware of the experiment, not one - prisoners included - questioned its morality. It was only when the situation was highlighted by an outsider that Zimbardo realised even he had become totally absorbed in it, to the extent of accepting its cruelties without question.

The Stanford Prison Experiment became a landmark in the field of psychology; a notorious exposé of the dark side of human nature whose ramifications are still debated to this day. Anyone wanting to learn more will find a wealth of information online, including film clips of the experiment and interviews with both prisoners and guards. A 2015 film adaptation titled 'The Stanford Prison Experiment' stars Ezra Miller and Billy Crudup as Zimbaro himself.

There is still a degree of controversy and criticism surrounding the experiment and its results. However, regardless of conflicting interpretations, one aspect that elicited universal shock was the actions of the guards. Given power over their fellow men, these students responded with a level of callousness and sadism many outside the experiment found hard to believe. It was this viciousness that compelled Zimbardo to write 'The Lucifer Effect: How Good people Turn Evil.' Published in 2007 and based on thirty years of research, Zimbardo describes the piece as 'a psychological account of how ordinary people sometimes turn evil and commit unspeakable acts.'

To be honest, I don't see what all the fuss is about as I've spent most of my life observing 'civilised' individuals acting in a deplorably cruel and prejudiced fashion without any provocation whatsoever. For all its horrors, Zimbardo's experiment yielded no truths about the human animal that the average outcast doesn't discover in the first few years of their existence, and without such an elaborate setup.

It has been said the Stanford study cannot be duplicated nowadays for moral and ethical reasons. I have to point out here that this is not entirely true as this particular experiment is being carried out every day in our schools. All any researcher needs in order to achieve comparable results to Stanford is to study one day in the life of any school reject *anywhere*.

A typical school is a far more effective prison than Stanford ever was. Unlike the students of that university, the prisoners in schools have no choice: their incarceration is a matter of law. The bullies are the guards of this prison and the prisoners are the students selected as their targets. The teachers fulfil the roles of ineffectual prison administrators who have little power and often little inclination to stop these particular guards from doing what they like (Zimbardo himself became institutionalised into accepting the brutality of the experiment; anyone who thinks teachers are unable to fall prey to such conditioning is fooling themself). As with their adult counterparts at Stanford, the bullies/guards become hooked on what professor Zimbardo calls 'the pathology of power' and seek to maintain this by establishing regimes of utter viciousness. The prisoners are subjected to regular acts of humiliation, intimidation, emotional and physical abuse; In time, they become accustomed to it.

These brutal dynamics were never the product of some safely-contained experiment. They are present in every school and have been acted out since the very beginnings of education. All Professor Zimbardo did was make them visible for a brief period by inflicting them onto a demographic capable of communicating their plight, and doing so under clinical conditions. And still it was not seen for what it was: a normal, everyday event for younger human beings trapped in their own prisons called schools.

I envy the students of Stanford. At least they were allowed to voice their pain, and were given understanding for the mental problems awaiting them afterwards. In that sense they received answers and perhaps even closure. Over the next few years, participants of the study were asked to fill in post-experimental questionnaires on the effects of their experiences. Students were also involved in extensive group and individual debriefing sessions. One of these can be seen in an online video clip. It shows a former prisoner confronting his guard and discussing his maltreatment.

I watched this clip and felt rage at seeing this 'privilege of recognition' being handed out to an adult in the face of what is accepted —and buried— in our schools. Regardless of its so-called horrors, the victims of Stanford didn't experience a *fraction* of the suffering or the damage inflicted on the average bullied youngster. Not one participant of the study has committed suicide, nor engaged in any shootings over it. As a person who experienced years, not days, of severe maltreatment at school, I can tell you that particular experiment sounds like a picnic. I would take Stanford over Whitehill any day.

The shocking events at Stanford are hailed as proof of the darker side of man's behaviour. The experiment has supposedly taught us much about our own capacity for brutality. It is strange then, that we have learned so little from the far greater abuses in our schools. Our society allows countless Stanford-level violations of human rights to be inflicted on the most vulnerable section of our population on a daily basis, and does so without batting so much as a moral eyelash.

Many would argue it's not the same thing. The answer to that particular myth is this: are children and young people any less human because of the number of years they have spent on this planet; are they less able to feel pain and fear; less vulnerable to oppression and any less capable of being permanently damaged by overexposure to it?

So why is it considered serious when it happens to adults and not when it happens to kids? Simple, the students of Stanford were adults with established personalities. They could not be denied an audience because their assertive skills had not been crushed by a lifetime of such treatment. The appalling truth is that recognition of plight within our society has always boiled down to how much voice you have before, and after, your ordeal. Children and young people —particularly socially maladroit outcasts— have very little, if any at all. Sadly there is scant hope of this ever improving. The victims of this abuse are seldom able to highlight the problem as there are no debriefing sessions or post-experiment questionnaires waiting for them when they leave school.

The adult society that awaits them is not interested in the truth. More often than not, the victims are culturally browbeaten into silence and accused of self-pity should they refuse to comply. A few years ago, a prominent Scottish newspaper printed an article on Deborah Scott, a young woman who lost a court case against her school for failing to protect her from a sickening catalogue of abuse at the hands of her fellow students. The same newspaper rubbed some salt in the young lady's wounds when its resident agony aunt suggested that the woman should just 'grow up' and 'put it all behind her'.

The assumption that we have voluntary control over the pain encoded into us is both insulting and damaging. For years, I was ashamed of my 'weakness' in allowing myself to be affected by my Whitehill memories. Since then, however, I've encountered many whose school experiences have left them total wrecks. Scars carved deeply into a child do not suddenly vanish when they become an adult.

And why should they? I'm only saying this because there seems to be an assumption that adults who were victims of chronic school abuse should be immune to their experiences since these occurred in childhood, and children and adults are different people; end of story.

I'm not sure at what point, in the transition between our juvenile and adult selves, we are supposed to lose all connection to the emotions of our past. It certainly never happened with me and, to be honest, I don't think it happens to anyone. I once challenged a psychiatrist to explain, in plain language, what he meant by 'come to terms'. I found his answer pretty vague (and more than slightly evasive), but from what I was able to glean, I was supposed to achieve this goal by cultivating some new interests and building myself a new life out of these. Eventually I was supposed distract myself from my past using the healthy emotions this new life would generate. That's all very sensible, but what if the very mechanisms required to do this building are the first things destroyed by your past? What if, despite your best efforts, your memories always remain louder than your present because the very building blocks of this 'new life' are completely poisoned by your earliest experiences?

This attitude of 'grow up' prevails in our society because the majority does not suffer, only a minority does. This minority suffers to a degree our culture cannot face, therefore, it denies it (Disqualification Heuristic, again). The resulting silence allows our society the luxury of burying the truth. We ignore it in the past and we ignore it when it happens in the present; as a result, we don't learn anything. Just as Professor Zimbardo completely underestimated the depths of viciousness in civilized people, so does our educational system. We allow another generation to suffer the same brutality, to take their roles as victims or guards and let the cycle of violence continue unimpeded. The Stanford University experiment didn't start in 1971; it began with the arrival of compulsory education and is still going on to this day. For some, it never ends.

I think we should use Stanford as another anchoring point to look truthfully at the norm in our schools and ask ourselves a very important question: if inflicting such a regime on a fully-developed human being, one who could walk away from it at any time, could cause so much lasting damage, then what would it do to inflict worse on a developing child or teenager denied even that basic right? A youngster whose developing personality could permanently assimilate the damage like a retrovirus? The answer is that it is *vastly* more damaging.

~~~

There is no way our society could maintain its illusion of morality when faced by a crime of this scale, so it is important for us to cultivate a couple of myths in order to render the whole obscenity palatable, and avoid any accountability for the results. The first is what I call the 'other country' argument. At an almost unconscious level, we distance ourselves from juvenile society as though it is some faraway country we are reading about in the news, one with customs we are not allowed to interfere with. It has no connection to our adult, our *real* world. Any abuses of human rights that occur in this other country are inconsequential and do not concern us as we adults no longer live there.

The second myth is that of 'childhood innocence'. A child cannot be a criminal, therefore there is no crime. If there is no crime then there is no victim. Children simply cannot inflict lasting damage on one another as everything that happens in childhood and adolescence, no matter how extreme,

The Unwritten rule within education

is simply a form of play, and nothing else. Violence between children - and by that, I include emotional violence - is not 'real' violence and has no long term consequences. A child is not a 'full' human being. Its lack of development and depth acts as insulation against trauma inflicted by its peers. Although able to experience brief, transitory pain, children are incapable of suffering true despair. Only adults have the depth to feel this (I touched on this idea briefly when I related my PE experiences in Chapter Six).

This isn't even the most extreme example of this type of thinking. As late as the early 70's, there are instances of babies and small children being given medical procedures - many of a surgical nature - without anaesthetics. These were carried out under the belief that the nervous systems of babies were not developed enough to feel pain. I know from personal experience this attitude wasn't confined to infants either. In the late sixties, when I was a small child, a dentist attempted to pull one of my teeth without anaesthetic; the pain was unbelievable. I struggled out of the chair and ran into the waiting room with the angry dentist in tow. After a brief argument with my mother, the man grudgingly gassed me for the rest of the procedure. The same dentist also attempted to give me some fillings without anaesthetic a year later. Anyone who has watched Laurence Olivier torture Dustin Hoffman in MARATHON MAN might understand what that felt like.

Around this time, I was also having my nose cauterised on a semi-regular basis to deal with my persistent nosebleeds. Cauterising involves burning away tissue to accelerate healing. I was fortunate in that my condition allowed me to distance myself from this lesser pain for quite a while (I focussed either on comic images or the ribbed surface of the arm rest on the clinics chair). Had I been neurotypical, I would probably have been in agony and been told to shut up about it.

A microscopically more enlightened belief held by many at the time was that, although capable of experiencing pain, a tiny baby or young child was unable to remember the experience and therefore unable to suffer any emotional trauma as a result. It is a modified version of this theory that underscores our interpretation of school abuse. Although we now acknowledge young people to be capable of feeling pain we limit this to the physical definition of the word. This section of our population are still considered infinitely flexible lumps of emotional rubber resistant to any level of stress inflicted by their own, or similar, age group. Proof abounds that chronic bullying can provoke suicide or increase the risk of psychosis. Despite this, the attitude, still held by many, is that kids cannot suffer profoundly because they are kids, and all kids are shallow until proven otherwise. There is absolutely no logic to this callous assumption. I call it the 'Conceit of the Adult': a form of society-wide ageism so extreme that it crosses the line into dehumanisation.

~~~

I can give you a personal account of what it's like to be Carrie White or any other kid at the bottom. I know I've covered this in the book before but I think it deserves to be reiterated here. I'll tell you what exists at the lowest levels of those pecking orders: another world.

It's almost impossible to describe the brutality of that place. I'm not just talking about physical abuse here. Take your life, your entire network of friends and associates, every experience that allowed you to develop into the person you are; now reverse all of it and imagine that every moment of contact with those around you, every spoken word and gesture occurs for the sole purpose of hurting you. Contact with others consists only of threats and insults, all intended to tear you down. You cannot speak back; any opinion of your own will be demolished the second you voice it. Standing up for yourself will only invite further attack from every direction. Your attackers never stop; they never run out of ways of putting you down. There is no-one to help you, no-one to listen because no-one wants to know. There is no place beyond your abusers and the suffering they inflict; no world beyond the fear.

This torture is perpetual motion. It goes on forever, an endless conveyer belt of pain and anguish. Every minute, every hour, every day, every week, every month, every year— all the years of your life, all of it steadily mounting up inside your head like pounds, then tons of pressure. You live a life of absolute helplessness. You go bed at night not wanting to wake up in the morning. You wake up in the morning looking forward to going to sleep at night. You face the coming day hoping you won't be noticed. Every corner in front of you may hide an assault on your body; every mention of your name may be the opening for an assault on your mind. This is what it is like to be the prey.

One short comic story that perfectly illustrates this is Paul Chadwick's THE UGLY BOY, a six page backup story in CONCRETE: ECLECTICA #1. (Dark Horse Comics, April 1993). The ugly boy is Arthur Harcourt, aged nine, who is cursed by a facial deformity that makes him a target. The boy suffers a hellish life consisting of one attack after another until, finally, he can take no more. Arthur runs away to die of exposure in the countryside, just as Steven Shepherd did in his strawberry fields. (I've often wondered if Chadwick had heard of little Steven.) Arthur Harcourt is not thinking of peace in his last moments, however. Like Carrie White, his thoughts are of vengeance, of slaughtering his classmates for their transgressions, their *crimes* against him. The tale is a heartrending example of innocent hatred spawned by school poisoning. Arthur is so polluted by the cruelty of his peers that he is inwardly deforming as well. Arthur Harcourt wasn't real but Steven Shepherd was. I often wonder what is wrong with this society that it allows such mutilation to happen in plain sight. That's a question asked by many.

Currently there is no effective method of protecting these youngsters. They are on their own and they know it. It is their place to accept this suffering because the ruling classes, the adults, say it is the natural order and they have no choice in the matter. But what if this section of the population is beginning to say otherwise? What if they have reached a point in their collective pain where they now recognise the injustice being inflicted on them and are prepared to do something about it?

A culture of abuse has always existed within education; it was only a matter of time before a culture of retaliation sprang up to confront it. Blinded as we are by the Conceit of the Adult we refuse to credit our youngsters with the capacity to inflict real damage on each other, nor with the emotional depth to experience the resulting anguish. Tragically, this blinkered attitude also seems to stop us recognising the mindset that this anguish can provoke: the mindset I believe we are seeing now.

DIAMONDS IN COAL

S trangely enough, I did encounter some professionals who rose above Whitehill's culture of boundless poison. The first of these was a Modern Studies teacher by the name of Mr Clelland. I first met Mr Clelland when I took (or rather, was given) his class in third year. Mr Clelland called me 'Mr Campbell' instead of 'Campbell' and I liked him for that. Almost immediately he recognised my interest in drawing and asked me to produce cartoons to advertise a school magazine called 'Scope'. Later, he commissioned me to copy some satirical cartoons onto large sheets of paper for the classroom wall; a task that educated me on the political points made by the cartoons. Mr Clelland gave me my first fibre-tip pen, a Tempo or Papermate fineliner with a cream coloured body. This led to me drawing with ink as opposed to just pencil.

He was a comics fan too. I found this hard to believe. Here was an intelligent adult, a teacher no less, who actually liked comics and did not ridicule their reading. His favourite cartoonist was BILL TIDY and his favourite painter was RICK GRIFFIN. Upon realising that I was a comics fan myself, Mr Clelland loaned me a number of books on the subject. These amazed me; there were *books about comics*. In their pages, I found images and stories from comics I had never even heard of. Some were so strangely or crudely drawn and possessed such oddball (and even 'adult') content I could not see how they came to be published. Mr Clelland explained these were 'underground' comics, printed by independent publishers who had no connection with the bigger companies.

Using examples from his collection he explained the concept of comic storytelling, likening it to the visual narrative of feature films. I found these discussions immensely helpful as this type of comparison had never occurred to me. Mr Clelland liked my artwork; although he did comment on the rather haphazard approach to shadows. He explained that since lighting, for the most part, came from one direction, shading should lie on the opposite. By way of demonstration he drew my attention to another of his books; this featured a black and white reprint of a classic Marvel horror story drawn by his favourite mainstream comic artist JIM STERANKO. Titled 'At the stroke of midnight' (TOWER OF SHADOWS # 1, September 1969), the story was a masterpiece of cinematic-level storytelling and chiaroscuro shading that opened my eyes to the power of rendering form through shadows alone. On the subject of direction, Mr Clelland also noticed I tended to draw motion and sequence from right to left. He pointed out that, for the most part, the human eye scanned from left to right which is why writing and comic strips ran in that direction. I took note of this fact and put it to good use in subsequent pictures and cartoon strips.

Amongst the many books he allowed me to read was THE SCIENCE FICTION BOOK by Franz Rottensteiner. This volume - a pictorial history of Science Fiction - introduced me to the work of one of the most influential artists of my life: VIRGIL FINLAY. Finlay was a 'Pulp' era SF and Fantasy illustrator renowned for his meticulous use of stippling - a time consuming drawing technique which produces the illusion of tonality via carefully applied dots (an effect that looked like a hand-rendered version of the old newspaper halftones I found so absorbing in early childhood). During the heyday of Fantasy digest publications many magazines were printed on cheap paper pulp. Stippling was one of the few methods of rendering decent shading on this low quality material, and Finlay was a master of the effect.

Finlay's textures were even more intricate than Nestor Redondo's. I just lost myself in them: gently undulating fields of tiny black dots that expanded, thickening into ordered yet somehow moving patterns of neat, round-tipped dashes; these kept the right amount of minute distance from each other as they eventually fused into even more intricate meshes of cross-hatching edged up effortlessly against little round-tipped white strokes on a black background; a negative pattern that sprayed out into the deepest shadows. His drawings were enmeshed by an ocean of vibrant textures that rippled and wove around any object they were used to render; totally absorbing and delicious to the eyes.

Stippling had a well-ordered, linear quality that was easily controllable since all it required was intense concentration and fastidious application. This was not threatening to me, far from it: the technique was intensely soothing for my natural stress levels (to the extent that even thinking about stippling could lessen them).

Creatively, it allowed me to produce and control the wonderful patterns that so absorbed me during my childhood and do so while rendering pictorial images. Naturally I fell in love with the technique and decided I had to master it too. From that point on I stopped working in pencil and moved over completely to pen and ink. I became completely obsessed with the technique to the exclusion of all other concerns. It was stippling and nothing else thereafter. I loved Finlay's work and wanted to become a master of it. I wanted to be Virgil Finlay.

~~~

Mr English was not an English teacher; he taught Biology. He had bright red hair and his nickname was 'King Carrot'. Mr English had a great sense of humour that, strangely for Whitehill, was devoid of cruelty. Although not a comics fan himself, he still liked my artwork and would always ask me about my latest piece or 'ghoul', as he occasionally called them. I remember him saying my drawings got better the more he looked at them. One in particular, a pre-TERMINATOR robot skeleton, drew considerable praise. He commented on its believability as, according to him, the various joints seemed perfectly functional.

For me, Biology was the easiest of the science-based subjects. Unlike Chemistry and Physics, Biology, for the most part, concerned itself with mechanical issues like the various organic structures required to keep life going. The subject was still taught using the same easy-to-understand diagrams which had made first year Science so accessible to me. The problems set in with the arrival of biochemistry. The pictures gave way to long chemical names and formula made up of numbers and chemical initials rather than the three dimensional surfaces I had been able to follow in the past. This made Biology impossible as I was unable to focus on anything that confused me or did not hold my interest (despite my best efforts, I have no voluntary control over this process; though I would dearly love to).

Things came to a head when Mr English looked at my attempts to follow a lecture in one of his classes. It was painfully obvious that I was incapable of understanding the lesson. He took me aside and asked me if I thought it was worthwhile continuing with his class. I told him I couldn't follow what was being taught. I tried to explain the gaps in my thinking, the white holes I blundered into when attempting certain trains of thought. We agreed that it would be for the best if I were to abandon Biology. He did not judge me, nor did he make any disparaging comment at my utter failure in his subject. I still kept in touch with Mr English after that; occasionally popping into his classroom to show him my latest 'ghoul'. On my last day at Whitehill he wished me luck and told me to 'Keep up with the drawing.' Thanks to him and others of his kind, I did.

~~~

'There is fair amount of difference between conflict and carnage,' said Mr Winpenny as we discussed the literary depths of my Hulk comics. Unlike Mr English, Mr Winpenny did teach English and was very good at it. Between lessons, we often discussed comics, classic Science Fiction films and writing in general. During this particular discussion (in which Mr Winpenny mentioned that he did *not* like 2001: A SPACE ODYSSEY, the best space film of all time, at least according to my SF film books) the topic strayed over to characterisation and conflict in stories. To be honest I had no time for such a thing; all I wanted from a story was for the characters to work with each other and solve whatever problem they were faced with.

Unless the main character was fighting a villain, human conflict was an ugly and unwanted addition to entertainment. I could not see why others were so interested in it. Mr Winpenny explained that drama often worked around people having different viewpoints and reactions in any given situation. These alternative attitudes often added realism and intrigue to a story. He asked if I had observed the differing perspectives of others in everyday life. I replied I had. Other people, by their actions, clearly did not think like me, something I considered incredibly stupid.

As an example of my deep understanding of conflict within drama, I mentioned my issues of the Incredible Hulk. In these, the Green Goliath spent much of his time pursued by an American General called 'Thunderbolt' Ross. Such pursuits usually ended with the General letting rip with every weapon at his command. The Hulk's response consisted of throwing a mountain or a sizable portion of a city back at him. The all important 'character conflict' was in evidence in such actions.

There were **books** about comics

Statements of this sort, from a seventeen-year-old, often prompted suggestions that I return to my building blocks. It is to his credit that Mr Winpenny never made such comments about the limits of my thinking and instead tried to point it in other directions. His response was simply to explain the fine difference between opposing philosophies and the act of dropping a skyscraper on someone's head.

The original KING KONG was his Favourite Fantasy film (he had no time for the recent De Laurentiis remake). During one conversation on the film's visuals, Mr Winpenny referred to an artist called GUSTAV DORE as one of its chief influences. I later discovered a book of Dore's magnificent engravings in the school library; this opened my eyes to the atmosphere that could be generated by subtle line-work found in such classic illustrations.

Although not a comic fan to quite the same extent as Mr Clelland, Mr Winpenny was familiar with the medium and had some favourite artists of his own. Chief amongst these was renowned TARZAN artist BURNE HOGARTH (or *Burned* Hogarth as I initially believed he was called). Mr Winpenny recommended I study Hogarth as a way of learning the human figure. By sheer luck, a British publisher had recently released a new volume by Hogarth which retold the origin of the King of the Apes. Apart from his slightly repellent method of drawing knuckles, I found Hogarth's work to be extremely impressive. His various books on rendering the human figure are considered essential reading for anyone with a serious interest in drawing without reference. I certainly learned a great deal about anatomy from his work.

Another area in which Mr Winpenny encouraged me was writing. I had real problems with this subject. Despite discovering prose, words were not my home territory. I had an intuitive grasp of structure and was capable of efficiently listing a sequence of events on paper but not with any regard for spelling, punctuation or grammar; these little add-ons were still Greek to me. Beyond the mechanics of writing, Mr Winpenny also encouraged my creativity. Since I always used templates when starting out, the works I produced in his class were derivative at every level. In fact, they were clumsy imitations of HARLAN ELLISON and ROD SERLING.

My first attempt at creative writing concerned a German soldier billeted with a French family during the Second World War (not that such a thing ever happened). It was a fairly paranoid piece, full of suspicions of betrayal that were beginning to make sense to me by this point. I chose to write this shortly after glancing through a war novel given to me by my older brother. This was by the writer SVEN HASSEL. Although I did not copy the text of the book, I studied the structure and dramatic pauses of Hassel's short sentences and attempted to imitate them for my story. This proved quite successful as I was given very high marks indeed. In fact, upon the return of my story, I discovered a number of complimentary notes about my use of these techniques in the margins. My second assignment was more ambitious by far: I was going to try a 'character piece'; one that used this all important 'conflict'.

The character in question was me. The tale I submitted was a semi-autobiographical piece concerning the tension between a young student and an abusive teacher by the name of Mr Walters. There was very little actual creativity involved in the story as most of it was based on real life. Mr Walters was a fusion of the more prominent aspects of Mr Wood, The Animal and my Art teacher. (Recombination happened with vile diseases; I saw no reason why it shouldn't happen with vile teachers.) A genuine effort was made to rationalize Mr Walter's dislike of the boy. I based his motivation on opinions voiced by The Animal and Mr Wood. Both men had frequently commented on my clothes. From this I deduced that they liked everything to be clean and neat and abhorred anything that was untidy. Both had suggested that I was of a low intelligence and implied I was a lesser class of person as a result. This obviously meant that they valued smart minds and looked down on those they considered lacking in this area. Lastly, both had made comments on my being strange or weird. This particular criticism was lost on me as I could not fathom what they meant by it, or even why weird was bad in the first place; for this reason, I decided to omit this latter streak of bigotry from my composite-teacher.

In the finished piece, Mr Walters was depicted as a neatness-obsessed bully who only had time for intelligent people. The boy, known only by his last name of Cowan, was badly dressed and slow-witted. The much desired character conflict was inevitable. Despite his appearance, Cowan was not really a troublemaker, and spent most of his time simply trying to get by. The events of the story covered yet another trial-by-class at the boy's expense. After Mr Walter's latest diatribe - in which we are shown all his vital character insights - Cowan is left seething with rage and, unable to take any more abuse, contemplates an unspecified revenge attack on the teacher in the near future. (Cowan's desire for revenge was not really based on my own feelings at that moment; it was something I felt was expected of him as I had noticed that characters in books became angry much more quickly than I could and for a far greater number of reasons.)

By seventeen, I was butting heads with more professionals than at any other period of my life; and doing so without the slightest inkling as to why. Thinking about it now, Cowan's plight may actually have been a cry for help on my part; that, or at least an attempt to rationalize things (much like my childhood comics depicting The Halfman and The Arm). Mr Winpenny probably had no idea of this when he read the piece. In all likelihood, he probably thought the characterization was something I had created. Whatever he saw in the story, he gave me the highest marks I had been awarded for any subject: twenty eight out of thirty; the highest in the class.

There was more to come As he handed these out, Mr Winpenny praised my work, saying the characterization was well defined and that the story reached a conclusion in which one of the characters changed. He complimented me in front of the class, something no teacher had ever done before. At the time, I felt only mild confusion. It would take the better part of a month for the impact to filter through. When it did, it hit me like a freight train.

I remember sitting in the common room, in my alcove, chewing part of a plastic bag, when it happened. I felt the rush of a strange feeling that I now know was pride. The emotions did not take me entirely by surprise as I had been aware of them creeping around inside my head for the last couple of days. They were not feelings I recognised, so I found myself wondering what they were as they drew closer. This type of observation was quite normal for me. My emotions were free-floating pieces of thinking that often collided with me when I least expected them. This was one of those occasions. As I gnawed the plastic into tiny pieces, they hit me with full force: Mr Winpenny had complimented me! I couldn't believe it. He said that something I had created was of value. Despite my not being a 'real' person, the product of my thoughts possessed worth. I became so excited I almost threw up. I can still feel this recorded pattern of emotions welling up in me. A teacher actually complimented me on my thinking; unbelievable. Years later, as I took my first tentative steps into writing it was Mr Winpenny's supportive words that were with me.

~~~

An English teacher, a Biology teacher and a Modern Studies teacher; it is ironic that I learned more about art (and my own worth) from these men than from the so-called Art teachers at Whitehill. They were open-minded about comics, and also open-minded about me. They must have seen I was different but never judged me for it. They actually encouraged me in my dreams. I would have buckled under the criticism of the other teachers and given up on art and most likely on myself had I not allies at Whitehill secondary.

Mr Winpenny, Mr Clelland and Mr English. In every sense of the word these men were true teachers, able to respect and nurture an isolated young mind, even in a subject that was not theirs. They were a credit to their profession. I wish I could meet them again, just to thank them for treating me like a human being, like a person with feelings, during a time no-one else did.

CRITICAL MASS

The cartoon was pinned to the common room notice board. It was a fairly recognizable representation of me so whoever drew it had some degree of drawing skills. The culprits were a new core group of bullies who had formed as I moved into my last year of school. (I had stayed on because The Rules said this was the correct thing to do if you wanted to be successful in life.) These boys hailed from the year under me but shared the common room with all senior students. They were academic over-achievers who were as vicious as they were bright.

This cartoon was the latest in their campaign. It must have been truly funny because everyone else seemed to get in on the joke. I could hear them all laughing as I looked at it. Acts of ridicule were constant now, jammed together and overlapping. I would feel the sting of a previous attack just as a new one commenced. In the senior years, abuse moved on from physical to verbal. Since insults and putdowns were no longer followed by fists and boots, just the occasional threat, it was a situation I could easily weather, or at least so I believed. In reality I was buckling under a new kind of pressure I had never experienced before. It may have had something to do with my being older and possessing a marginally greater inkling of what was expected of me within society.

One thing which managed to hammer this point home was a poster I discovered in the school library. This was rolled up with a wall chart on dinosaurs. Neither had been put up on the walls so I was considering asking for the latter. The poster in question was an educational comic strip covering the subject of young people's health. The first few panels advised young people to eat well and stay away from drink and cigarettes. There was no reference to drugs or safe sex as this was still the pre-AIDS 70's. Successive panels advised young people to indulge in regular sports. The last panel depicted a group of young people enjoying each other's company in what looked like a rather dated 60's or even 50's-style coffee bar complete with a beatnik guitar player. The caption advised the young reader to cultivate a social life and relax in the company of friends. The poster in the library said I was supposed to fit in. The cartoon in the common room said I never would. A dull sense of abnormality was creeping into my life. The sense that I was once again failing to live up to The Rules, by virtue of being an outcast, was unnerving.

To tell the truth, I was not entirely isolated by this point. In my own limited way, I was mixing with a handful of other students in the common room. These tended to be the less popular kids with whom I shared a tenuous interest in SF and Fantasy. Despite this, I was still considered a grotesque by the rest, an object of disrespect and derision. They were 'real' people and I was not, it was as simple as that. Prior to the cartoon, I had read a leaflet on bullying. It stated that only a minority carried this out. Looking at the cartoon and listening to the giggles behind me, I wondered what it was called when everyone picked on you. There had to be another leaflet, but I never found it.

~~~

'Look at me! *I* SAID, LOOK AT ME BOY!!'

I still could not look The Animal in the eye as he leaned in close, shrieking. He had no respect for personal space, and his pronunciation of the pronoun was as repulsive as ever. For some reason, known only to him, the creature had taken to giving senior students his idea of pep talks. It clearly enraged him that I had been perverse enough to stay on and continue to ruin the look of his school. I was given the distinct impression he believed badly dressed pupils were not deserving of the privilege of education. He made this clear in a number of verbal attacks carried out in front of other students. This latest assault actually started on a reasonably positive note with his comparing my drawing efforts to those of an artist called HIERONYMUS BOSCH (I had never heard of the man and wondered what comic or book company he worked for).

Unfortunately, the speech took its usual, hostile turn with The Animal ranting about my abysmal academic record, my appearance and inability to fit in. Midway through the diatribe I started to white out and found myself focusing on the curved surface of a pen I was holding. I kept this on my person to help me deal with stressful situations. I returned to the world just as The Animal reached the point of his denouncement.

'You're a MISFIT Campbell, and there's NO PLACE for misfits at this school!'

Having seized his pound of flesh, he returned to his lair. It was then I realised the back of my left hand was covered in tiny droplets of his saliva; a little stippled pattern.

Misfit!

I had a word to describe me now, a bad word. A misfit was a bad thing. I was a bad thing. Lesson learned.

~~~

I was walking with another boy when we encountered Mr Wood. He was leaning against a wall talking to a group of students. On the occasions I encountered him by himself he would express disgust or make a sly dig at me. When he saw us, he waved to the boy to stop. Naturally I did the same. He looked at me and said: 'No, not you.'

Even for me, there was no mistaking the open hostility in his voice, so I did as I was told and walked on. I looked back to see him discussing something with the group, some of whom were looking over at me and laughing; I had a bad feeling about that. Minutes later, the boy caught up with me.

'What did he want?' I asked.

'He said I was too smart to hang around with a weirdo like you,' was the reply.

So that was it: no more hiding within humour. No more jokes, just honest in-your-face bigotry. Mr Wood was sending his diseased message far wider than the History corridors now. I had proof of this as I approached the Art department a couple of days later. Standing outside the Metalwork door was a group of younger boys (Art and Metalwork shared the same wing of the school), two of whom had been standing with Mr Wood. They started whispering and chuckling as soon as they saw me. As I entered the Art class they called out 'WEIRDO!' It was the beginning of a new chapter of humiliation during my final year at Whitehill.

Weirdo!

This new term was cropping up with an increasing regularity the older I grew. My Art teachers had used it occasionally and so had The Animal. I had been called weird in the past but it had little meaning to me. Somewhere along the line, weird became 'Weirdo' and weirdo was clearly a dirty word, a new type of derogatory term used by adults to describe the likes of me. Hanging out with a 'Weirdo' was apparently a bad thing; this lesson imbued the term with even deeper shame than 'Misfit'.

Although ASD children are prone to patterns of behaviour radically different from their neurotypical counterparts no one places expectations on them to conform to the norm due to their age. The case with teenagers is somewhat different. Along with individuality and rebellion there are a whole range of 'normal' attitudes and interests expected of them as they enter this period of their lives, most associated with socialisation. A strange child is not always noticeable, a strange teenager usually is. Our society accepts the former, yet is less inclined to tolerate the latter. It is in the teenage years that 'different' often becomes associated with shame. This was definitely the case at Whitehill.

The contempt of authority figures had sharpened my sense of abnormality. I was different. The pupils, and many of the teachers, did not like me for this crime. I had spent most of my life dodging hostility from one side, now I was dodging it from both for reasons completely beyond me. I was not aggressive; I did not start arguments or fights, nor did I destroy property, yet I was apparently considered as bad, if not worse, than any unruly or violent student. What was it they loathed in me? Did they think my weirdness was contagious like some kind of plague?

I recently discovered that, in many cases involving ASD children or young people, bullying by teachers is quite common. Until recently these youngsters have not belonged to any recognized minority and, as a result, have not enjoyed any real protection. I was a quarter of a century from my diagnosis and had no idea why I was being targeted. Perhaps it was because I was mad.

During several of my encounters with The Arm, The Halfman informed me that 'They bastards' would have access to my disgraceful psychiatric records. 'They bastards' was his description for anyone in a position of power, including teachers. Perhaps this had already happened I wondered? The image of Mr Wood, The Animal and perhaps even my Art teacher hunched together, chuckling over written proof of my insanity was a horrible one (particularly when combined with the picture of Mr Wood oiling up old Beelzebub in the process), but it did seem to explain their dislike of me. I was mad, this was written in stone - well, ink - and their attitudes suggested that a mad person was a *bad* person. It occurred to me that my terrible secret was possibly the subject Mr Wood had been discussing with those kids. If this was the case, was it possible that everyone knew I was insane and had spent time in a 'loony bin'? Nowadays of course I know that I was not insane, nor was there any way my teachers could have seen my medical records. Unfortunately, being a product of Little Russia, such thinking was second nature.

The hostility of these adults contributed to occasional bursts of wild anger I was beginning to experience. It was during one of those moments of sharp-edged thinking that I realised I wanted them to be hurt in return. I wanted them be hurt badly because it was now clear, after years of observing brutal human interaction, that only through being hurt badly could such enemies be made to 'go away'.

For once, I got my wish. As it turned out, old Beelzebub wasn't the only thing getting well-oiled. Mr Wood had started to drink during school hours, I just hadn't noticed. It's ironic that, despite hailing from a household crippled by drink problems, I was unable to recognize alcoholism in the man. (The idea that teachers could malfunction at such a human level was just too much to grasp.) Mr Wood's imbibing increased and his behaviour deteriorated over the next few months. During this time he indulged in activities that were fondly remembered by every student privileged to witness them. Eventually, it was announced he was leaving. Shortly afterwards, a going-away card was passed around the common room to be signed by all the senior students as a gesture of appreciation for a respected teacher's years of service at his school. There was nothing on the card to suggest the despicable truth behind the man. I didn't sign it, I wasn't asked to.

~~~

I was sitting in the common room, rendering a stippled pattern on a robot drawing when a loud click at my left ear startled me. It was one of the new core group; he had snuck up behind me and driven a staple through the epaulette of my army surplus jacket. The jacket wasn't a fashion statement; I wore it because it had several large pockets to store the pens I was collecting. The watching audience roared with laughter. As I turned in shock, the stapler pulled the material to one side and the collar ripped; this elicited even greater cheer. I threw my jacket off and looked at the damage as the boy backed away, dropping the stapler. I picked it up and chased him into the small English class which sat to one side of the common room toilets. I don't think the boy had the slightest idea that he had crossed a line by this physical contact, that he had become *The Enemy*.

These responses, dormant for almost two years, snapped back into full alert in less than a second. I cornered him in the room, near the exit. He turned to look at me as though expecting me to back down. I could not. I was terrified of him and the threat he represented. I was moderately malnourished, physically weak and acutely aware of this. Despite being younger and not a particularly aggressive sort himself, this boy was tall, well built and almost certainly capable of making mincemeat out of me; in addition he had a room full of cohorts mere yards away. I could not boast such a thing.

During the senior years, attacks against me had been of the verbal sort. This contact was a step back to the bad old days of physical intimidation and abuse. I could not go back there; not to that changing room, to The Event; not under any circumstances. At an instinctual level I knew that if I let him get away with what he had done then it would have been an invitation for anyone else to take similar, or worse, liberties. This could have thrown me into a new, dark age of physical abuse and I couldn't allow that. By his actions, he had given me no choice, I had to hurt him, to make him 'go away' as quickly as possible and send a message in the process.

I threw the stapler at his head as he ducked down to one side. It was a very large, old-fashioned device made of solid metal, and I threw it as hard as I could. He managed to dodge. It missed him by a hairsbreadth, striking the edge of a chair, cracking the hard plastic, before bouncing off to impact against the door frame, putting a sizable dent in it. Had it struck the boy where I intended, it would probably have hospitalized him. I didn't care, it was the only thing I could do. There are idealists who would argue my actions were unjustified; that there had been other options besides violence. If that is the case, then perhaps they should have taken the effort to be present at the time in order to suggest one to me. After throwing the stapler, I found myself experiencing an intense kind of elation, an odd 'high'. This brought a sense of freedom and relief, as if nothing mattered anymore, absolutely nothing. I can only describe it as the feeling of having let go of a burden.

The boy scuttled away, leaving me confused at this unfamiliar state of mind. After a minute or two, I wandered out to hide in the toilets situated between the common room and the Science wing. The new feelings faded to be replaced by the more familiar fear and agitation. As these started to sweep over me, I sat rocking back and forth in the cubicle, biting myself hard on the base of my thumb, drawing blood. I couldn't think about anything, not even comics. I felt a pressure mounting in me, a dull throbbing and slight nausea that was pressing on the left side of my throat. After a while, the agitation dropped to a level I was able to deal with. When I returned, most of the other pupils had gone. My jacket was where I had dropped it. Someone had ripped the tear on the collar wide open.

Constructive criticism from my Art teacher

~~~

I have to add a note in here about changes that were occurring in my home life around this time. This is the most shameful part of the book for me: the period I became physically abusive towards Mum, my younger sister and brother. I don't have the courage to describe the things I did. Suffice to say, my actions were not out of place in our Little Russia.

~~~

'Campbell... what did I tell you?!!'

The Art teacher had ordered me to blend the paint again. Despite years of questioning he still refused to clarify what 'blend' actually meant. The metal on the side of the huge space ship I was copying was a smooth green-blue mix. I was trying to reproduce this tonal gradation using stippled blobs of poster paint. After years of avoiding colour I had worked up the courage to tackle the subject once more.

Cautious as always, this latest experiment was an extension of tried and true drawing methods I was familiar with. I could stipple in black and white, so why not in colour? The effect for this latest effort was fairly neat and gave me a sense of control which appealed to me. I took pride in inventing this completely new technique of 'colour stippling'.

Being unaware of art history, I didn't know that Pointillism - pioneered by such artists as SEURAT, VAN GOGH and PISSARRO - had been established for almost a century. It seemed I wasn't the only one basking in such ignorance. The teacher voiced the opinion that the effect was not really painting at all; it was more akin to 'potato printing'. My response, as usual, was to go into autopilot and continue with the picture. This was a copy of the splash page from my 1974 Fleetway DAN DARE reprint annual. The title of the story was SAFARI IN SPACE. The ship was the awesome 'Galactic Galleon', magnificently rendered by artist FRANK HAMPSON and his team of assistants. It was a combination of airbrush colouring and meticulous line work.

After finishing the colour, I began copying this using a black fibre-tipped pen. Though nowhere near as slick as the original (the pen bled slightly into the soluble poster paint), the picture was by far the best piece of colour art I had ever produced. Had I been allowed to finish it, I would have achieved my first anchoring point for breaking into the field. When the teacher discovered I was still working on my 'potato-print', he tore into me once again for my stubbornness. I don't consider it paranoid to observe that, as I grew older, his opening volleys of criticism had shifted away from my work and onto me as a person. For the crime of attempting to learn - in my own fashion - I found myself hauled over the coals as a villain once again. Having crucified the criminal, he returned, as usual, to deride the crime.

'Look boy! This is just painting by numbers.'

Line and colour was hardly a new technique, having been favoured by the likes of WILLIAM BLAKE, ARTHUR RACKHAM and ALBRECHT DURER. Again, I knew nothing of these men (apparently neither did the teacher); all I could do was let him look at my copy of the annual. Hampson's work on Dan Dare represented the zenith of 50's comic illustration. The strip was a studio effort, painstakingly assembled using a combination of posed actors, costumes and meticulously built props. Combined with Hampson's superior drawing ability and that of his assistants - a team of talented artists and colourists - individual panels alone often boasted as much preparatory work as classic paintings or frames from feature films. My teacher didn't see this as he gave the pages a cursory glance. After a moment, he sighed to the whole classroom:

'If you think this is any good Campbell, then you truly are a lost soul.'

It certainly felt that way as I listened to the suppressed giggles around me. Who was I trying to fool? Everyone knew my work had no worth, including me. All of my tentative attempts at colour had been shot down humiliatingly by this man during my years in Whitehill; this was the last straw. The Galleon was my final foray into the field. I gave up after that, only returning to the medium years later, in college. I would never forget the smell of the Whitehill Art classes: Gum Arabic, the smell of despair.

~~~

I was still burning over this latest humiliation as I sat in the common room a week later. Whitehill's judgments had been mounting up for years. I felt them flowing around inside my head. I was a misfit, I was a weirdo, I wasn't a man, I was stupid, I was talentless and therefore worthless. It was official, all of it.

Art had been my protection against this world; a shell which had just been smashed to pieces. My ability to retreat from this pressure had been smashed along with it. The students didn't like me and teachers didn't like me either. Why was everyone so hostile? What was I doing wrong? How did I become such a bad person? These teachers said I was wrong therefore The Rules were saying I was wrong. This was worse than The Halfman telling me I was mad. *The Rules were saying I was in the wrong no matter what I did.*

I could hear the rest of the students tittering about something as I sat with these thoughts. I ignored them until someone called to me. 'Hey Campbell, check this.' They indicated the notice board. There was something on it: another cartoon.

THE PATH OF HATRED

This second cartoon was much more extreme and much more vicious than the first. It repeated the message of the previous in a far louder voice: 'You are not one of us and you never will be. You are different and we hate you. We can do anything we want to you and no-one will stop us because what we are doing is right.' The tittering of the students behind me grew louder and a group of boys gathered around me to enjoy my pain.

The largest of the boys told me I would be attacked if I touched the cartoon. Acutely aware of my own isolation and weakness, I decided to leave. As I turned to the door he hit me across the back of the head to the laughter of the rest. It wasn't even a hard strike, just a slap to remind me they could do anything they wanted. This contact, as my back was turned, and the closeness of the others was enough, and I found myself back in the changing room, at

The Event. I was surrounded by The Enemy, all of them stronger than me and all of them able to touch me again after all these years.

They could do anything they wanted to me. The fear was overwhelming. As it peaked, it was momentarily replaced by something else: a vertigo-filled rush that was almost elation; the same feeling - though far more intense - I experienced after throwing the stapler. I stepped out of the common room and turned towards the exit stairs expecting more blows to fall at any moment. Two of the laughing boys - though not the largest - followed a few footsteps behind. This was it, I thought. I walked a few more feet when suddenly the fear and the anger vanished completely, leaving only the rush. I felt nothing apart from it. It lasted a minute or two and then fell away again.

I am able to look at it from different angles now. What I see is quite frightening. This emotion doesn't feel like one of my own. (It was similar to, though not exactly the same as, a sense of abandonment I experienced in adult life while contemplating suicide.) Although prone to momentary outbursts, my temper was still limited in its ability to distort my overall thinking. This was not the case here. This emotion, which I can only describe as a horrible joy, dwarfed all ordinary feelings. It justified the anger, made it right, stopped it hurting and stripped away all fear. Concepts like responsibility and consequence ceased being part of my mental makeup at that precise moment. Nothing mattered, neither The Rules nor anything. There was no right or wrong. There was only what I wanted, and I wanted the students to go away, to cease.

Had I been armed, I would have shot the two behind me first, then the rest in the common room. I would have shot them all, not just the bullies but students who had caused me no harm, possibly even the teachers who had been good to me. One of the sad things about the outcast and paranoia is that believing everyone to be against you becomes second nature when most of them actually are. In this state of mind, killing everything that crosses your path makes sense since nothing has any value at all. All that matters is the desperate need for freedom through immediate power over everything around you.

I doubt if anyone would have understood such a reaction on my part. As I mentioned in the introduction, the students probably considered their efforts a harmless prank against someone who deserved it. All they saw was the joke of the moment, not the life of abuse behind it. They knew nothing about the pressure of countless attacks bubbling inside me, pressure they had just tapped into.

Fortunately, there was no gun culture in Britain, at least back then, and I had no specific interest in such things. Had any method of mass slaughter been put into my hands, I would have used it. But I had nothing. I was an underdeveloped scarecrow, empty handed, in the company of peers, most of whom could have wiped the floor with me.

The popular name for this state of mind is *school rage;* this is a wholly inaccurate and two-dimensional term, indicative of a deliberately blinkered approach to this problem. According to popular theory school rage is behind school shootings. Based on my own experiences, I don't think this is the case. The mental state I experienced may have been triggered by fear and anger, but as an emotion it would not be accurate to call it rage. I was to return to this state twice more in early adulthood. From what I have seen, there are others, kids included, who experience it far longer than I did, long enough to carry it to its tragic conclusion. I think this is due to their experiencing an emotion my autistic mind was incapable of feeling back then: hatred.

~~~

I spent my remaining school days sitting in an alcove across from the toilets. I didn't venture out after this experience, and took to carrying a sharpened screwdriver inside my bag of superhero and robot drawings. I lay low and hoped that no-one would notice me. Eventually I came to the end of the term and sat my exams. Despite my best efforts, my marks were miserable. I tried my absolute best and barely scraped by; two low passes, one on appeal. Stupid as usual.

Then I left. I remember where everyone was at this time, where they will always be for me. Mr Winpenny is entering the teachers' common room. I want to call out to him to say goodbye but I am afraid of who else might be in there. Mr Clelland is talking with a group of kids and, once more, I am too embarrassed to say anything. I have more success with Mr English. He is the last person I speak to in the building. After saying goodbye, I take a side entrance, step out into one of the car parks, cross the distance to the gate and leave Whitehill Secondary School for good.

Or so I thought...

~~~

It was the end of the 70's. In the next few months the 80's, the era of big hair, AIDS and Techno-Rock would arrive. This decade had a few surprises waiting for me. One of them was my last meeting with Mr Wood a few months after Whitehill. This took place on a main street that was his regular haunt. I had seen him lurking around it in the past (and managed to avoid him on most occasions) so I suppose he had something approximating friends, possibly drinking buddies there. I didn't realise it was him until I glanced up. He was standing at a bus stop outside the old Dennistoun abattoir. He was neat, sober and did not seem all that bothered to see me. He just glanced at me then looked past at something he presumably thought more interesting. There was no great confrontation, no triumph on my part. I suppose I was entitled to such as he was now a disgraced failure incapable of waving authority over my head. (He hadn't been fired as I had presumed, just forced to accept a lesser post at another school.) Perhaps he was aware of this and felt embarrassed. I will never know.

Thank God he had no idea of the truth: that I still considered him my superior. Had he known this, he could have flayed me alive with a few choice words. I could not have lived with the coming years had that happened. I hurried away from him as quickly as possible because I was still afraid of him. I left him where he belonged: at a place of dead meat.

To me, he will always be at that bus stop and at that position in his life. His last confirmed sighting in the area was being dragged insensate from a local pub wearing a pair of ghastly tan slacks, with a healthy stream of urine running down one leg. Ray Wood, BA (Hons), alcoholic failure waiting for death; beautiful. And death found him. A drink related accident a few years later resulted in his hospitalisation It was there, his badly-burned, booze-ruined carcass gave up the ghost. I hope he wasn't alone in his final, agonising, hours. Who knows? Perhaps he had Beelzebub to hold, well-oiled, in a loving embrace, as his organs shut down one by one and his liver ran out of his body through plastic tubes. Perhaps they lie together in a forgotten grave.

In case you're wondering what I'm doing here, I'm gloating. I'm gloating over the death of this bigot and I don't apologise for it. (Just because I don't approve of killing, doesn't mean I can't enjoy it when the idiots do the job themselves). More than his death, I'm gloating over his disgrace. I feel not the slightest shame over this ability to derive intense pleasure from the suffering, the losses and the deaths of any who wrong me. Far from it, I am proud of the fierce delight I experience at the failure of this man's life, his suffering, his loss, even the physical agonies and indignities of his bodily collapse. These are all slivers of meat I will try to claw back from his cheap ghost.

~~~

Anyone still operating on the assumption that autistics are timetable obsessed automata incapable of true feelings is sorely mistaken. We are fully able to experience a wide range of emotions, many of which are more complex and deeper than those felt by neurotypicals. If abused, these emotions, like yours, can be twisted into terrible scars. The Halfman was proof of this; and, as you are perhaps beginning to understand, so am I.

As it was for The Halfman, there is no distance in time for me. Right now, I am stuck in the History corridor in the old Whitehill, tasting fear in my mouth. I am thirteen-years-old and have an autistic spectrum disorder. For this crime, Mr Wood calls me Bushman, and likens me, in public, to a degenerate who eats raw animal flesh. He is doing this because it gives him pleasure to hurt a child incapable of defending himself. He knows full well he is teaching the other students to look on me as a target for abuse. I have done no wrong to this man; I am incapable of even considering such a thing. He wants to hurt me because I am different and nothing else. He is doing this in the knowledge that Bushman, that ugly, stupid little lower-class runt, who cannot even look up from the floor, will never amount to anything and never be heard. He is having his sport with a frightened, friendless boy he has judged from day one as something less than a person.

Had I been neurotypical, I would have hated him back then and there. Fortunately I could not feel that emotion at that stage in my life. I was just stupid and naive, with a head full of robots, textures and drawing techniques. It would take years of mental development for me to process my school experiences into the emotions that burn me as an adult.

This betrayal by professionals has caused me far more problems than my abuser father. The teachers who bullied me did so from positions of authority; they represented *The Rules*. Their judgments were 'official' in my eyes. And yet, the full scope of Whitehill's attack was far more insidious than even the efforts of these bigots. Through mechanisms designed to help ordinary young people I had been taught terrible things about myself. Six years of PE had hammered home that my body was ugly, unmanly and something to be deeply ashamed of. My mind fared no better. Having a brain that processed information at a different speed from normal marked me with the lifelong stigma of stupidity. Because I assimilated information at a visual, as opposed to verbal, level and expressed my creativity through a form of art not recognised by education, I was taught that I was talentless and told openly I would never amount to anything. Through socialisation difficulties, I found myself a focus for endless hostility and criticism from all quarters; hostility that was to cripple my dealings with the human race.

For the outcast, primary education teaches a general sense of worthlessness. In secondary school, these Dark Lessons become more specialised, able to generate a more sophisticated and intense sense of inadequacy. This can cut through a vulnerable young mind like a scalpel. Golfhill taught me the shame and fear of a child; Whitehill taught me the hatred of an adult.

By far the worst thing however is simply this: Whitehill Secondary, that sick place, was an ordinary school, nothing more. Its teaching ranks boasted some particularly shoddy specimens and also some exceptional individuals; yet, for the most part, they were simply the usual collection of academics found in such institutions. Its students were an ordinary cross-section of young people who would go on to define normalcy within our society. Many would enter the teaching profession themselves. Whitehill was normal; and, as I discovered, this was its most awful feature. For if you are different, normal, with its inbuilt intolerance, is *terrible*. Normal hates you; and often all you can do is hate in return.

Contrary to popular belief it does not take monsters to teach us this hatred, society's everyday intolerance will do just fine. Mr English once told me how pearls are created: a tiny piece of sand becomes lodged in the tender flesh of an oyster. The oyster, in order to protect itself, coats the sand particle in a substance called *nacre*. Successive coats of this substance result in the creation of a pearl. The emotional equivalent often happens inside the heads of outcasts.

An unacceptable fact or sequence of events can be lodged in the sensitive flesh of their feelings. The only way for them to deal with this is to violently reject it. Many insulate themselves from the pain by the mechanism of anger. In time, this anger can become second nature. It can increase in intensity and harden to become hatred. This emotion is often the only protection available to those crippled by lifelong pain and helplessness. Far from being unnatural, it is one of the key components of our emotional immune system. Hatred is one of the most effective glues for holding a mind together should it come under persistent attack. Sadly, it usually ends up more extreme than the forces that shaped it.

And this hatred is all I have left now. It is the only insulation I have against my school experiences. Whitehill is The Enemy. It has never left me. Its judgments are recorded onto me. They play out inside my head, finding fault with me at every level. Nothing has stopped them, neither medication nor therapy.

I have spent my entire adult life with my back against the wall because of that twisted place. Every day I have to reject it and curse it for all I am worth. By doing so, I am able to keep it from my throat that little bit longer. This is true hatred, not the pitifully small emotion experienced by most people. This is a feeling so extreme that it has congealed into a permanent part of my life; a path I have navigated for the last thirty years. I will try to keep it out of the book as much as possible, but that may be easier said than done. If it creeps in every now and then, I hope you will recognise it for what it is and make allowances.

It's a myth that we shape our own personalities. Apart from the genetic component, human beings are mostly the sum of their experiences. Anyone who insists they alone guided their early development is fooling themselves. You are the person you have been *allowed* to become. No-one would argue that you may have some say in the later direction of your life, but the build-

I left him at the place of dead meat

ing blocks of your personality were fashioned by the attitudes and actions of those around you. What is true is that we all have the potential to become a certain person, if allowed. Sometimes however, we are denied this basic right.

The person I could have become died at Whitehill and something far uglier was born. There is nothing unusual about this type of school poisoning, it happens to countless thousands of innocents every day. It has been part of education from the very beginning and walks hand in hand with the lessons on paper. As a society we never hear about it because we do not consider its victims important enough to recognise.

There are those within education who would argue I benefited from my time at Whitehill. They would be lying. The educational system has always lied about its Dark Lessons, and every year, innocents pay for this dishonesty. Should you allow a developing mind to be reduced to a human dumping ground for the collective negativity of its peers, be prepared for some spectacularly ugly results. The path of hatred creates monsters. But who is really to blame: the innocents who have this warped emotion thrust upon them or the cheap and cowardly minds who cultivate it through regimes of unchallenged brutality? Who do we condemn: those forced to walk the path or those who lay it; the poisoned or the poisoners?

HALF LIFE

DOTS... DOTS... AND MORE DOTS

S uicide; the idea never crossed my head while I was at Whitehill. Strange it should occur only months later. Even stranger was my method of holding it at bay...

~~~

My careers officer took one look at my bag of robot drawings before sending me off to my first place of employment: a youth training program in a community arts festival situated in an area called Easterhouse. Easterhouse is a large housing scheme situated at the Eastern outskirts of Glasgow. As with many isolated urban environments, its early reputation was marred by poverty and crime.

During the 70's, a number of organisations had sprung up for the purpose of improving the look and spirit of such areas; one being the Easter-house Festival Society. 'The Festival', as it was known, employed a number of school-leavers in a government funded training scheme called the 'Youth Opportunities Programme'. The areas covered by this ranged from photography, murals, drama to printing. The trainees were known as 'Yops'. As a result of my obvious interest in art, I was dispatched to the print shop.

Unable to face public transport, I walked to work every morning despite the distance of several miles. I avoided main roads, people and even breakfast since I occasionally threw up on my way to my destination. This was the Festival print shop. Upon commencing work, it was suggested I make several changes to my lifestyle, i.e. washing. After 18 years of none-to-subtle hints it had gradually filtered through that I was physically repulsive. Getting a haircut and a change of clothes was logically the first move at this point. (Of course, it wouldn't occur to me for a while that, having changed my clothes once, I had to change them regularly thereafter, but that was a problem for a later date.)

Moving into this totally new environment was also an ordeal. For all its viciousness, Whitehill was still known territory; the Festival was entirely unfamiliar and all the more frightening for it. I was unable to mix socially or relate to the other trainees or supervisors. Much of what they said passed completely over my head. I had a reputation as an oddity, and earned some interesting descriptions in the then-fashionable rhyming slang used by the other Yops: 'Hammer shaft' (daft/insane), 'Dolly dimple' (simple/insane) and 'Radio rental' (mental/insane). Despite such familiar labelling, I found that working in an environment bereft of violence and constant ridicule did make a welcome change. For the first time in my life I was known by my Christian name in public. After the initial shock, it came to feel like a rare privilege, one which could be withdrawn at any moment.

Unfortunately, there were some who took a dislike to my being different, and, in a now-familiar pattern, decided to make me the focus of their mirth. I was a non-drinker and non-smoker who did not touch drugs - which were very much the vogue in the Festival. (I'd learned about the evils of drugs from an episode of KOJAK.) When this was discovered, one of this group spiked my tea with hallucinogenic mushrooms and sat back with the rest of his buddies for the show. Whether he didn't use enough, or he boiled the mushrooms for too long, or the ASD brain is just that little more resistant to this type of drug, I don't know; but he didn't get the entertainment he was looking for. I tapped my foot, apparently.

I was useless when it came to the actual printing. The vibrations of the presses unnerved and revolted me just like the lathes in the Whitehill metalwork shop. Unlike the other trainees I could not get to grips with the machines, despite the best efforts of the supervisor. My attempts resulted in some dangerous accidents; one of these being a near-disaster with a loose aluminium plate. At that point it became clear I was a total liability on the floor. I was subsequently banished to a side room to produce the artwork instead. It was then I found my true calling: graphics. There were no computer artwork programmes back then. Everything was done by hand, which suited me fine as I possessed a paradoxical aptitude for neatness and precision in this field. In time, I became completely obsessed with my new calling. Graphics was my passion; graphics defined me. I decided on my course for life: I was going to be a graphic designer. Using the print shop, I was going to develop my portfolio to study this wonderful field in college.

~~~

It was in the print shop I discovered I had not left Whitehill and never would. My feelings during this period were a source of considerable confusion. If things ran smoothly, a sense of safety would result. If they didn't, terrible drops in mood occurred. These persisted long after my normal agitation had abated. As the days wore on they appeared with increasing regularity, often swamping me. These were not the feelings of Little Russia; those had been fading as I grew older. These were considerably more powerful and possessed an entirely different, but not unfamiliar quality. It came as a real shock when I realised they were the emotions of Whitehill. They had the smell of the place, the fear, the despair, the sense of failure and futility, of inescapability and helplessness.

The memories came flooding back. They were around and inside me: their boots and fists driving into me, their voices stripping me to the bone. Every comment, every verbal and physical blow played out in perfect detail. I was ugly, unmanly, talentless, stupid and worthless. There were images too: an Art teacher laughing as he turned to address his audience, an entire classroom he was using to humiliate me; a rain of fists slamming into my face; a PE teacher pointing at his crotch; a crowd rushing me. Worst of all, there was a sense of being judged and found wanting by something much larger than myself – something *official*.

The absurdity of this confused me. Whitehill was in my past, not my present. There were no groups surrounding and attacking me now; no teachers telling me I was a weirdo. I was no longer attending the school, and therefore had no logical reason to experience such intense emotions. During her years of inebriation, Mum often whined about The Halfman's brutality. I felt no sympathy for her during those pathetic weeping sessions as - so far as I could see - she was physically removed from his presence and therefore had no ex-

Heading into ever-darkening territory

cuse for feeling bad. This was sound logic, so it came as a surprise when I was unable to apply it to myself.

In some horrible way, my Whitehill experiences had followed me into my adult life. Looking back now I can see they had never left, just been temporarily displaced by the trauma of moving to a new environment. On a bad day these feelings could intensify to the point that they interfered with my ability to work or even think straight. Often, in the middle of conversations, I would be struck by the sudden knowledge that anyone speaking to me knew I wasn't a 'real' person. Then the helplessness swept over me and I would be back, facing the punches and hatred of the playground and the changing room, and know, with a certainty greater than any other, that people could do anything they wanted to me. I had accepted long ago that I had no worth, but I hadn't expected the fact to hurt so much as I grew older. I was leaving my teenage years behind. The adult world was in front of me and I wasn't good enough for it. Whitehill's lessons were reaching me more effectively as an adult than they ever had while I was a student.

These states of despair were terrifying. They clogged my thinking wherever I went. At their worst, I could only see an endless vista of misery stretching out in front of me. Around this point, the escape of suicide started to look pretty tempting, worse, it started to look sensible. I had always found the idea of self-destruction to be stupid; after all, as I had heard: 'You only have one chance at life, why throw it away?' (Particularly since escapism allowed you to walk away from a source of pain and into a pile of comics.) Unfortunately, I now had an answer to that question. Life was like a bus ride. If you were lucky, the bus took you through nice areas and nice experiences. In my case, it seemed to be heading into ever-darkening territory and there was nothing I could about it, apart from stepping off before things got too painful.

I tried everything to escape these feelings, even attempting to discuss them with the printshop supervisor (the idea of talking to a shrink carried too much shame). He laughed and told me to grow up and put it all behind me. From that point on, I knew the feelings were stupid and I was in the wrong for allowing myself to experience them. That didn't stop them hurting though, nothing did. I desperately needed protection from this pain. I found it at the end of my fingertips: dots, hundreds of thousands of them.

I discovered I was able to counter an attack of Whitehill misery by rendering ever more intricate patterns of stippling. Upon realising this, I started to lose myself in the technique, using it on absolutely everything; on artwork which need no such gilding and even the margins on newspapers and magazines. I often worked through the night and into the morning to obtain results.

Whitehill said I amounted to nothing, a skillfully manipulated pattern of dots said the opposite, taking away my immediate sense of shame. (It required constant effort though, like a ping pong ball held underwater: the slightest slip in concentration and the feelings shot to the surface almost instantly.)

The quality of my actual drawing suffered badly as a result, becoming stilted, half-hearted and amateurish; little more than an excuse for stippling. At the time, I didn't realise this was only a short-term solution. The increasing sophistication of my despair in the coming years meant it would eventually work its way around my protective dots. In the meantime, however, it sufficed and I gained a reputation for my obsessive preoccupation with the technique. Even to this day, if I meet someone I knew during the period I'm often asked 'Are you still doing your wee dots?' Everyone thought they were my hobby. No-one seemed to understand they were actually an anaesthetic, the only one available to me. Some turned to the drink to numb the pain of their lives, some the drugs, for me it was the dots.

JACK

I encountered two individuals at the Festival who had significant effect
on my thinking. The first of these was the most tragic person I have
ever known. For the benefit of his privacy, I'll call him Jack. Jack
started in the mural section some time after I had begun working in
the print shop. Initially, I was wary, even frightened of him. He was a thickset,
round-faced boy with a slightly deep voice, who wore tinted glasses of the
type sported by TV villains or hard-nut heroes. The first thing he said to me
was a joke of some sort. I didn't know what he meant and suspected he was
making fun of me. Later, I realised he was just attempting conversation and
was even worse at it than I was.

After this initial misunderstanding, we began to talk. I learned quite quickly that Jack, like me, was someone who had suffered extreme rejection in school. I can't say I liked him, no-one did, but I did enjoy our occasional meetings as he seemed even more stupid than me. This left me with the novel feeling of superiority over another human being. Jack was a compliant soul who, unlike others, would listen to me talk endlessly about my pet interests. The fact that someone was actually giving him time of day seemed to be enough for him.

The subject of these conversations was mostly comics as I knew little else to talk about and he knew even less. Jack had an unusual, perhaps very Scottish, pronunciation of the name Spiderman - favouring a heavy emphasis on the sound 'EI' as opposed to simply 'I' - which I found to be intensely annoying. For this reason, I directed our comic-based conversations away from Marvel's Wallcrawler and onto the Hulk and even more importantly the Glob and its matchless strength.

Inevitably, I brought up the subject of Virgil Finlay and stippling. I demonstrated the technique as Jack watched, probably not following me at all. During these lessons, he would occasionally interject with comments which bore no connection to the important information I was imparting. These interruptions annoyed me as, so far as I was concerned, his place was to shut up and listen, nothing else. Things came to a head during a demonstration of a particular technique. After looking at the patterns of dots, Jack mumbled that he had heard the singer Deborah Harry was a heroin addict. I didn't know how to reply to this. Perhaps the fool was becoming bored with the all-important information I was imparting. I changed tack and drew him a picture of the Silver Surfer instead.

Looking back now, I can see that Jack was the most isolated individual I'd ever met. Sad to say, he wasn't particularly bright either. The extent of the boy's plight became appallingly obvious after a meeting in which his supervisor told the other trainees to seek him out in the event of any problems. Jack did just that. I overheard him asking the supervisor a tentative question as I stood behind them in the queue for the canteen.

'Can you do anything for Yops who are lonely?'

I thought that had to be one of the dumbest questions I'd ever heard (unlike the 'sensible' ones I'd been asking my boss), apparently so did the supervisor as, from that point on, he proceeded to humiliate Jack mercilessly. He was not alone in his efforts as most of the other Yops and several other adults joined in. Over the next few months, these ordinary people happily reduced this awkward, helpless boy to something like a bear at the end of a rope. It's quite difficult for me to write this, as the particular supervisor I'm referring to had always treated me with respect and I liked him for it. In fact, I actually considered him to be a good person, at least for a while.

From a distance I watched Jack gradually crumble under the abuse being rained on him. It was an odd experience to observe the processes which had shaped me being directed towards another. It was equally strange to realise there were rungs even lower than mine on the social ladder. Though considered an oddball by most in the festival, I had some acceptance due to my status as the 'graphics guy'. I knew who I was, that I had some function and I drew strength from this whenever I could. Graphics was the crutch which allowed me to stand in the company of others. Jack had no such support, no such protection and he paid for it.

~~~

The second important character, I'll call Lem. He was the most useful idiot I've ever talked to. Lem was the first adult I beat in an argument. It was an incredible experience which turned sour fairly quickly. Though not an actual employee of the Festival, Lem seemed to know the staff and could often be found hanging about the building. We first locked horns after I heard him criticise another artist's work for its supposed sexism. He then challenged the 'sexist' nature of comics in general. This was over a cartoon produced by the artist and a Horror anthology comic called EERIE (produced by the American company WARREN COMICS) which Lem happened to flick through. The advertisement pages of the comic featured a poster of the company's buxom heroine VAMPIRELLA rendered by Spanish artists PEPE GONZALEZ and ENRICH. It was the depiction of the blood-drinker's statuesque anatomy upon which Lem draped his argument. Like many I encountered, Lem affected an interest in morality, intellectualism and left-wing politics. He expressed a total disrespect for Fantasy, particularly comics. One of his cohorts often voiced a phrase which perfectly summed up their collective opinion of the field.

'Vampires... pphhhttt!'

Their assertion was that anyone showing interest in such a childish field was clearly emotionally retarded. 'You should grow up, be into real life' was a sentiment bandied about in their company. I knew all about real life: it was a malevolent force which sought you out for the purpose of hurting you. Real life was a thing to hide from in corners, under beds, old buildings and even between paper pages. I wanted nothing to do with it and did not consider myself to be a criminal for doing so. After Lem finished his little lecture, he asked my opinion on the subject.

'What about you? D'you not think these comics are sexist?'

'Errrrr!.. Aahhhhh'.. Ummmmmm!..' was my reply, since the finer points of gender stereotyping were as far beyond me as rocket science. I suspect

An amoral louse

Lem took this to be a sign of weakness as he then tried to impress me with a long-winded, and frankly absurd lecture on the nature of imagery and sensory experience which had nothing to do with sexism. The gist of his lecture was that people blind from birth possessed a full range of internal visual imagery which allowed them to imagine a world they could never see.

'...so, even if a tree falls in the forest an' there's no one there to see it, then a blind person can see it in their head,' he concluded.

To the best of my knowledge this was not the case.

'I don't think they can.'

'How no?' ('Why not?')

'Because, discounting race memory, all internal visual imagery is derived from external visual experience. So far as I know, were a person blind from birth given sight then they would need a period of readjustment to come to terms with this completely new sensory experience. It would be similar to you being somehow given the ability to see or hear electrical or magnetic fields. Certain animals and fish can do this as they have a different sensory range from humans. Since you share a common ancestor with these creatures, it is theoretically possible that your brain holds the latent capacity to process such information. That being the case, can you say that, in the absence of such faculties, you can still tell me what an electrical field looks like?'

He looked at me for a moment.

'What's race memory?'

'I don't know much about it, but from what I have read (from a copy of the, then popular, science/SF magazine OMNI) it's the theory that all living creatures carry some form of memory locked in their genetic structure. I think it's an idea which is very much in controversy.'

'Right,' he said and walked out the room. A day or so later it occurred to me I had done something unthinkable: I had beaten an adult in an argument. I was aware of the emotion of pride welling in me as I processed the fact. It took a couple more days to reach me but it was worth the wait. I was smart. I was invincible.I could take on the world.

~~~

Lem got his revenge shortly afterwards. As I was drawing some cartoons for a variety show flyer (on which I misspelled 'surprise' as 'suprise'), he and one of his associates engaged me in a conversation about my intended graphics career. This ganging up approach was much favoured by Lem and his compatriots. I disliked it intensely as it brought back uncomfortable memories of Whitehill and there were too many of them rattling around inside my head as it was. Unable to follow a line of questioning which jumped from person to person, I found myself on the defensive relatively quickly. Eventually, Lem asked me:

'So, would you work for someone like NESTLE?'

'Yes, I suppose.'

'So you'd work for a company that exploits third world babies, would you?'

'What?'

'Oh, aye, that's what they do. How come you don't know that if you're so f*&^ing clued up eh?'

(Clued up = Aware, Informed)

I was as far from 'clued up' as possible. I knew little about politics apart from the fact capitalism was bad and communism was good (a truth that Marvel comics were forcing me to finally question). My knowledge of worldly affairs was appallingly stunted as I only learned in a narrow bandwidth, along lines of specific interest. I knew nothing about the practices of this company apart from the fact they made condensed milk and chocolate. As I was still prone to interpreting things literally I was not sure whether Lem was joking or not. Adult communication persistently confused me with such open-ended statements. Although continuing on his thread of attack, he did not enlighten me on the basis of his opening question. Now his cohort joined in. Thereafter, it was pretty much a good cop/bad cop-style interrogation.

'Who else would you work for, then?'

'Would you work for ICI, then?'

'ICI?'

'I bet you would.'

'Aye, I can see you wouldn't have problems working for a company that did stuff like that to the rest of the world.'

'Did what?'

'Aye, you wouldn't have a problem.'

'What?'

'D'you know about Nicaragua then?'

'Nicaragua?'

Despite his earlier defeat, it was actually easy for Lem to run rings around me. My approach to an argument was simply to plod along in a straight line towards a logical conclusion. Lem's initial mistake was to stick to a specific (and mistaken) point. Now he was adopting a different approach by jumping from subject to subject and throwing in a series of unrelated facts, or in this case accusations, to throw me off track. It wasn't a genuine political argument, more a series of concealed character assassinations, but it was entirely successful at knocking me off my feet.

The upshot of the lecture was I now stood revealed as a stupid, amoral louse; a potential stooge for every corrupt corporation on the planet. I couldn't answer this and was forced to concede that my lousehood was, in fact, entirely deserved. Mission accomplished, Lem and his henchman departed, leaving me the bad guy once more (and a *stupid* bad guy at that). After a few hours, I realised the conversation had been manoeuvred for the sole purpose of making me look bad. It was not the last time I would endure this type of denouncement for my political indifference. Later that week I was derided for my 'bourgeois sentiments' by a hard-line communist who knew of, and respected The Halfman. The accusation was taken up by Lem and several of his acquaintances. Looking back now, there was a certain irony in being accused of bourgeois values by the type of people who had ridiculed my clothes and derided me as 'tramp' a handful of years earlier.

It is perhaps uncharitable to describe Lem as a genuine idiot. From our conversations, I was given the impression of an average mind saddled with a bad habit of expounding theories quite beyond it. Nonetheless, I was told by others that he was 'thick' and there was no way on God's Green Earth I was going to let anyone 'thick' beat me in an argument. If Lem could play his little game for his moment of gratification, then so could I. Besides, I deserved it more than he did.

Before anyone sees fit to comment, I know this reveals a desperate pettiness on my part, but, having won a moment of intellectual pride after a lifetime of 'stupidity', I was loathe to part with it. Lem had to pay for his crime. Because I feared him, I needed a weapon to even the score. I was prepared to use anything, even another person.

The person was Jack. I didn't choose him because his plight meant anything to me; he was simply convenient to use. In this boy there was a perfect opportunity to beat Lem on his home territory, his so-called morality. By virtue of diatribes directed at me, I had begun to grasp the basis of Lem's supposed principles. They seemed to be a fine tuning of the broader ideas of right and wrong. Yet, despite a repertoire of arguments hinging on such noble ideals, I had observed Lem ridiculing Jack quite viciously (Jack had a hopeless crush on a girl trainee and was eventually warned away from her. Lem seemed to find this hilarious and continually dredged it up in front of the boy and others).

There was another, less honest, reason for choosing Jack. In the company of these politically-relevant sorts I was also an object of contempt for my 'weird', non-drinking, non-smoking, non-womanising and frankly non-masculine lifestyle. I couldn't see why they thought of me in such disrespectful terms since I now dressed in decent clothes and even washed (occasionally). Nor could I grasp how they reconciled this attitude with their much-touted concepts of responsibility and equality. Using Jack as an example of someone being denied respect (without having to mention myself), I would beat Lem by showing him he was no better than the bigots he had decried in my presence. At least that was the theory.

I got my chance a few weeks later when I cornered him in the drama office. It was during lunch break when the building was almost empty. He was reading a newspaper, apparently waiting for the drama supervisor. I asked him if he wanted a cup of tea, hoping he would accept so I could sit around and crush him. It was an ideal situation. He was in a light-headed mood, having smoked some dope. In my eyes this made the fool especially vulnerable to the unleashed power of my great mind. I was not capable of manipulating the conversation as effectively as him, so when I broached the subject, Lem asked me what my problem was. I replied there was nothing wrong, I was just thinking about the things he had said.

When I confronted him on the subject of Jack, I discovered he had an entirely different interpretation of his treatment of the boy: he refused to recognise his words as being anything other than good humour and insisted they were bereft of any hurtful or serious content. He also reasoned that if Jack didn't like the things said to him, then he would have objected; the fact he didn't proved there was no problem. This was perfect, I was going to use Lem's own ideals as new anchoring points for this argument; and this argument was going to flatten him. Everything was going perfectly up until the awful moment when I fell through an all-too-familiar 'hole'.

It was the same hole I'd encountered with the guidance teacher and the lady psychologist at Whitehill, the same hollow space full of vague ideas for which there were no words. It hadn't filled itself in over the last few years. The first problems arose when I tried to describe Jack and found there seemed to be no specific phrase to communicate just how the boy differed from all the others (who, by their actions, clearly saw him as being different). The only description I could muster to cover him was as 'one of those people who don't know how to talk to other people', a definition which hardly established his intense vulnerability or explain why contempt for this characteristic was in any way a bad thing. Lacking correct language, I found myself unable to bring this blurred sense of injustice into sharp focus for Lem's enlightenment.

At that point I discovered that attempting to communicate an idea without adequate language is as futile as trying to assemble something out of wisps of gas. Lem had no interest in any of my half-baked ideas and dismissed them as quickly as I voiced them. It was clear he wasn't an intellectual giant who established his own moral definitions. In this area he, like most others, seemed to do little free thinking. His reasoning went like this: if a subject were truly serious, then a word would exist to confront it, as was the case with racism and sexism (although it was obvious from certain comments he had made in the past that no-one had educated him about the evils of homophobia). Since there was no word to establish that the devaluation of a person 'who didn't know how to talk to other people' was in any way wrong then it couldn't be, and that was all there was to it. My argument, bereft of the verbal and intellectual ammunition needed to challenge such perfect pseudo-logic, collapsed quite quickly. The worst thing about the defeat was I knew that I was right and that Lem was wrong, yet I could not clarify how, even to myself.

I was mortified that this half-cut, half-wit had effortlessly wiped the floor with me by virtue of a closed mind. The irony was that Lem did not even grasp the scope of his victory since, rather than sitting around to gloat, he then left to 'cadge a joint' (smoke someone else's dope). I was confused and slightly frightened by the experience and ended up leaving early. As time wore on, I fell into obsessive rage over the defeat and ended up cursing him constantly (behind his back of course). The content of the argument was unimportant, winning was all that had mattered and I had lost, disastrously. I was enraged at the swine for beating me a second time and avoided his company thereafter because I was even more scared of him than before; not at a physical level, I was frightened of his limited thinking and the humiliation it could inflict were I to engage it again. I doubt if he ever realised this was the case.

Lem taught me there were areas of thought you didn't venture into because there was nothing there to stand on. Trying to open his eyes had led me back into The Blindspot and shown me more of its awful depth. However, being a patient and stubborn sort I would circle this particular void for another couple of decades before venturing in once more.

Eventually, I finished my stint at the Festival. I had prepared a portfolio which had earned me a place on an illustration course at a local technical college (I lacked the qualifications for Art school). I was going to mix with other artists now. Everything would be perfect. I would be taught to paint, be accepted into society, and make friends with whom I could discuss Virgil Finlay and stippling. I left my first place of employment marginally wiser than I had entered. During my time there, I had met many different sorts, some pretty decent, others not so. Although I had been hopelessly inept and dangerously clumsy in some areas, I had shown excellence in others. I had given the Festival a higher standard of artwork than it had seen in the past, and used the place to learn a craft, which is what it had been intended for.

It was just a shame not everyone saw my potential. During my final days at the place, the Festival secretary confided a little nugget of information concerning the call from the careers advisor who had interviewed me; apparently the man had been very specific in his recommendations.

'We've got a right strange one here for you. Want our advice? *Don't take him.*'

And that was official.

DIDN'T HAVE FUN AT COLLEGE

The college annex was close to my house, which allowed me to avoid travelling. Apart from that, the whole experience was a waste of time. Firstly, no-one wanted to talk about Virgil Finlay, secondly, we weren't taught illustration. After a brief introduction to technical drawing (enough to fill an A4 leaflet), students were thrown into a series of projects, expected to produce professional results and criticized when they couldn't. Since many of these projects were in colour, this left me in big trouble. I asked the main tutor how to paint. This was still a sensible question to me, although by now I had refined the description of my actual requirements.

'How do you render a tonal gradation without visible brushstrokes in an opaque, water-based medium?'

His response was an expression I recognized from my comics as a stupid grin.

'Ohh… what a question,' he replied and simply wandered off. I never did get an answer, although I suppose I should have been grateful he didn't call me 'retarded' for asking. This was pretty much the level of teaching for the rest of course. Not one useful painting or line drawing lesson was taught in the two years spent at the college. Students clumsily rendered pictures using little sets of watercolour paints and techniques they brought with them from secondary school; when they graduated, they were using the same paints and the same techniques.

There was worse to come. Parts of the course made no sense no matter how hard I tried to fathom them. This became obvious during my first typography lesson in which the tutor tried to teach me the correct method of measuring text. Although the rest of the class mastered the skill quite quickly, the lesson was completely lost on me. When it became clear I had failed to grasp what she had said, the tutor explained it to me once again. She might just as well have been talking in Latin. After the third attempt, she gave up in frustration.

The most confusing thing about typography was that it was there in the first place. From what I'd read, the course was in illustration; why other, unrelated subjects had been jammed in as well, made no sense. Instead of being taught the necessities of illustration - slick, professional painting, line art technique, anatomy - I found my time wasted on compulsory PE lessons (in an illustration course?), bookbinding, craftwork, printing and hot metal typography using machines and methods obsolete for decades.

I could not see the point of such academic padding. After all, printing and bookbinding students weren't taught illustration, so why should illustrators be taught their craft? Genuinely angry at this absurdity, I asked the tutor to explain the reasons behind this time wasting rubbish. He replied that it was intended to give students a balanced educational experience.

As I was to learn, this 'balanced educational experience' (as opposed to usable skills and a decent portfolio) didn't find any of the students work in the real world. What it did give them was a qualification and that looked good on the records, good for the college and good for the tutors. Any problems faced by the students after graduation weren't important.

An illustration course that didn't teach illustration. I couldn't grasp how such a contradiction could exist at an official level, nor how education could be so badly and irresponsibly designed to waste a young person's time in such a fashion. It was around this point I began to entertain the hitherto unthinkable suspicion that the people behind the course, behind education, behind even The Rules might not actually know what they were doing, nor for that matter, care.

~~~

The overload of returning to a classroom triggered anxiety that made it hard for me to sit still. I took to wandering again, dropping into the other classrooms occasionally. This greatly annoyed some of the tutors. In actual fact I did very little work in college. Almost everything was done at home, during the evening, since I had very little else to do.

It was at college that I discovered adult social behaviour was essentially no different from that of children and adolescents. The same divisions and stratifications were there. These were based on confidence, aggression, attractiveness and advantage. They weren't maintained by violence, but they were there.

This came as a shock since I had been led to believe that people acted in a more civilised (perhaps fairer) manner in adulthood. The future looked bleak thereafter. I'd been at the bottom of the ladder in juvenile society, these codes of expected behaviour meant I would be occupying a similar rung in its adult counterpart.

My first inkling that something was wrong came when I discovered that, despite being artists, my fellow students did not want to talk about stippling or any other drawing method which interested me. My attempts to integrate proved futile since my journey into early adulthood had not honed my social skills in the slightest. Although capable of short exchanges with one or two individuals, social groups completely baffled me. Listening to a gathering of young people engage in conversation was the equivalent of watching manic channel-hopping over areas I barely understood. In a few minutes of normal discourse, I would hear subjects bandied back-and-forth, suddenly dropped (as the conversation inexplicably shifted onto entirely different tracks), and just as suddenly returned to, before I was even able to grasp the first lines of the opening statement. Unable to keep up, I would drift out of the conversation and out of the group, lingering on the periphery like unwanted greens on the edge of a dinner plate.

My occasional attempts to include myself into the rapids of these conversations were both awkward and pitiful. One student stopped me mid-sentence with the blunt statement that I 'talked a load of s***'. He was right, but I had no idea what to say to him or any of the others in order to get them to talk to me. The white spaces of my childhood and adolescence were still present in my head when I opened my mouth. My only recourse was to fill this void with random, made-up rubbish in the hope that at least some of it would prove interesting enough for them to want to hear more. It didn't, it just earned me a reputation as a weirdo who 'talked a load of s***'.

The 'illustration' course

I was tremendously immature in my early twenties, really still a teenager and a young one at that. Sadly this was on show for all to see. My clumsy floundering drew attention from a number of students who reacted with caustic dismissal. Eventually one particularly aggressive individual told me to 'F*** off!' After this, I learned from a student in another course that this attitude was shared by many of the others. I took the hint and stopped attempting to mix. It was then I understood I would never be accepted into normal society, and that most of the doors of human experience and opportunity - taken for granted by almost everyone else - were forever closed to me, a fact that brought me into conflict with The Rules once more.

The shame of isolation, a dull thing during my teenage years, had begun to grow into a terrible gnawing ache. There was clearly something wrong with me and my solitary lifestyle. I could find no term to indicate this was anyone else's fault so I deduced it was mine and hated myself for it. An ironic little piece of insult was added to this isolation when an older student - another socialist no less - criticised me for working too hard. According to this character, tutors had cited me as an example in order to justify the course's intense workload when other students had complained. This was indeed the case since, lacking a social life, I had all the time I needed to complete any project set out before me. I was lonely and miserable. Discovering, once more, that I was the bad guy into the bargain was an unwanted bit of salt rubbed in just when it wasn't needed. Mr Wood certainly would have approved.

I can see the emergence of my mental illness during the isolation of my college years. My programmed worthlessness was returning with a vengeance. My moods, which had stabilised slightly at the Festival, were now swinging back and forth like a pendulum and stippling was doing little to halt them. The fact that my expectations both creative and social were obviously going to remain unfulfilled, possibly forever, was weighing heavily on me, too heavily.

Things were dire on the home front as well. In the intervening years, we had been forced to leave Firpark Street as the building deteriorated through neglect and vandalism. Our new home, situated in a small inner city scheme, was a horrible place. As an outcast family, we were recognised as being different from day one and persecuted accordingly. Constant harassment was the norm as we walked the streets; both our door and garden were vandalised and bricks were thrown though our windows on a regular basis. As the years passed, this intensified to violent attacks on the males of the family. I distinctly remember this period, glancing out though the gaps in my curtains at The Enemy, young sub-humans prowling around for prey. More than anything, I wanted them to go away; and the only way their type of evil could be made to go away was for it to die. I wanted them to die, all of them.

It was now clear that there was a connection between youth and evil. I'd once read that there were certain insect species whose larvae were predatory. This was obviously the case with humans. Young people were selfish, vicious, cowardly and evil to the core. There was no getting away from this. My dislike for youth intensified into a loathing that wasn't quite hatred, but was getting there. What had become obvious was that the lives of all young people, young *evil* people had no value, none at all.

~~~

This sense of enmity was to extend to my limbs. I had always loathed them for being so pale, underdeveloped and weak, now it looked as if they were going to let me down once more in a catastrophic fashion. A persistent pain in the fingers of my right hand was misdiagnosed by the family's senile doc- tor. (His sons were doctors of advanced years themselves.) He examined the middle fingers of my hands - both of which have always curved outwards in a shape similar to the swan-neck deformity of arthritis - and pronounced: 'Yes, well, there definitely seems to be some arthritis there.'

At the time, I was unaware that such a diagnosis required a series of X-rays and a blood-sedimentation test so I took the old fool's diagnosis as gospel. This was crushing, as my brain dealt in absolutes and malfunction of any kind was unacceptable. As a child I'd found a rubber bat and played with the thing until, one day, I noticed a slight tear on the wing. To me, this meant the bat was finished as it could no longer be trusted. It was utterly repulsive and I couldn't even touch it after that. My hand was no different; I began to look at it as a separate entity, one which had betrayed me. Even after this medical blunder had been corrected by a specialist, I became fixated on the malfunction of my body. This was to mar my last months at college, a fact a number of my fellow students found hilarious.

On the day of the certificate examination I didn't show up as there seemed to be no point (to tell the truth, I couldn't have passed anyway, since the examination involved elements I was still unable to grasp). Although I did not gain the qualification, my portfolio was the only one up to a professional standard. When the marks of the individual assignments were tallied up I was left the leader, with a clear gap between me and the others. Yet it counted for nothing in my eyes.

Course completed, I left with a deep sense of resentment for the absurdity of education and The Rules. A few weeks later, I received a secondary qualifi- cation - a college diploma in design (not even worth the paper it was printed on) - through the post. I tore it to pieces and ate some of it. The word 'Diplo- ma' was inscribed in gold ink; it tasted disgusting but I ate it anyway, because I wanted to destroy it and all the incompetence it represented.

ALAN MOORE THINKS I'M DEAD

Comic fandom abounds with countless I-met-Alan-Moore stories, but mine beats all others hollow as it ends with my death.
Moore's ground-breaking writing career debuted in the early
80's when he quickly gained a reputation for complex and highly dramatic storytelling coupled with the innovative reworking of comic book
clichés in strips like THE BALLAD OF HALO JONES, CAPTAIN BRITAIN
and eventually DC's flagship horror title, SWAMP THING.

To comic readers of the middle 80's, Moore's work was as revolutionary
as Stan Lee's Marvel explosion of the early 60's. In many ways, mainstream
comics were entering their adulthood.

Moore wasn't the first writer to produce 'clever' comics. Writers like
STEVE GERBER and others had been subverting the medium years before
with stories that subtly (and sometimes not so subtly) satirised and re-exam-

ined their very roots. What Moore managed to add to the mix was to make such an approach fashionable; he achieved this with writing that was clever and intensely exciting at the same time. He was a real comics fan with a penchant for dredging up long-forgotten characters and imbuing them with new life. In addition, he displayed a real talent for emotive and often lyrical-sounding captions.

As the 80's progressed, other writers - assuming that such captions were a fast track to high art - imitated his approach to death, churning out comic panels choked with blocks of ornate, redundant and pompous wordage. I found this to be something of a step back as it left pages looking like certain old-style comics I'd glanced at in my early childhood: the type that sat tiny panels atop huge, unhealthy looking blocks of dense text. I was to become leery and distrusting of this new type of comic writing as it felt as though the reader needed a degree in English to get the point of every story. They left a bad taste in my mind, the impression of a snobbish writer trying to impress his audience rather than simply entertain them.

Moore was different. He was genuinely talented and his work always intensely dramatic. Many cite WATCHMEN as his masterpiece. For me it is V FOR VENDETTA. VFV, as I will call it here, debuted in 1982, alongside Moore's other strip MARVELMAN, in a new British anthology magazine called WARRIOR. I have to admit it was Marvelman - a dynamic re-invention of the superhero genre - that grabbed my interest first. VFV turned out to be slow burner whose brilliance would take decades to reach me.

Initially I didn't even like VFV, as it seemed to be a reworking of a strip I had read years before, called V FOR VENGEANCE. In reality, this was a minor and ignorant niggle. What really put me on the defensive was the story itself. VFV featured deep characterisation, subplots and complex themes all locked together like a Chinese puzzle. If this wasn't bad enough, its pages were laced with ironic references to culture, both classical and popular that indicated the dreaded presence of intelligence. Since there was nothing better than intelligence to make me feel stupid, I read the strip grudgingly, taking several months to become engrossed in its mystery.

Moore was a guest of honour at ALBACON 84, a Science Fiction and Fantasy convention held at Glasgow's Central Hotel (which was part of Glasgow's Central Station). I drew a portrait of him for the convention programme book. Although I shied away from such conventions due to the overload of people, noise and events, I still participated in them through the production of artwork, particularly portraits of the various guests. (The American writer Harlan Ellison had also been scheduled to appear but couldn't make it at the last minute. I had produced a picture of him using a modified version of 'No Scream' which featured in the same programme book, nonetheless.) Moore's portrait was a parody of his Swamp Thing covers which depicted him as an amalgam of his various creations. I imbued the image with as much Virgil Finlay-like detail as possible, and hoped he got the joke.

I had the chance to ask him during the first day of the convention when I saw him signing autographs in the corridor outside the art show. Under other circumstances, I wouldn't have dared approach Moore or any other celebrity for that matter, but as I was the one responsible for his image in the programme book, I figured I was entitled to stand in his presence at least once.

I was still leery of approaching him as he was clearly intelligent and this meant there was a possibility he could detect my stupidity early on. I resolved to stick to technical matters with lots of quotes from his work designed to keep him from detecting my lack of mental worth. (Quoting is second nature to the ASD brain as we usually remember things we like in perfect detail. As it turns out, nothing will creep-out a writer more than some obsessed oddball regurgitating wholesale chunks of text or dialogue they had written, and forgotten in years past.)

Taking the obvious route, I also asked for his autograph, clumsily slipping in the fact that his portrait was my handiwork. Much to my relief, he did like it and bought me a lemonade by way of thanks. We started talking. My initial trepidation about not knowing what to say vanished instantly with his astonishing opening comment.

'You must really like Virgil Finlay.'

Moore had no idea that he had just trod on the verbal equivalent of a landmine by bringing that name into the conversation. Delighted, I launched into an immediate and lengthy lecture on the subject.

'...so, it's obvious Finlay was using a wide range of techniques ranging from crosshatching and feathering combined with scraperboard to render the effects in his pictures rather than just stippling alone. The scraperboard handles the denser areas of the shading while the stipple is used for lighter. You can see this in his illustrations for A. Merritt's 'The Face in the Abyss' and Robert Abernathy's 'The Rottifers' where the strokes start off as scraperboard lines to become feathering and finally lighter stippling. I use Rotrings and Marsmatics to render line work. According to what I have read, he drew using a 290 lithographic pen. I'm not exactly sure what that is but I have asked my local art shop to try to obtain one for me.'

'Right,' said Moore and glanced around quickly (doubtless for an escape route).

I stopped, realising my mistake. I had discovered over the years that waxing lyrical about my favourite artist's techniques was a sure route to a sleeping audience. *Show interest in other people's thoughts, regardless of how pointless they seem to be,* I reminded myself. I quickly changed the subject to comics,

Portrait of Alan Moore

and we conversed on the subject for a short while before he left to helm a panel. Before going, he thanked me for the picture, and complimented me on its quality. I have to say that it was one of my better memories of that period. It was shortly after this that I died.

I was not aware of my demise until someone pointed it out in a local newspaper featuring an article on the Polmont rail disaster. On July 30, 1984 a high speed express train travelling between Glasgow and Edinburgh struck a cow which had wandered onto the track at Polmont, near Falkirk. The impact derailed several carriages, resulting in 13 deaths and 61 injuries. A small paragraph at the bottom of the main column in the article stated: '...one of the victims was Thomas Campbell, a recently graduated graphic artist from the east-end of Glasgow.' Considering I was Thomas Campbell, a recently graduated graphic artist from the east-end of Glasgow, I found this obituary somewhat surprising. There was more to come: this Thomas Campbell was roughly the same age as me (he was a year older), had left Art college around the same time as me and was commuting in the direction of Edinburgh.

During my college years I had been told about a number of illustration studios in Edinburgh and had intended to look these places up for possible employment (this was prior to the emergence of my health problems), a fact I had mentioned to several parties. Given this string of morbid coincidences, it was inevitable that many assumed the poor guy was me. One local comic fan and shop owner informed Moore of the tragic news; his response was to commiserate my loss both as a person and an artist. The same fan nearly jumped out of his skin when I walked into his shop, very much alive, a few days later. I have often wondered who that other Thomas Campbell was. Although our paths never crossed, it is possible they came very close.

During one of my first-year Science classes at Whitehill we were asked to give samples of our blood for slides. I was reluctant to prick my finger with the tiny scalpel so the teacher let me see the blood of someone with a little more courage, someone from the year above me: his name also was Thomas Campbell. The slide had a fairly impressive smear on it. 'Your namesake wouldn't stop bleeding, Campbell,' said the teacher. At the time, I was deeply unnerved by the notion of someone else walking around with my name. These days, I am more affected by the grotesque irony that holding a glass slide stained with blood was perhaps the closest I got to meeting my tragic doppelganger.

~~~

My next encounter with Alan Moore was during a comics mart held in the city's largest library a few months later. I hadn't really wanted to go, but it was a chance to get away from my street and lose myself in some cheap comics. As usual Moore was surrounded by a gaggle of fans and looked fairly unreachable. I was surprised when he recognised me and called out to me with the appallingly clichéd line:

'Tom Campbell! I heard you were dead!'

I replied that I was not and walked away. I suppose I could have responded with some equally hokey, comics-style reply like: 'That was just an android duplicate!' or 'Fool… you only saw what I wanted you to see!' but speed of reply was never my forte, besides, I hadn't all my wits around me by that point. Isolation was wearing me down, and my Whitehill-induced sense of worthlessness was steadily returning as the days wore on. I had been receiving treatment for depression and it wasn't working. I was despairing and totally obsessed by bodily malfunction. I spent my waking hours convinced that fate held some dire biological surprise just around the corner. That fear was totally justified, as I discovered some months later, when the doctors took a look in my eyes.

CLIVE BARKER OFFERS ME A JOB IN THE MOVIES

'Chronic pain is the most fearful of all burdens.'
Vernon Coleman MD

~~~

O ur tears, we take them for granted as symbols of sorrow, joy or even rage. We may give them marginally greater attention should we use them to wash out a small piece of dust or insect unfortunate enough to fly into our eye. Very few ever realise they are a thin layer which separates us from a lifetime of agony. I certainly never gave mine a second thought until we parted company a week before my twenty-third birthday; they couldn't have picked a worse time.

~~~

My problem was discovered during a routine test for another condition which had manifested shortly after leaving college. I'd always had slight double vision but, as my work towards the end of college became more intricate, I found myself beset by headaches and bouts of blurriness. I ignored the problem for over a year before getting it looked at. The ophthalmologist identified it as 'Ocular Drift' - a weak convergence reflex. I was given a range of exercises intended to strengthen this and admitted back on a semi-regular basis for check-ups.

The doctor who detected my new problem was a polite young Asian. During the middle of a convergence exercise - during which he spent more time than usual examining the surface of my eye - he told me he wanted to try another test. This was excruciatingly painful as it involved placing two plastic strips under my lower eyelids. When it was finished, the doctor told me that my tear production was extremely poor, particularly in my right eye.

'That eye is producing almost no tears at all,' he said.

Dry-Eye (Ocular irritation) Syndrome, the condition was unknown to me, although I had noticed my eyes had become sticky and irritable over the last few weeks. During my first years I believed the condition to be the result of stress. The discovery that my cousins suffer from it also suggests a genetic component. (In fact, a possible link between congenital eye problems and ASD was noted by child psychoanalyst, Selma Fraiberg, as far back as the 70's.) I asked the doctor what was to be done.

'There is very little that we can do,' was his reply. He explained that I would have to use artificial tears to lubricate my eyes from now on and that I would probably find myself more susceptible to eye infections as a result of the condition. I asked him what would happen were I to stop using the drops.

'Small ulcers would develop in your eyes,' was his reply.

I didn't ask any more questions after that. I felt sick. First my hands, now my eyes. My career, my life was under attack.

~~~

A month after my diagnosis, I was assaulted on the main road near to my house by a football thug. Shortly afterwards, my older brother was badly beaten by a local gang on our front doorstep. As the little sub-humans who picked on us grew into big sub-humans, so the persecution of our family began to escalate. It felt like the whole world had returned to that changing room. I couldn't stand it any more; I had to be free of this life of oppression and terror. I had to escape.

In my own, desperate fashion I'd always struggled to follow a dream cleaner than the emotional and physical squalor of my background. Unfortunately my means of escape seemed under threat by some form of insidious erosion. For the first time, I began to truly understand what it meant to be trapped. This accumulation of malfunctions, in the face of my needs, had started to seem strangely deliberate, perhaps even conspiratorial. I'd always seen patterns in the events which occurred around me before but never *malevolence*. Now such a thing was becoming obvious, perhaps even logical. After all, if human beings were basically evil then why shouldn't the universe which created them also harbour some innate enmity? I explained these theories to my new GP during a particularly despairing - actually, near-suicidal - visit and promptly found myself hospitalised at Glasgow's Gartloch Psychiatric Hospital for the next few months. It seemed The Halfman was right after all: I was mad. (Actually, it is estimated that 31% of all adults on the autistic spectrum develop mental illness at some point in their life.)

Discussions with psychiatrists were amazingly frustrating and virtually pointless. Time and time again I was forced to explain I did not hear voices except through my ears. The professionals I encountered persistently focused on Little Russia, while ignoring my attempts to explain my isolation and paralyzing sense of school-induced worthlessness. (As usual, communication was hampered by a lack of language.) After being given some impossibly naïve life advice - I was told to 'stop' being an outcast – the shrink informed me that I had grown up in something called an 'emotional vacuum' and that the solution to my problems lay in my 'coming to terms' with what had happened to me. I had no idea what 'coming to terms' actually meant; thirty years later, I still don't, not really. From what I mentioned before, it seems to be some form of neurotypical alchemy involving the transmutation of one emotion into another through an act of sheer will. Had I been capable of such a thing, I would have employed it on the spot.

Unfortunately, my brain, like The Halfman's, lacks such flexibility; it will rage back and forth against an unacceptable situation for hours, years or even decades without losing one iota of energy. When it became clear I wasn't responding to their 'treatment', the psychiatrists simply had me medicated and dumped in a corner. At the time, I accepted their words as gospel. I now recognize them as stock phrases; verbal band aids slapped over a person's life by professionals too lazy to do their jobs properly.

I have read a fair amount of literature on other people's experiences with the stigma of mental illness. Perhaps through shame, several have tried to glamorize the experience, even attempted to depict it as some kind of fashion statement. I can't say I have ever thought of it on those terms. There is nothing more terrifying than being in the grip of pressures larger than yourself, forces that can bend you out of shape until you are unrecognizable. The summer of '86 was the most nightmarish period of my adulthood. I felt totally helpless.

For the first time, since leaving Whitehill, I had become a passenger in my life again.

~~~

The middle 80's may have been a bleak period for me but they were quite opposite for a young Liverpudlian author by the name of Clive Barker. Skilled in a multitude of fields from writing to feature film production, Barker's arrival on the Fantasy scene was nothing less than explosive. He first reached public awareness through a series of anthologies titled CLIVE BARKER'S BOOKS OF BLOOD. These, often surrealistically twisted tales, pushed the boundaries of what was considered acceptable in mainstream supernatural fiction with their combinations of physical perversity and often comic-style imagery. (In Barker's short story, SON OF CELLULOID, a young filmgoer engages in a bout of fisticuffs with a carcinoma which just happens to be impersonating John Wayne.)

Barker was the guest of honour at Albacon 86. Shortly before my admission to hospital I'd produced a stippled portrait of him for the programme book (done, of course, in the style of Virgil Finlay). I posted this to him, along with a moderately incoherent letter, via an Editor by the name of Steve Jones - a friend of Barker's and the unit publicist for his up and coming feature-film debut, HELLRAISER.

I'd been in correspondence with Steve for a while after submitting some work for his supernatural anthology magazine FANTASY TALES. I'd produced the cover and interior illustration for the main story of issue No. 15: Fritz Lieber's 'In the X-ray', for which I'd received excellent reviews for rendering yet another Finlay-influenced piece. (I'd chosen this magazine with its pulp-style presentation as part of my attempts to follow in Finlay's footsteps.)

On the date of the convention, I was allowed out for the weekend to attend. This was on the understanding I stuck to my medication. I met Barker at the art show. Like me, he was exhibiting several pictures there. I only realized who he was from the crowd of fans clinging to him. He was a neat man of boundless enthusiasm. Having gone from struggling writer to overnight Horror celebrity and film director, his world must have been moving in fast-forward. Using the tried-and-true method of asking for his autograph and hoping he would recognise my name, I introduced myself. This approach worked for Moore, I was surprised to find that it worked even better with Barker (I called him Clive at the time. These days, such familiarity sounds like name-dropping).

'Tom Campbell. Oh good! Pleased to meet you. Got a minute? Loved the portrait by the way.' (No mention of Virgil Finlay. Bah!)

He led me into the art show. I couldn't walk very fast as the medication was affecting my balance. We stopped at the display featuring my own work. He indicated one of the pictures.

'Is this one for sale?'

The piece in question was a painting, not a drawing. I'd taught myself to paint during the latter months of college, with no help at all from the tutors. Like writing, it was not a gradual process, rather it simply happened. After this, my colour work went from the bottom of the class to the top. Once I'd got the hang of producing tonal gradations without brushstrokes, I used this long-sought anchoring point in my conquest of colour. In time, I refined the technique to the point that many assumed my work was rendered by airbrush and not by hand (although in the case of this piece, there was a small amount of airbrushing on the background sky). This finish was necessary, since even the slightest uncontrolled brushstroke, would have been an admission of defeat, and driven me into a terrible rage.

The painting was a paperback-style image depicting a gangly, space-suited alien striding along a mountain ledge with the inevitable planet and moons hanging in the background sky. It was titled 'Rhubarb Alien with Ceramic Jockstrap;' it had originally been called 'Alien Astronaut' until my older brother commented that the creature's gangly body and purple suit made it look like a piece of walking rhubarb (sporting a ceramic jockstrap no less). This piece, in particular, seemed to impress Barker. It was part of a portfolio I'd been assembling to find work in the paperback field, at least until the dry-eye bit down and things began to unravel.

'How much is it going for?' he asked.

My mind drew a complete blank; worse than usual, due to the drugs. I had no idea how much to charge for a painting, having never sold one in my life.

'Ah... um... Fifty pounds,' I replied.

The figure seemed to surprise him. I wondered if I should have charged less. I was about to suggest twenty when his next statement nearly knocked me off my feet.

'Listen, are you interested in designing for feature films?'

I thought he was joking. Things like this simply did not happen to me. I froze for a minute. After a while it occurred to me that I should reply.

'What?.. er... yes... I mean, of course... um... certainly, uh...'

'Well, I'm working on several projects at the moment and I'll be looking for someone with your abilities.'

I thought it best not to mention I was on day release from psychiatric hospital. My guts were in the grip of a growing nausea and I was having problems with the overload of the convention. Despite assurances from my psychiatrist, the side effects of the medication were not going away, if anything, they were getting worse (autistic brains are notorious for unusual and often extreme reactions to certain drugs). These manifested themselves as a state of hair-trigger agitation accompanied by slight, but persistent visual distortions. Over the last few days I'd noticed a number of objects located around my peripheral vision were bulging towards me. I'd hoped this disconcerting illusion would clear up by the time of the convention. It hadn't. Worse still, it was joined by yet another: the ground underfoot had begun throbbing slightly. Since the hotel hosting the convention was next to a train station, I'd assumed this was the result of approaching trains. However, it was becoming clear the resonation I was feeling through the soles of my feet could not be put down to any approaching vehicle. I tried to ignore all this as Barker continued talking about his various projects. In the middle of everything, I was struck by a sudden, horrible thought.

'*What if he can smell me?*'

To put none too fine a point on it, I was stinking. I hadn't showered for quite some time. Having witnessed violence and public defecation in the washroom of the ward, I had steadfastly avoided the place. I was also sporting a tatty and matted beard after discovering the shaving equipment given to patients was used and reused by just about everyone. Since the ward often admitted people with drug problems - and this was during the 80's AIDS scare - I declined the use of the dirty, often bloodstained razors casually handed out by the nurses.

The idea that my big break could be undone by poor hygiene upped the volume on my already jangling nerves. There was the added problem of the visual distortions encroaching on my vision the longer I talked. Feeling attacked on several fronts, I succumbed to sudden panic and decided I had to leave. I made my apologies, promised to keep in contact with Barker and left the building. Outside, I tore a strip of paper from the programme book and started to chew it to help me collect my thoughts. Experiencing sudden hunger, I decided to find real food. A nearby cafe provided me with a fish and chips meal. The rest of the convention passed in a haze. *I was going to be a film designer.*

I could see it all: I would design the most astonishing creations for multi-million dollar feature films. These would be brought to life using the most advanced makeup and animatronics available (CGI was still years away) and look as good as the Alien or The Thing. The status of such achievement would be overwhelming, far outstripping that of my teachers and peers at Whitehill. Reaching such heights would allow me to escape the place and the rest of my old life: the brutality, poverty and isolation. Everyone would want to hang around with a film designer, no matter how weird. There was going to

Portrait of Clive Barker

Rhubarb alien with ceramic jockstrap

be a happy ending to the nightmare after all. I was finally going to become a 'real' person.

Barker and I corresponded for a few months after the convention. I sent him the painting and he replied with a card adorned with one of his excellent drawings. In it he reiterated his intention to use me as a designer on his approaching film projects. He paid me £200 for the painting, four times what I'd thought of charging for it. The all-too-brief weeks which followed were unlike any I'd ever experienced. For the first, and last, time in my adult life I was not trapped in the corridors of Whitehill. Looking back now, this state of mind seems so removed from my norm as to be hallucinatory. I try not to think of such freedom nowadays as I find it too painful.

~~~

Of course, it didn't happen or this book would never have been written. The one thing the young Asian doctor had not prepared me for was the *pain* of dry-eye. The condition had manifested itself during the colder months. Since heating was never used in our house, I had no idea how my eyes would react to raised temperatures. As it turned out, they didn't react well at all. In the months after the convention, the weather brightened with spring's approach. The warming of the world was welcomed by everyone except me. The irritation in my eyes, particularly the right one, increased to a persistent burning that felt like soap or hot fat. Applying the drops did nothing to stop this. In fact they actually seemed to make the pain worse as I experienced a sharp sting every time one was applied. At first, I was able to ignore the pain. However, after a few weeks, the opposite occurred and it started to bother me constantly, eventually eating its way through to every level of my awareness.

Autistics have a problem with chronic pain. In her book LIFE BEHIND GLASS, Aspergers writer Wendy Lawson describes a similar reaction: an ability to ignore pain that transforms into an obsession with the sensation if it does not go away. The medical term used to describe this alteration of the pain process is 'Perceptual Inconstancy'. In his book UNDERSTANDING THE NATURE OF AUTISM AND ASPERGERS DISORDER, Edward R. Rivito MD discusses the problem, suggesting: 'Brain systems in autism filter out the pain at certain times and thus the child does not respond appropriately, while at other times, the brain amplifies the pain and makes it worse.'

This was certainly true in my case. As a child, I'd fallen and slashed my leg on a piece of glass. Discovering the limb had been opened up almost to the bone only elicited mild interest on my part. Both the injury and the accompanying pain were ignored as I returned home to watch an episode of LOST IN SPACE. (After the episode, I told The Halfman I had injured myself and was thumped before being taken to hospital for stitches.).

Unfortunately, this little Aspergers wrinkle isn't just limited to children. The pain of my childhood injury was only transitory, gone before I was able to grasp it was there; in that sense it was not real to me. This stinging in my eyes was another matter entirely. It was constant and therefore very real. It drove me into a state of despair that painkillers and artificial tears did nothing to alleviate. '*Why now?*' I thought. This was my big break, my chance to escape. It couldn't be taken from me like this. At my insistence I was given another appointment with an eye specialist to look for a solution to my problem. I wish I hadn't gone.

During my bouts of ill-health I'd encountered some crummy professionals and some good ones. The young man who had diagnosed the condition had been very polite and almost apologetic. The woman ophthalmologist I found myself facing that particular day was from the other end of the compassion spectrum. She seemed to have forgotten that the organs she worked with were attached to people. I realised things were not going well when she evidenced confusion over my fears concerning lifelong pain. I explained I was an artist and that the condition was interfering with my work. This seemed to mean very little to her. In fact, she hinted that I was wasting her time.

'It's a minor condition,' she said.

The pain wasn't minor, it was horrible. By this point in the summer it felt as though ground glass were being rubbed into my eyes on an hourly basis. It robbed me of my ability to concentrate, to think straight, and drove me mad in the process. I was no stranger to physical suffering. It had been part of my existence from earliest childhood. My first sensory memories were blows from The Arm. Yet even with that brutality, there had been periods of respite.

Dry-eye was different. The pain was every moment and, for me, in the worst area imaginable. I could not work with it, nor could I distract myself from it. I explained this to the doctor, yet it still didn't seem to mean anything to her. Her attitude was something all too common in the caring profession: specialists who dictated to patients whether their condition was serious or not, regardless of what effects it had on their lives.

Telling an artist that debilitating ocular pain is a minor condition is the equivalent of saying a paralysed foot is not a problem for a runner. Sadly, during my later years meeting other patients in pain clinics, I found this incredibly insensitive - in fact near sociopathic - attitude towards pain to be a widespread problem in the health service.

'What's causing it?'

'Your tear-film is very bad. In the right eye it's lousy.'

'I mean the condition. What's causing it? Will it get better?'

'No, changes of this sort are usually permanent.'

She was saying that this was forever? She had to be joking.

'What caused it?'

She replied with a series of vague and incomplete answers that only confused me. I responded by asking the same questions over and over again. Annoyed, she indicated a bottle of artificial tears.

'Look, your tears lubricate and protect your eyes. You secrete them every time you blink. Even the manual application of a more viscous solution cannot match this.'

'What caused the condition?' I asked. The malfunction of any portion of my body was something of a concern for me. She seemed to find the question silly.

'It could be anything, central heating; anything.'

I later discovered this was not true. While exposure to central heating can certainly thin a tear-film, there is no evidence to suggest it is actually capable of causing full blown Dry-Eye Syndrome. Were that the case, the condition would be far more widespread than it is. Genuinely afraid, I pressed the point again. This annoyed her even further.

'Can we find out what caused the condition?'

'There's no point. We wouldn't be able to do anything about it.'

'I would still like to know what caused the condition.'

'There's no point.'

'What's going to happen?'

'That eye is going to sting like *blazes* from now on. Even putting in the drops will cause pain.'

'How do I stop the pain?'

'On a hot day, you may have to go through a bottle a day.'

This was the closest thing she gave me to an answer on the subject and, as I discovered, it wasn't an answer at all.

'What if I stopped using the drops?'

'You lose the eye.'

Lose the eye? That couldn't be true.

'Has this anything to do with my ocular drift?'

She checked my notes.

'No it's not related.' Then she dismissed me with an all-too jocular comment: 'You just have to accept you have the wrong body for the kind of work that you do.'

And that was it.

~~~

'*You lose the eye.*' I was numb as I left the ophthalmology department. Blindness was one of my greatest fears. The idea of my eyes requiring manual maintenance for fear of wearing away was beyond appalling and would haunt me from that point on. The full impact of the doctor's words would not hit home for a few weeks, but even at this dulled level the shock was enough to stagger me. The hospital was a short distance from Firpark Street so I took a detour there before returning to Gartloch. Finding the wall where Mum used to wait, I sat and tried to 'come to terms' with my situation.

'*You lose the eye.*'

'*You have the wrong body for the kind of work that you do.*'

'*You lose the eye.*'

'*On a hot day, you may have to go through a bottle a day,*' or '*You lose the eye.*'

How often did that mean I had to use the tears? Taking out one of the spare bottles I'd been hoarding, I squeezed the contents onto the back of my hand and counted out seventy-four large drops which I rounded off to seventy. Seventy drops a day on a hot day. Assuming I rose at seven or eight in the morning and retired around eleven at night; that meant my waking day consisted of approximately sixteen hours. I tried to sub-divide these by seventy to arrive at the exact times in which to apply the drops. Since my arithmetic hadn't improved in the slightest since my primary years, this turned out to be a futile exercise. I calculated and failed then re-calculated and failed once again. Eventually I crashed, whiting out completely. The burning in my eyes brought me back to an awareness which was nine-tenths despair.

'*You lose the eye.*'

The doctor's callous, evasive and contradictory advice was the worst medical sloppiness I'd ever encountered. For starters if, as she told me, using the drops would actually cause pain, then how was emptying an entire bottle into my eyes expected to stop them hurting? A few months later I learned from a student ophthalmologist that applying drops so often would break up the existing tear-film and actually do more harm than good. I recently discovered that applying any solution containing the toxic preservative Benzalkonium Hexachloride – a component of all drops prescribed me at the time – more than four times daily would have damaged my eyes by scarring the cornea.

There are plenty of online horror stories about this debilitating and often nightmarish condition, mine is far from the worst. The most terrible thing is just how little seriousness the medical world attaches to it, even in the face of sufferers committing suicide. To this day many within the medical profession refuse to recognize chronic ocular pain as a condition deserving of study and proper treatment. In all my years I have never encountered an eye specialist who regarded the condition as anything other than 'minor'. I've met other sufferers; the one thing we have all observed is that only doctors say this.

At this point in my life, I didn't need to be told by someone who represented the medical side of The Rules that I had the 'wrong body'. I needed an ally against the world, not another enemy. In the weeks that followed, my mental state slipped further. The pain ate me alive. The knowledge that it was forever plunged me into pits of despair I hadn't dreamed possible. My confidence crumbled to the extent that even basic tasks terrified me. My eyes were not going to get any better, ever. The prospect of a career in films, based on these compromised orbs, now inspired despair where it had once generated hope. I felt I had no choice but to inform Clive Barker of this. '*You lose the eye.*' '*...go through bottle a day,*' seventy drops, or else '*You lose the eye.*'

'Good God!' he said over the phone.

It all went to pieces after that. I couldn't face the pressure of his offer and gradually fell out of contact with him. Barker's career was only just beginning and it soon became obvious to me that I would be a liability to anyone in a professional situation. This was my decision. The responsibility to stay in contact was on my side as his time was taken up by a multitude of creative projects. One day I decided not to phone him, nor to send another letter. It was probably for the best as, looking back now, some of my last calls, made from the ward, probably sounded just a little bit on the crazy side. (My reaction to the medication still hadn't abated and my psychiatrist's reaction was to simply increase the dosage).

I kept Barker's card, I'm not sure why. Every few years I summon up the courage to bring it out and look at it. It's a window into a life that never was, much like my paperback career. Still at least I touched the big time, even if I couldn't hang onto it. Not bad for someone who would 'never amount to anything'. I suppose I should thank Clive Barker for at least giving me one moment of freedom from Whitehill.

After a few months, I was discharged to a place called Huntley Lodge. This was a halfway house for ex-psychiatric patients located in Glasgow's West End (situated directly across the street from the apartment of emerging comics mega-talent Grant Morrison) run by a mental health charity called the Richmond Fellowship. It was there I tried to pick up the pieces of my life. It didn't happen. I was like the proverbial lion with a thorn lodged in its paw. The atrocious stinging followed me wherever I went, ruining every waking moment with its reminder of what it had taken from me. I was young, supposedly with my whole life in front of me; yet there could be no foundations of any sort built on such unending agony.

I began to suffer from terrible panic attacks and my already damaged sleeping patterns disintegrated completely. During my time in the Lodge, I tried to undertake some commercial work to make a little money. It was then I discovered that the pain increased the more I used my eyes. (The tear-film is sustained by blinking, reading or producing artwork results in a reduced blink-rate which thins the film. This is not a problem for a normal eye. For a compromised tear-film it is disastrous.) I could not stand the burning and was forced to abandon the project halfway. For the first time in my life I let an employer down. At that point, I realised my career as an artist was finished.

Art was my life. It was the crutch I'd spent years building just so I could stand in the presence of others. It defined me and gave me my occasional moments of worth. Art was my only real link to the world. Without it, I had nothing. I had spent the last six years stippling and painting just to hold Whitehill at bay. Now that protection was gone and my old school closed its jaws around my throat forever. I was worthless; I was 'Campbell'; I was 'Bushman' once more. Finally, I had an inkling of what The Halfman must have felt after losing his arm. Dry eye, this 'minor condition' had taken an entire world from me. It had erected a barrier of pain that forever separated me from the life I had worked for, a life I needed to live because it would have saved me from the demons of my past. Now there would be no such salvation.

~~~

Around this time, I would visit Mum in the East End where I drove my family to despair by talking hour after hour about my condition. During one such excursion, I bumped into Jack, or rather what was left of him. This was not our first meeting since leaving the Festival. I'd encountered him in the street during my second year at college. On our first meeting, he asked if I was still drawing pictures of Spiderman (his pronunciation of the 'I' in 'Spider' still annoyed me). He was gardening for the Glasgow Parks department by that point. I have to admit that, despite my problems at college, I felt more than a little smug on seeing this. He was involved in manual labour whereas I was in the process of being 'educated'. As usual, this doesn't sound particularly nice, but all I can say by way of defence is that I was desperate not to admit I was in the same boat as him.

On this second meeting, things were very different. The last few years had been bad for me, I was taken aback to see that they had been even worse for him. He had deteriorated badly, was far heavier than before and wobbling from foot to foot. I knew this was due to medication as I'd seen this type of movement and weight-gain on those prescribed major tranquillisers. (I'd even experienced the same type of physical agitation after being prescribed similar drugs.) We were near a psychiatric clinic called Karswell House; this was situated just behind Mum's so I suspected he had just left the place.

Jack had never been the world's greatest conversationalists but now his attempts at speech were reduced to a few halting comments, many of which made no sense. During our attempted discourse - in which I was only interested in talking about my eyes - a woman walked past. Jack's reaction astonished me. Upon seeing her, he made a gurgling sound and immediately turned away to face the wall at our side. I didn't know what to make of this, and almost laughed as I found it both disturbing and slightly funny. *Loony*, I thought, then remembered my own situation. Once the woman had passed, Jack turned to face me again, mumbling an apology that he 'Had a thing where he couldn't be around women.' After that, the conversation pretty much ground to a halt.

The Halfman once told me how he witnessed a young horse being broken on a Canadian farm. Looking at Jack, I realised this process was not limited to animals. I had time for my own hell and nothing else, so the presence of despair that exceeded my own elicited no sympathy on my part. If anything, I felt a stab of anger that Jack dared indulge himself in such a state in the face of my problems. Making my excuses I left, hoping never to see him again. I got my wish, I never did. Looking back, I wonder if I should have stayed. I may be paying lip service to conscience by saying probably not. In all likelihood he wouldn't have benefited from another malfunctioning mind in his life. That said, I think I at least owe him some recognition for abandoning him. For that reason I am writing this.

Like most on the autistic spectrum I was not born with the complete range of mental software issued to neurotypicals but I was able to acquire an approximation in later life. Amongst this was a sense of responsibility and fairness. With these in place, I began to understand that there is something very wrong with the way our society treats certain types of human being; looking back over my last memories of this crippled innocent, I am convinced of this. More than anyone I have encountered, it was Jack who started me thinking in this area. His tragedy became my ultimate anchoring point, a human one.

Describing Jack as 'one of those who don't know how to talk to other people' is hardly an effective way of communicating the scope of his problem. More specifically, he has severely deficient social, communication and assertive skills. I discovered a perfect term to describe this in a review of Martin Scorse's TAXI DRIVER. In this classic film, Robert Deniro plays a young man driven to acts of violence by a life of isolation and frustration. In the review, I chanced on a term that lodged in my mind. The text described Deniro's character as a 'social inarticulate'. I remembered the term and realised, over a decade later, that it perfectly described Jack, myself and so many others.

Outcasts like Jack exist in countless numbers. People see them in every walk of life without seeing them for what they are. The worst thing is that he entered this world with as much right to life as anyone else, and this is the first thing our society has denied him. The life most people take for granted as normal is something he will spend the rest of his existence looking at from a great distance. Through no fault of his own, he faces a life-sentence of mockery, dismissal and ostracism which could not be inflicted on a convicted criminal. His future will be an endless cycle of isolation, illness and hospitalisation. The numerous psychiatrists and professionals he will pass through will have neither the courage nor the language to offer him any real help. They will drug him, break his symptoms down into medical terms and, all the while, avoid the awful truth of what he really is.

In actual fact there is very little wrong with Jack (at least there wasn't to begin with). He is simply reacting to the forces that shaped, and continue shape him. Despite this, you will find no mention of his plight in any literature concerning our interactions or any impassioned speech on human rights; doing so would mean highlighting an area of our behaviour so shameful our society has chosen to deny its existence.

Jack is a socially inarticulate person existing - not living - in a culture in which the devaluation of his kind is an unchallenged social norm. He is something which cannot exist in a civilised society but nonetheless exists in ours: an innocent denied status and even basic acceptance within the human race.

Jack, like most social inarticulates, is a second-class citizen.

THE BLINDSPOT

E quality is an absolute. It's for everyone or it's a lie. I can tell you from experience it's certainly not for everyone In my book that makes it a lie.

One of the more popular myths of recent years is that second-class citizenship is impossible in a civilised society like ours. According to lore, we employ a range of laws to prevent any minority falling prey to such a thing. The problem lies with these laws only covering recognised prejudices and recognised minorities. Our everyday social behaviour is vastly more complex than is acknowledged by such two-dimensional regulations. The true laws which underscore our interaction are far from fair and have never been committed to paper. They are much too animalistic for that.

This brings us to another myth: that second-class citizenship is solely the creation of corrupt governments. Sadly, this school of thought does not recognise the possibility of such things being brought about through the collective amorality and ignorance of the people themselves. The second myth is hardest to confront as it clashes with the almost-sacred notion that the majority of our citizens, left to their own devices, are basically fair in their attitudes; itself leading to the assumption that this society's most destructive prejudices are safely marginalised onto specific, easy to identify groups. Nothing could be further from the truth. Second-class citizenship is as real as the ground beneath our feet and those who enforce it are the ordinary people who walk that ground, uneducated and educated alike.

~~~

Most humans are social animals with a basic need for integration within the ranks of their own. Recognition, acceptance and respect are as important to the stability of the average mind as food is for the body. Denial of these needs can lead to a range of appalling emotional and mental consequences. Unfortunately, social acceptance is not guaranteed simply because an individual happens to hail from the same species as their peers. One unpleasant aspect of our society is that the majority of our citizens, with few exceptions, have an automatic tendency to close ranks on any individual lacking certain characteristics. The most prominent of these (apart from physical attractiveness) are called *social skills*: this is the ability to casually communicate with others in a fashion they find interesting or entertaining. The presence of social skills - and the confidence they bring - indicates to others that you are worth listening to and, at a more animal level, you are 'one of us'. The greater these skills, the higher the position an individual may achieve in company and, to a certain extent, within society itself.

Sadly the opposite is also true. A lack of these all-important skills, and accompanying confidence, communicates that an individual is neither deserving of an audience nor even basic respect; in animal terms they have no 'pack status'. (Incidentally, vulnerability and social inarticulacy are not the same thing, but they usually go hand in hand. It is true that there can be emotional vulnerability without social inarticulacy but where there is social inarticulacy there will always be vulnerability.) Regardless of what many say, these are the true laws which shape the majority of our interactions even at the most educated and enlightened of levels.

Social skills are a learned behaviour. The average person acquires them during childhood and adolescence through play and other forms of contact with their peers; for this reason, they are taken completely for granted. Unfortunately this learning is not a universal experience. Many young people, through no fault of their own, are denied the development of these abilities during their formative years. A lack of social skills in a youngster can be a devastating thing; it is no less so for an adult. Yet another irresponsible myth cultivated in our society (and I know because I've been handed this nonsense on more than one occasion) is the notion that once a young outcast leaves school and enters adult society, they are immediately accepted by the 'responsible' adults they find there. An extension of this is the belief that, by virtue of reaching adulthood themselves, they spontaneously acquire a full range of social skills; said skills, and the presence of mature company allows the ex-pariah to live a life of acceptance and fulfilment; happy ending.

This is complete rubbish. What really happens is that the young outcast finds themselves just as much an object of dismissal and disrespect in the company of adults as they were during their childhood. (True, the spectre of violence fades, but only to be replaced by a slower and subtler form of damage.) Rejection of this sort usually leads to a vicious circle of isolation and mental deterioration from which there is little chance of escape.

When I describe outcasts as second-class citizens I'm not exaggerating, nor am I using the term in any metaphorical sense; I'm saying they are literally second-class citizens. Mainstream society openly devalues, ridicules and abuses these awkward, friendless pariahs to a level that could not be inflicted on any recognised minority. These marginalised weirdoes/nerds/geeks/dweebs are the one class of individual still considered a legitimate target for universal mockery to this day. At an unspoken, animal level, their inability to integrate is looked on as some kind of failure, one deserving not of understanding, but contempt.

Another deplorable fact I've observed is that the more maladroit and helpless an individual is in the social arena, the worse ordinary people will treat them. (Jack was by far the most vulnerable outcast I have ever encountered. The level of cruelty inflicted on him totally clashes with any picture we may cultivate of our 'civilised species'.) I call this behaviour 'the cruelty curve'; it's the result of another questionable attitude normalised by our culture: prejudice against vulnerability. This is the oldest of the prejudices, predating all others. It motivated our animal ancestors to weed out and destroy their weaker own. In juvenile society, it is primarily physical vulnerability that is targeted. In adult society, it is largely the emotional vulnerability of the outcast and oddball that is seized upon.

~~~

In theory and on paper, Jack is a member of this society, a full citizen with just as many rights and social opportunities as the next person. The reality is quite different. Were a cross-section of our society - say a hundred 'morally aware' human beings - plucked from their everyday lives and placed in social contact with him, most wouldn't even give this damaged young man the time of day. Virtually all would ignore him. A very large number would treat him openly with disrespect. Many would go out of their way to ridicule him (often as groups). A few would subject him to outright hostility. No-one would have a problem with any of this, at least not enough to do anything about it. For the last three decades, I've observed this behaviour to be one of the most reliable human constants. If it isn't second class citizenship in action then I don't know what is. This is the world Jack lives in. It's the one that destroyed him.

One comic piece which illustrates this point was created by the British artist/writer RICHARD COWDRY. I've included a mention of it here as it functions as perfect companion to this chapter. In his self-published magazine THE BEDSIT JOURNAL (www.bedsitjournal.com), Cowdry often displays a preoccupation with the subject of social isolation. His most striking piece can be found on the back cover of issue #2 of the publication. Titled HOW TO SUCCEED AT FAILURE: A STEP BY STEP GUIDE.

This, possibly autobiographical, story charts the life of an outcast from his earliest experiences of social rejection all the way to his mental breakdown in adulthood. The strip is a blackly humorous, one-colour affair drawn in Cowdry's distinctive cartoon style. Despite its apparent simplicity, it manages to pack more truth about social rejection into its nine panels than can be found in any hundred books attempting to cover the subject. In many ways it is the flipside of that callous library poster from Whitehill, and a more truthful piece for it. The image from panel seven in particular - that of the young outcast lying drunk and despondent in a shabby, rented room - packs a punch that is both grotesquely funny and deeply tragic. (This is comic illustration at its finest: communicating an idea - in this case a truth - at an intellectual and emotional level and doing so with a minimum of clutter.)

On the subject of mental illness, our health service has a particularly spineless way of tackling the damage arising from this type of isolation. During the early stages of my deterioration, I passed through a number of psychiatrists who listened to my tales of isolation and woe. Eventually I was dispatched to something called 'social skills classes'.

In these, I found myself surrounded by several other young outcasts, most suffering mental illness and many bloated on the types of long-term medication used to suppress such a thing. The tutors at these classes attempted to teach these young pariahs all the necessary communication codes and observational skills needed to open society's doors. One of the lessons specifically handed out to me was to lower and raise the pitch of my 'monotone' voice.

My memories of that most tragic of all classes are shared misery and shame; shame for being different; shame for being a failure and for needing this type of help. At the time, I was grateful for the efforts of these tutors (not that they did me any good, I had problems grasping most of the points they were trying to make). Now I feel only the deepest contempt for them.

During my years of mental illness I talked to many who attended such lessons; none seem to have benefited from the experience. My belief is that these classes are close to pointless. The comparison I would draw here is with attempting to cultivate verbal skills in feral children. Apparently there is something of a 'launch window' for doing this as, after a certain age, a child cannot be taught spoken language.

Teaching social skills to young adults is, in my opinion, similarly futile, although for different reasons. You cannot ostracise and devalue a human being throughout their formative years without irreparably crippling their confidence. This lack of strength is not easily masked by a few weeks feeble training. Such an exercise probably looks great on paper. In the real world, it's hopelessly naive because it does not take into consideration the still-active attitudes which denied their development in the first place. In practice, these artificial and somewhat fragile skills usually fare badly against these attitudes, leaving the outcast back at square one. I suspect this supposed solution is really little more than a symbolic gesture, our health service's way of saying, 'At least we tried.' The truth is, they could have tried a whole lot harder.

There is an oft-used STAR TREK scenario in which Captain Kirk encounters an apparently idyllic society hiding a terrible flaw at its core. This usually manifests as the maltreatment of a section of the population. The inhabitants of this society, due to their programming, cannot grasp the moral dichotomy in their midst. Captain Kirk, being an alien, lacks this conditioning and is able to see the invisible injustice happening before him (and striving to end it before the credits roll).

Autistics have, to a certain extent, an alien perspective on human matters. We are often missing certain inbuilt codes of 'correct' behaviour, the type that tell us what to see and what not to see. This is definitely the case with me. Like the good Captain, I lack my close-your-eyes-and-don't-see programming. From my point of view, I see the species-wide devaluation of a section of our population by an attitude which is clearly a prejudice, one the society around me appears wholly blind to. This observation brings me to the reason behind my contempt for the professionals I encountered during this period. I am contemptuous not of their naivety but their cowardice.

I'd never heard of social skills classes before being sent to them. Meetings for Alcoholics Anonymous, group therapy for gamblers or other forms of mental or personal malfunction, yes, I'd heard of those; read the occasional reference to such things, but not classes where damaged young people were taught communication skills in the hope they might be accepted by the society around them. This is an area in which our culture displays an unusual degree of ignorance, perhaps deliberately so. At a stretch, I can accept that the average citizen lacks objectivity as regards this injustice but the psychiatrists and councillors who have to deal with its victims on a daily basis are a different matter.

These professionals are well aware that a percentage of the people who end up in their hands suffer psychiatric problems simply because of the disrespect and isolation inflicted on them by their peers. I would have hoped these caring sorts might have realised they could do their jobs, and help their charges better (then again, perhaps those are *two* different things) by focussing their efforts on identifying and educating the young outcasts about the evils that had shaped them in the first place, telling these young people what was happening to them was not their fault, that they were victims of the rest of society. An opinion of this sort, voiced at a professional level, might have helped with the shame that walks hand in hand with a life of isolation; though such a thing is perhaps too much to ask for as it might require these professionals to form – and voice - an opinion on the society which practices those evils, and by an opinion, I mean a *moral*, not a clinical one.

Should a person find themselves subjected to this level of disrespect due to their ethnic background, their devaluation is not broken down into medical terms; it is called racism and condemned as such. On the other hand, if a member of a non-defined minority complains of mental health problems arising from the same type of abuse there is always a rush to classify and medicate them, to change them while ignoring the attitudes that shape their misery. Upon hearing my tales of isolation and woe, my psychiatrist's response was to offer me antidepressants, when this didn't work I was prescribed tranquillisers; when this didn't help me, the dosage was upped which simply made me worse. This approach is the equivalent of a doctor treating a man for shoulder pain while ignoring the fact he has an arrow embedded in it. It's complete irresponsibility on the part of the medical professionli.

Perhaps I'm reading too much into this situation but, in all my years, I've never encountered a single psychiatrist or councillor who seemed interested in confronting this particular external cause. It looks to me as though someone is deliberately avoiding the issue at a professional level. Attempting to protect a minority from maltreatment by altering its characteristics, rather than confronting the prejudice it suffers, is the equivalent of trying to deal with racism by covering black people in a layer of white paint. It's a gutless approach that could not be described as preventative medicine by any means (and as they say, bad doctors treat only the symptoms). Still, these classes did open my eyes to the scale of this evil and the culture of avoidance that surrounds it. The woolly thinking behind this irresponsibility is not the Aspergers way. I prefer things to have a clear definition, which is what I'm going to attempt here.

The devaluation and marginalization of the social inarticulate (and any non-defined minority for that matter) is as wrong as racism; this is not open to debate. Regardless of their lack of communication skills, these are human beings with as much right to a place in the human world as the next. (It might be argued that to categorise this group in such a fashion is to insult them. My answer is that such a thing is necessary since they are already categorised and judged by the society around them.) You cannot incorporate second-class citizenship into any model of a civilised society no matter how much you try. You cannot paint over it or attempt to blend it in with any number of social skills classes. The maltreatment of this minority is an injustice to be confronted, not hidden. The first step in doing such a thing is to give it a name; here we encounter our first problem. The same I faced while arguing with Lem.

To the best of my knowledge, there is no word in our language to admit to – and challenge - prejudice against social inarticulacy, nor is there a word to recognise prejudice against vulnerability. Neither of these deplorable attitudes is looked on as being particularly wrong. In fact *they are not recognised as prejudices at all*. Over the years, I've read a wide range of literature purporting to examine the mechanics of our society. Not once have I come across a single analytical look at these attitudes, only the vaguest references to the outcasts they create. At first glance this 'effect' without 'cause' makes no sense until you recognise that, unlike the victims of racism, sexism and homophobia, the vulnerable and inarticulate have no voice. Those who do, those who shape our language, are the very ones who embrace and normalise these attitudes in the first place.

Prejudices are never spontaneously recognised as evil. History has shown it takes an articulate minority, usually the victims, to force an awareness of their plight. Racism, sexism and homophobia were only recognised when they were highlighted and condemned by their victims. Doing so was an uphill struggle for these people, often covering several decades. Strange as it may seem, this is the one area in which other groups have a clear advantage over social inarticulates: identity.

Many minorities only come under attack as fully formed adults with an established sense of self, able to resist, at least at a verbal level. Others who experience it during childhood tend to hail from well-defined groups (usually race) who cultivate a sense of community and support for their youngsters. Their children grow up into adults able to define both who they are and why they are being attacked.

Social inarticulates are defined only by damage. They are brutalised and isolated from earliest childhood, to an extent far greater than any other group.

The Social Skills classes

Under this type of attack, it is the very mechanisms of assertion and self whose development this minority are denied.

Another complicating factor lies in their very definition. Nowadays, it is relatively easy for an individual to assert recognition of their racial status, gender, sexuality or religious beliefs and similarly easy to highlight prejudice against it. Physical disability is similarly easy to establish and champion. Had Jack been physically, rather than socially disabled, he might have been treated in a more civilised manner (although hate crimes against the physically disabled are, sadly, on the increase). You can be black and proud, gay and proud. It is harder to proclaim that you are an outcast with deficient communication skills and proud.

Social disability and the bigotry it provokes are based around behaviour rather than clear-cut, easy to establish facts. Trying to communicate that Jack is the victim of an unnamed prejudice for being 'vulnerable' only works assuming the listener is prepared to accept his vulnerability in the first place, and therein lies the second problem. This part of the argument is open to interpretation based on which side of the line you have grown up on. Since most hail from the side opposite Jack's, their viewpoint tends to be slanted against recognising his status. Attempting to suggest that a bias against this unproven 'vulnerability' is something which deserves to be named and shamed is a proposition almost universally rejected and ridiculed. (Without sounding cynical, another reason this subject is not taken seriously is simply because it might not be fashionable. Unlike other prejudices, there is no articulate minority generating the momentum required to make supporting it attractive. It is always easier to jump on the bandwagon and back an established cause; it is rather harder to bring a new one into being.)

I've noticed that even those who display high levels of moral awareness have extremely selective definitions of right and wrong in this area. One thing that truly horrifies me is the number of intelligent people who will attempt to justify these attitudes while making light of the cruelty which goes hand in hand with them. On more than one occasion I've had the difference between Jack's maltreatment and 'serious' issues like racism explained to me in great detail. My intellectual limits are probably showing here, but I still cannot tell the difference between the two. The principal seems the same and so do the effects. Clearly others can see something I can't but I think that says more about them than it does about me. So far as I am concerned, the seriousness of a prejudice should not be determined by its political clout but rather by the damage it inflicts on its victims. If this particular prejudice is less serious than others then this would suggest social inarticulates are less important than all other minorities which brings us back to their second-class citizenship.

An attitude that marginalises an entire section of our population, often resulting in lifelong mental heath problems; and this is not as serious as racism? If you are prepared to accept this bigotry then why not accept all the others while you are at it? Recognising this prejudice is the test as to whether or not we can call ourselves civilised; up till now, it is one we have utterly failed. In this area, our entire society, even at the most educated levels, is still in the moral dark ages.

THE SACRED COW.

'Not everyone's like that.'

Human society is its own sacred cow. Suggesting that the majority of its citizens are neither as responsible nor fair as they paint themselves is never a popular idea. The above quote is the almost universal response when the notion is voiced. Not everyone accepts these attitudes. This is true. There are exceptions, but *most* do, and that is enough.

'Not everyone's like that.'

This is another of those unpopular questions, but how exactly is this so? Where is the logic behind the assumption that the majority cannot be questioned, that truth and innocence lie in numbers? History has shown that entire societies are perfectly capable of standing on questionable moral foundations. Most of the prejudices we condemn now were practised openly by entire populations long before they were confronted and shamed. In what way is this not possible now, simply because the majority say so? Entire societies can develop moral codes and then fail to live up to them. It's easily done. I know many will cite examples of the wealth of compassion also found in our ranks. I would never deny the existence of such, only point out that this rather selective caring, like love, that supposedly selfless emotion, never seems to reach the likes of Jack.

This often feels like a reversal of the Emperor's new clothes scenario. I've spent all my adult life seeing this injustice while no-one else does. I watch people walk and talk around this gargantuan moral blindspot as if it were not there. Trying to highlight it meets with an astonishing degree of rejection, even from the supposedly open-minded. (When dealing with such opposition my anchoring points are my memories. Those social skills classes, and Jack, a boy broken like a dog or a horse, so hopeless, so desperate that he was reduced to ask his employers for help with his loneliness.)

I do wonder about this reticence. For a phenomenon most seem blissfully unaware of, touching on this area results in a suspicious degree of defensiveness. Most moral or enlightened people —and by those definitions, I am not being sarcastic— show a strong desire to avoid discussing it, others will immediately attempt to dismiss the notion. The most resistant are those quickest to bring morality into the conversation for the defence of recognised minorities. These groups in particular take umbrage at the notion that the very people whose cause they champion may themselves harbour attitudes as vile as those of the bigots they condemn. Their most extreme reactions tend to occur when they realise even their own attitudes stand to be cast in a dubious light.

I suspect many of the people I have broached the subject with are, at some level, aware of this void. Perhaps it is considered a kind of moral no-man's land; here be dragons and the dragons are us. Possibly, as a culture, we are still too embarrassed by the power of our pack instincts.

To recap: The formula for this particular prejudice is a simple vicious circle that goes something like this.

1. Prejudice is not second nature to human beings en masse, it is *first* nature. Far from being some external evil which crept in from the outside, it is encoded into man at the genetic level. Casual interaction between ordinary people incorporates a wide range of attitudes that, if viewed with any objectivity, would be recognised as being prejudiced. These types of attitudes are only ever seen for what they are when their victims force this awareness. If a prejudice is not identified, enough members of a society will practise it to the extent it becomes a social norm.

2. Prejudice against vulnerability is the oldest of all prejudices. It is present within many animals, including the human one. This particular prejudice is usually at its most intense in children. Given the chance, most children will pick on their weaker or 'different' own.

3. Certain children become the focus of this abuse to the extent that their developing personalities suffer permanent damage, particularly in the areas of assertion and the skills required to integrate into society. (Other children may have problems with these skills due to conditions which affect behavioural development.) There is a degree of variation to this. Some will end up with difficulty integrating, while others will not be able to integrate at all.

4. Upon leaving school, these maladjusted youngsters are ostracised and openly devalued by adult society who, in contrast to popular belief, are just as exclusive and often as callous as their juvenile counterparts.

5. By nature of the damage inflicted on them, these 'social inarticulates' are unable to form a cohesive minority and force an awareness of their devaluation as being morally wrong. If, as isolated adults, they attempt to highlight the abuse which damaged them, they are shamed into silence by accusations of self-pity. (Abuser societies always shame their victims.) Should they even possess the ability to suggest that certain accepted attitudes are unfair and imply that, by virtue of embracing these, the entirety of society might be in the wrong, they are automatically branded cynics or cranks and their 'antisocial' arguments dismissed as unreasonable – a particularly easy process when there is no real vocabulary to say otherwise. In addition, lacking the assertive abilities required to make a stand, they are often extremely susceptible to being told what has and hasn't happened to them. As a result, this particular minority remains forever voiceless and the prejudice remains unnamed.

6. Since there is no-one and no language to tell members of this society that their attitudes are wrong they continue as social norms and are passed down to the next generation; which leads us back to square one.

~~~

From my own experiences, I think it is during the early twenties - when the myth of adult acceptance wears off - that most outcasts get the first inklings of the rejection that lies in front of them. In the initial stages you experience confusion because you find no advice to help you, no literature, no

Trying to highlight the blindspot

language to stop you slipping away into a marginalised existence the like of which you have never read about. (My strongest memories of college consist of looking at groups of young people and wondering what it was that stopped me from being able to mix with them the way they mixed with each other, knowing there was something wrong with my life but not having the means to properly define this.)

There is the ever-present shame of being 'different' without actually knowing what this difference is. You feel a desperate, almost terrified need to belong because that is what life is about. But you can't; these 'normal' others seem able to talk in codes you cannot decipher. You have no idea what to say in their company and so you wait for what looks like an opening in their conversation to add your piece. Sometimes you are lucky and get your opportunity. More often than not you outstay your welcome or, in desperation, say something really stupid and feel foolish for it. Usually others remind you with the wrong kind of laughter. Some will make it clear you are not welcome. As the minutes pass the conversation becomes faster and harder to follow, it slips away from you. How can people do this, and why can't you? Why are you different? By this point they are closing ranks; they have forgotten you, and why not? You have nothing they want to hear. You are not one of them; not a 'real' person. You can't have what they have. The doors of opportunity, open to all others, are closed for you.

Life, beautiful life is being dangled in front of you every day, enjoyed by all the others, rubbed into your face by those who refuse to share it with you. The pain of being on the outside is terrible. The knowledge that your failure marks you as a figure of contempt adds salt to this suffering. This is your lot, it's all you had behind you; the realisation it's all you have in front clogs you with a terrible sense of despair, inadequacy, abnormality and most dangerous of all, the feeling that you are being *denied*. It becomes clear after a while that this is exactly what is being done to you. After all, this is a civilised society, is it not? It says so on paper doesn't it? We are all meant to live together? It's what you have been told to expect from day one and yet still, these people refuse to accept you. As your thinking and perceptions buckle and distort, you slip into paranoia. *These horrible, selfish people refuse to accept you because they are all against you.*

It is difficult to communicate the helplessness of the outcast. In many ways it feels like drowning, like suffocation; being denied air, life. You drown, without dying, every day. Of all minorities, the outcasts are truly lost. There is still a glimmer of hope for alcoholics and drug users since they have the option - no matter how hard - to give up their addiction. This is not the case if you are a pariah of Jack's type His ostracism is not in his hands; it is enforced by others who will never allow him to live any other way. For the outcast, existence is a prison, a life sentence.

It's an appalling state of affairs for anyone to find themselves in, particularly young people with their entire lives in front of them. I'd hoped by now that someone would have done something about it. Unfortunately, I'm *still* waiting for a name to highlight this injustice. I've a horrible feeling that, at this rate, we'll never see it. Why is this? Why is it so hard to recognise that disrespect for one type of person is just as bad as disrespect for others? The answer is that classifying such widespread attitudes as prejudices would mean condemning massive areas of our ordinary behaviour, something few, if any are prepared to do, not when they have the luxury of rendering the problem invisible simply by ignoring it.

Keeping an evil unfocussed does not make it any less wrong or any less destructive. Many of the attitudes we consider harmless are intensely damaging. Yet, on a daily basis, they are inflicted onto an entire section of our population with no recognition of their seriousness or their consequences. Since these attitudes are practised by the majority, their targets often experience little else. In time they become saturated by it. This 'blanket disrespect' is appalling in its ability to mutilate. It can twist a person into something inhuman, and do so in plain sight. Again, I'm relying on my own experiences, but I can tell you that living a life composed of a million and one acts of disrespect and dismissal can make you hate your jailers – the entire human race - with ferocity only the drowning and the desperate can.

KILL THEM ALL!

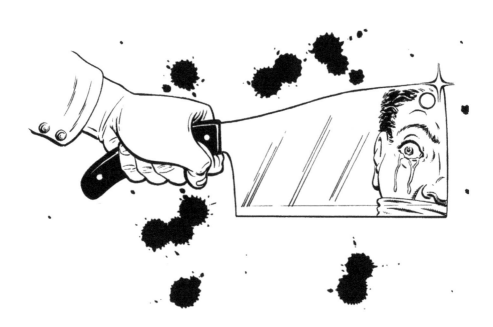

The giant red robot stopped the bridge from collapsing. The cover of the 1969 HURRICANE annual - featuring 'The Juggernaut from Planet Z' - was an image of power which had delighted me during my early years. I'd wanted this particular book for a long time and now had enough money to buy it, but there was no point. It meant nothing now. I glanced briefly at the cover before leaving the comic sale.

I'd attended to take my mind off things. It hadn't worked: the pain followed me even there. My interest in comics had waned over the last few months and now, was disappearing completely. Comics had entered their most exciting period for years. Titles like Alan Moore's WATCHMEN and Frank Miller's DARK KNIGHT RETURNS were being excitedly gobbled up by fans but I was falling away from it all. These fantastic tales no longer meant anything. Everything was coloured by the stinging in my eyes. I couldn't watch films or read comics because the pain stripped the experience of even the slightest joy. There seemed no point in looking at anything or doing anything; nothing meant anything in the face of the pain. I could neither lose myself in plots nor in textural patterns. My last refuge had fallen.

Nothing soothed me, not even recalling the texture of the wall on which Mum sat. The feeling in my stomach as I walked out of the building was the most awful emptiness I'd ever experienced. I was locking down onto a single despairing point and nothing else. The doctors' response was to simply bury me under antidepressant and tranquilliser medication while insisting I 'come to terms' with my condition. I couldn't. The emotions churning in me felt worse than the death of a loved one. There was horror, disbelief, despair and a sensation of unending panic. I'd experienced such feelings before, but only on a transitory basis. This new state did not diminish with time; it intensified with each passing week. I woke up every morning, opening my eyes to pain, knowing all that lay in front of me was another day of suffering. My waking hours were blighted by terror over my future; I dreaded the coming years.

The overload of the condition was taking its toll. I could not think straight, couldn't concentrate. I was beginning to shut down and pull away from a world I had no reason to hang on to. Everything I had worked for had been taken from me. There had been no point to any of the effort, the struggle I had put into my life; it was all for nothing. The book covers I was going to paint, the films I was going to design, all of it was gone. It wasn't fair. After Little Russia and Whitehill, after all the emptiness of my past, what lay in front of me was a lifetime of the same. No future, no escape. This couldn't be forever, but it was.

I had dropped away from comics and Science Fiction fandom by this point. I'd bought my way in and established tentative social contacts by producing artwork for various programme books and fanzines. Now, bereft of such currency, I found many of these people avoiding me like the plague. I was no stranger to being shunned, though such a thing following on from my loss just added to my revulsion with the bigoted, exclusive and thoroughly selfish world I saw around me. Everything was worthless, rotten, diseased and foul. Everyone and everything was against me.

I had still managed to hang on to one or two associations with other outcasts; these could only be called friendships in the most strained sense of the word as they involved no small amount of domination from more aggressive and forceful personalities. In all fairness, I must have been equally hard to tolerate by this point. My mind, formerly fixated on drawing techniques, now locked itself onto the idea of my eyes wearing down. My conversations during this period revolved around this and nothing else. My sense of self was disintegrating, fighting back desperately before collapsing under the weight of misery. One minute I was a genius - cursing a world that refused to recognize me - the next I cringed and hid from view, knowing full well I was a mental midget. The presence of heat worsened this instability since it meant dehydration of my already thin tear film. Dehydration meant pain and pain generated immediate despair. I was, and still am, one of the few people who can be driven into the depths of total misery by a radiator or convector heater.

The inability of my family to deal with my deterioration only added to my paranoia. In recent months I had began to focus on them as another aspect of the conspiracy growing around me. I was at my most vicious and antagonistic towards them during this period; causing rifts that would take years to heal. I reacted to small comments and slights as though gargantuan in scale. Such things were clearly part of the same evil which was eroding my life and as such, had to be recorded, logged in terms of time, place and content, and stored in my rapidly growing library of slights. I was joining the dots now, seeing patterns to events and people, a process that was completely involuntary.

The timing for my illness was bad. I had matured to the extent that I was now able to process my Whitehill experiences. With my last defense swept away, I was fair game for every poisoned memory recorded onto me; these played out every hour of the day and in perfect detail. In an appalling imitation of The Halfman, I would list and curse every person who had crossed me in all the years of my life; what was said, when and where their crimes were carried out. I would quote, without deviation, entire exchanges of hostile dialogue from years ago for the simple reason that it was not in my past; it was *still* happening.

Whitehill was alive inside me, eating me from within; the changing room; the poster; the cartoon; the students; the teachers and, worst of all, The Rules, all eating me alive. More than ever I couldn't live up to The Rules and felt all the more trapped because of it. Every moment of pain was obviously my due since I was bad, stupid and ugly; a lesser quality, worthless person. Perhaps Mr Wood was right and weirdoes deserved this kind of suffering.

And yet I knew I didn't. Another part of me recognized, at a very basic level, that I had done no wrong and was as deserving of respect as the next. This part raged against Whitehill's lessons. The knowledge that this conflict, this loss of self-worth, was the legacy of an institution which was supposed to help me was sickening. In my new, highly paranoid state, I reviewed my memories of my old school. It was then I realised that everyone *had* been against me there. I was presented with an ever-darkening picture of their bigotry and, in the case of my teachers, their betrayal. *They had let all that happen to me.* Thinking back to those social skills classes a more awful fact clicked into place: *they let this happen to people like me all the time.*

This wider perspective affected my anger. It focussed into something longer lasting. My moments of rage lengthened to hours then days. My thoughts, which had been churning for months, cooled without losing one iota of antagonism. This new thinking was methodical and patient, capable of scrutinising circumstances and memories in intricate detail. It burned slow, could counter any argument it didn't want to hear and was able to sustain itself. It made sense and became a way of life. It was hatred, true hatred. With the arrival of this emotion, another change occurred in my thinking. I will discuss this in chapter twenty-four; it was the final alteration of my perspectives and would shape my attitudes from this point on.

The picture that began to materialise was of a totally corrupt society. Everyone was potentially The Enemy. As this conviction intensified I found myself switching flicking back and forth from black despair to the rush, that awful, vertiginous, sense of freedom I'd experienced when standing before the cartoon at Whitehill. It was during these moments of grotesque elation, and not despair, that suicide became the logical course of action once again. Life was just going to be pain and nothing else. It was worthless. There was no point in living it, so there was nothing to lose by throwing it away. I realised extinction was on the cards after a phone conversation with Mum; this ended with her saying she loved me. The inability of that feeble emotion to make me feel better only served to make me feel worse. It was like the giant red robot, a painful reminder that nothing could help me now.

~~~

As my desperation increased I turned to faith healing and alternative medicine with no success. I started looking at literature dealing with pain control around this period. Much of this was bleak reading that I consigned to the bin after a few pages. The best of these books was NATURAL PAIN CONTROL by Dr. Vernon Coleman. An easy to read book of medium thickness, it attracted me immediately. Although an accessible volume with one or two useful tips, the book offered little immediate help as none of the physical treatments - from massage to heat treatment and the TENS electrical machine - were applicable to dry-eye. Only the chapter titled 'Use your imagination' offered any real outlet for my despair. This part of the book dealt with the psychology of pain and suggested a number of techniques to manipulate the mental side of suffering.

Coleman's approach broke down into two types: passive and aggressive. The passive involved a person imagining themselves in a tranquil setting, a place beyond pain and concern. I found this approach useless as I could never be alone in such imaginary places. Trying to slip into this type of fantasy only relaxed the mental restraints that kept Whitehill at bay, allowing my old school to invade any mental refuge I formed. It became obvious my problem was more than just physical. I was being attacked by a combination of problems; one physical, the other emotional, each reinforcing the other and placing it beyond conventional treatment.

The aggressive approach was another matter. It required the subject to actively imagine their body combating pain. The book instructed the reader to picture an army of miniature surgeons at work inside them, cutting the nerves transmitting the pain to their brain. The image of these tiny, scalpel wielding creatures met with marginally greater success. However, one suggestion in particular - a rather adversarial one - struck a definite chord: this involved seeing the pain as a small invading army of dirty brown cells. The exercise was to picture your own immune system destroying these invaders (hopefully with their vicious little scalpels). The imagery of one line stood out above all others: 'Imagine that the brown cells are littering your tissues with their rapidly decaying corpses.'

Rapidly decaying corpses! The vicious, destructive nature of that image held an exciting thrill that comforted me but left me wanting more. The invaders had to suffer for their crimes. It was through this I arrived at a more effective fantasy method to help me cope with my pain: inflicting it on others. (By pain, I mean both physical and emotional.) Although I could not see it at the time, my real problem was not just my eye condition, it was the Whitehill-induced damage that allowed the pain to eat me alive.

As a result, my visualizations took a slightly different form from those suggested by Dr. Coleman. They did not use faceless micro-organisms but the people who had crossed me in my life, mostly those from Whitehill, my teachers and fellow pupils. They were hurting me. They could still hurt me therefore I was afraid of them. I was afraid of them therefore I hated them. They could do anything they wanted to me so I had to do even more back to them.

I was still living at Huntley Lodge at this point. Part of the daily programme was a series of workgroups in which residents either prepared meals or tidied and cleaned the place. After this, we attended meetings in which we were invited to discuss our feelings; I kept mine under wraps as I had a suspicion they might give people the right impression of me. I would sit, chew paper and pretend to listen to the problems of others while picturing myself wrecking vengeance against my old associates. Each scenario had to be properly prepared and timed for effect. Often I would repeat the opening or a specific point, rewinding them like The Halfman's recordings, just to get them right.

Though exceptionally violent, my fantasies were bereft of firearms as I'd been brought up in a culture in which gun crime was virtually unknown.

The attacks were prolonged and sadistic

(True, by this point I'd seen TERMINATOR and TAXI DRIVER but shooting someone was a method of retribution too distant to relate to.)

My imaginary instruments of righteous vengeance were an assortment of hammers and blades. For this reason I never entertained any concepts of mass slaughter. All attacks were focussed onto individuals. The first targets in my imaginings were the two core groups of my past: the brutal young-sters of my early years and the viciously sarcastic teenagers of the later. Most were trapped in isolated locations, mutilated and bludgeoned to death after being struck from behind. Attacking them in this way seemed cowardly but I didn't care. These creatures were stronger than me, even inside my own head. Striking in such a fashion was the only way I had of realistically opening such scenarios; besides, there was an added excitement of using what others would consider a 'rotten' method.

The attacks were prolonged and sadistic, always focussed on destroying my enemy's evil, sneering face. Often they were made to drink acid or it was poured into their open wounds (I'd heard, mistakenly, that the wife of the silent Horror star, Lon Chaney, had committed suicide by imbibing this particular brew on stage, so it seemed a perfect method of silencing a mock-ing voice). Once they had been executed, their heads were crushed. This was accomplished by placing them under several large concrete slabs and jumping on them until they split like over-ripe melons.

The next to receive my justice was my Art teacher. For his crimes, he was blinded and his fingers severed by a large guillotine before his head was flattened. The Guidance teacher and the lady psychologist who had ignored my pleas at Whitehill also received summary executions. From her lack of reaction to my plight, it was obvious the psychologist accepted and perhaps even approved of what had happened to me She probably considered it normal. It was even possible that she was annoyed I dared question my place and treatment. Perhaps The Halfman was right and she was 'One of those bastards who liked to talk'. She probably had a good laugh at my expense after getting rid of me, sitting in some expensive coffee bar, joking with her educat-ed friends about the 'weirdo' she'd had to interview that morning. The lousy, smug, snide, shrink-bitch was not joking now, as her educated head went under the slabs.

The Animal's demise had a slightly cartoon quality. It occurred during one of his yelling and spitting sessions. The moment the word 'misfit' reached his lips I lightly prodded his purple, swollen face with the tip of a pin. At just the slightest touch of the metal, his internal pressures did the rest. His face would disappear in an explosion of hate filled blood followed by his skull falling out of the remains of his deflated head.

A certain PE teacher was worked over with a claw hammer. With a criminal this robust, it was not enough to simply strike him from behind; he had to be disabled first. This required severing the tendons in his arms and legs while he was down, leaving him to flop about like a fish out of water. There was an urgency to the alterations carried out on this man. Even as an adult, I was afraid of him and the masculine contempt he represented. I could feel it radiating from him as he lay helpless, contempt for the weakness I knew was inside me. Despite being hackwork with no finesse (bones yanked out, etc) there was a certain satisfaction to the results of my labours. Before going under the concrete, his face and the manly tuft of grey hair poking out the top of his open tracksuit were set on fire for good measure.

In sharp contrast, I took my time with Mr Wood. I had no problem facing him as his drinking made him seem weak. (I'd had firsthand experience of the vulnerability of drunks with Mum.) All fantasies dealing with his demise therefore started off with Mr Wood being inebriated - not a hard thing to visualize. When he recognizes me, he becomes indignant, even sarcastic, demanding to know what I am doing in his house. His sarcasm disappears when I get to work on him with a surgical scalpel. (In a variation of this scenario he attempts to defend himself using Beelzebub; the gesture is so pathetic as to be beautiful.) I have to do this because he is still attacking me. No matter what I do, I will never be anything other than trash in his eyes. He, and the world he represents, will always call me worthless. In order to protect myself from the pain this causes, I have to destroy him as often and as viciously as possible.

I apply the same level of care and precision to Mr Wood that I once lavished on my art. Unlike the PE teacher, he is a flabby man who howls like a baby and pleads for mercy as I slice him up. This is better than stippling. This makes me feel strong for the first time in my life, no longer helpless, a man, better than a man.

Mr Wood's kind are cleverer than I am. They can talk rings around me, even when ignoring or distorting the truth. They use the weight of their learning to shut me up. Hurting them horrifically is the only way I know of punching through such deliberate ignorance. That is what I am doing now: showing him the truth - that it is he who is in the wrong not me. I am doing this in the one language he cannot sneer at, the language he and the rest of Whitehill Secondary School taught me: pain. I am not just avenging myself here, I am communicating with him, I am *educating* him.

If, as I have been told, I am a bad person, then I have nothing to lose by being something far worse. This becomes obvious as the work on Mr Wood reaches ever more sophisticated and imaginative levels. Now he understands that 'Bushman' is no longer the worthless little nothing he made such sport of; now I am sick, twisted and vile. Being vile is good. Thanks to his kind, I've no chance of ever being a 'real' person; being a monster though, is well within the reach of my imagination. It is the difference between a slug and a wasp: respect. Mr Wood's respect, terror and revulsion are wonderful They are the most clean and beautiful emotions I have ever felt; basking in them makes everything that has happened worthwhile, makes the world a brighter better place. Once justice has been done and there is nothing left of him to suffer, his head is crushed and he too is consigned to the fire. (Ironic, considering the hamburger halfwit had cooked himself for real by this point.)

It wasn't enough. My sense of injustice demanded more. These worthless pieces of trash needed to recognize their part in their demise. They had to see that they deserved what was coming to them because it was their own fault. They had to understand they were criminals, that they were *wrong*, in much the same way they had told me I was *wrong* all my life. This prompted a new range of scenarios in which these miscreants were subjected to prolonged interrogations and denouncements for their crimes (a great deal of which were modelled on my own experiences in Little Russia) The further I went into these scenarios, the more ritualistic they became.

Eventually, I saw these imagined tortures being carried out for something larger and more important than just myself. There was a principle here. My former classmates and teachers had to see that their punishments were necessary for a greater good. Often they were coerced into signing documents legitimizing their horrible deaths. These were described in considerable detail and usually with accompanying photographs. This was to help them understand the seriousness of their situation. I called this understanding 'Fundamental Communication', communication through pain, fear and death.

Other examples of this new language began to emerge to legitimize vengeance meted out to those who had wronged me. The various quasi-surgical tortures carried out on them were given deliberately sinister titles like 'Corrective Enhancement' or 'Compassionate Modification', As I saw it, titles of this sort were necessary to balance the books, to give my vengeance weight, make it legitimate and even *official*; after all, school had used terms like 'Physical Education' to describe the various forms of torture it had inflicted on me. The scenarios that followed the development of this language cannot be put on paper. They involved obscene surgical mutilations surpassing the greatest excesses of the currently fashionable 'torture porn' genre.

~~~

Despite offering a temporary diversion to my despair and direction to my rage, these visualisations proved to be a short-term solution with some major drawbacks. Firstly, each scenario had less effect each time it was used, leading to an ever-greater need for sadism that was taxing my imagination. Secondly, the longer I spent in them, the worse I felt when returning to the real world. Most disturbing of all, indulging in the visualisations seemed to increase the frequency of the elevated moods I had begun to associate with suicide.

Life was still unlivable. Drugs could not help, therapy was useless. I needed something else, something real. I needed an escape. Since the only avenue of freedom open to me was self-destruction, things looked bleak until someone suggested an alternative. It was the best advice I'd ever been given: try to get back into films, this time through writing.

Driven by desperation, I started penning my first screenplay.

THE SURGEON

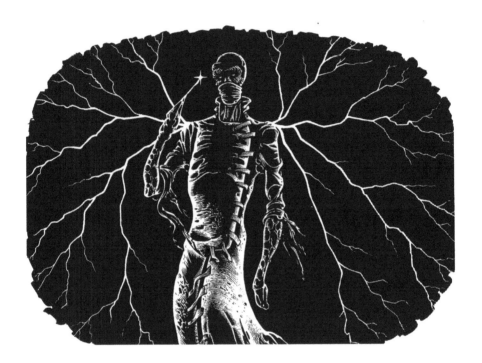

The popular notion that those on the spectrum possess completely linear thought processes is somewhat simplistic. My observation is that our brains often lack imagination and flexibility in some areas - particularly when dealing with incoming information - but can compensate by an overabundance in others. There are countless examples of intensely creative ASD minds in our culture. We might be late developers in this area, but when we get started we can compete with the best. I was showing considerable originality with my revenge scenarios, now it was time to use this talent for something other than immediate gratification.

During the early days of my illness, as an offshoot to my drawing, I'd developed a series of Horror stories in conjunction with another collaborator. These were intended for an amateur Horror comic titled 'Penny Dreadfuls'. I'd even produced an advertisement which was printed in a Glasgow 'fanzine' (a non-professional publication) of the period. The comic never materialised but it did leave me a taste for the Horror genre. There was one small problem. Despite some aptitude in the field, writing terrified me. I still couldn't spell (prior to publication of the comic ad, someone pointed out I'd spelled 'Dreadfuls' as 'Dreadfulls') and the abstractions of punctuation and sentence structure were as impenetrable as they had been a decade before. A page of hopelessly inept text would serve only to humiliate me in a way a pattern of dots never could. When it came to restoring my career, prose, therefore, was out of the question. The suggestion I work on a film script seemed the ideal solution.

Like all my early efforts, my first foray into screenwriting was a collaboration. Considering my fantasies about skilfully altering my old school friends and teachers, it is no coincidence this piece - entitled THE SURGEON - was an SF/Horror story based around fear of going under the knife. The tale concerned a time-travelling serial killer whose mode of traversing the centuries was to surgically assemble disposable time machines from living human flesh. Like all 80's screen monsters, the eponymous creature - described as a 'walking operating theatre' - was designed to incorporate a repertoire of distinctive visual gimmicks all based around surgery. (It had no hands, just severed stumps from which a variety of surrealistic surgical instruments could sprout.) The Surgeon didn't just kill or torture its victims. It made people into things, things it used and then discarded. The horror and tragedy of the story stemmed not just from the surgery but from the ghastly and pitiful objects these innocents had been transformed into. The promotional tagline read: 'Time Heals No Wounds'.

The 80's heralded the return of 'surgical horror' in Fantasy filmmaking. (There had been an endless stream of mad doctor films since James Whale's 1931 classic FRANKENSTEIN but the genre had largely fallen out of favour since the late 60's.) The early video market had unleashed a slew of notorious, low budget flicks based around surgery. These were mostly of the 'Nazi experimentation camp' sub-genre and were as incompetent as they were brutal. At the respectable end of the spectrum, the Canadian filmmaker David Cronenberg had carved his niche with his groundbreaking work in the 70's, but his films had failed to produce a distinctive monster for popular audiences. David Lynch had come close with the grotesque Spacer's Guild and Family Harkonnen featured in his adaptation of Frank Herbert's epic DUNE and Clive Barker was about to spring his torture-obsessed Cenobites on us with the release of his film HELLRAISER. The field, therefore, seemed large enough for another monster.

In order to avoid comparisons with other films, I decided - at least in initial drafts - to focus on the SF elements of the premise; one of these being the psychic side-effects of time travel. The first draft of the script was heavily influenced by Hammer Films QUATERMASS series, brilliant adaptations of classic BBC SF serials of the 50's, and a major influence for me.

At this point, my racing thoughts actually began to work for me rather than against. The world stopped being such a terrible place now I had a new future ahead of me. Everything that had happened had obviously been for a reason. The pattern was clear now. Fate had diverted me away from art and towards writing since the latter was a far more prestigious career than simple design (so I told myself at every opportunity). The Surgeon was a great idea (so I told myself at every opportunity), a first-rate monster with an original gimmick. Freddy Kruger attacked through dreams, The Surgeon attacked through time itself, slicing and stitching its way across human history. It was a new slant I thought, yielding endless franchise possibilities. The creature had an infinite range of permutations and, being a time traveller, could be injected into any number of scenarios and periods. There was no way such an idea wouldn't be snapped up by Hollywood; it would become a great success, spawn many sequels and start my new career (so I told myself – desperately - at every opportunity).

I could see it all. Magazines would feature wonderful colour spreads of the production, pictures of the creature and the various special effects used to render it onscreen. There would be interviews with the cast and crew. I would render Virgil Finlay-style illustrations which would feature in these publications. Film scripting would give me everything I could have got from art and more. Despite being unable to type and having handwriting that was an unreadable mess, my work would shine and attract attention from all quarters. Producers would rush to get their hands on anything written by me when they discovered the quality and originality of my work. The sheer prestige of working in such a glamorous field would banish Whitehill forever. A grubby life of isolation and pain would be swept away and instantly replaced by something far cleaner, something worth living for. The name 'Campbell' would no longer be a derogatory word; it would be something to be proud of. I wouldn't just exist, I would *escape*, I would *live*. This all made sense; it had the smell of *destiny* to it.

My enemies, those who had wronged me, became mere irritants. My revenge fantasies diminished overnight as the energy behind them was directed towards these new imaginings. Carried along in this new rush, I began to look and plan beyond the immediate for the first time in my life. One such scheme involved a more aggressive method of dealing with the pain. I was going to see the end of it regardless of what the doctors said. Once I had amassed enough money from my film career I would have surgery to desensitise my eyes. This would consist of using micro-surgery to selectively sever portions of the sensory nerves leading from the conjunctiva membrane - the part of the eye which generated the burning sensation - while still leaving enough of the rest of the optic nerve to see with. I had discussed this with a young GP who categorically stated that no-one would perform such an operation as it would almost certainly result in blindness. Dr. Coleman's book had similarly advised against surgery on the grounds of its ineffectiveness. This information was ignored as it did not fit into the logical pattern of fate I sensed around me. I was now armed with the knowledge I was on the cusp of ending the pain; this meant that, although it was still debilitating, it no longer possessed me to the extent it had before. With my new dream in place I had a future once again, and that made all the difference.

Those were incredibly intense, exciting days. I can still remember the emotions, the air was buzzing with an impatient excitement. *I was going to be in films.* The worse my eyes felt, the more I dreamt in response, balancing the inevitable despair with ever greater and desperate hopes. The pain had a purpose after all: it was a rocket intended to drive me to greater heights of achievement.

Many I discussed my new ambitions with expressed scepticism. Several advised me not to get my hopes up. I know this was genuine concern on their part as they didn't want to see me come crashing down once again. They were wasting their time. I was haunted by the loss of my moment in the light and had no time for anything that tried to block my regaining it. Besides, I'd reached the film world with art so I saw no problem doing it with scripting.

I would have my eyes fixed and, even with reduced sight, make a new career for myself as a top Hollywood scriptwriter. I would write the smash-hit multi-million dollar sequel SURGEONS, which would out-gross even James Cameron's ALIENS. My films would keep a seat for me in the world no matter how little effort I put into it. They would be my new credentials: the ultimate bag of robot drawings. All my rotten teachers and schoolmates would see how brilliant I had always been... *And* be in awe of my achievements... *And* be sorry they had treated me the way they had... *And* I would be free of poverty... *And* live in luxury... *And* security forever, in a nice house in a quiet area away from my old street where no-one would pick on me... *And* Life would be like the credits of MIAMI VICE... *And* the brightly lit streets in the video for the BANGLES 'Manic Monday' single (which I had gazed at as I sat medicated in Gartloch hospital). *And... And...And...*

~~~

With hindsight, the naivety behind this seems almost comic. (A similarly hilarious desperation is evident in Dustin Hoffman's tragic dreams in the film MIDNIGHT COWBOY.) Yet I had no choice but to think like this. I was trapped with an illness and a past I could not live with (one perhaps, but not both). I needed a light at the end of the tunnel even if I had to make it up. Walking towards an imaginary goal may have been a fool's errand but it was better than standing still and 'coming to terms' with my new life because such a thing meant suicide. My ambitions were fuelled by the same need that had driven me all my adult life: to undo my past, to rise above its predictions of my failure, to numb the pain of my worthlessness through achievement and social status. It was the pure and desperate drive of seeking lifelong anaesthesia.

Of course there was a little matter of getting the script written and sent off to the appropriate filmmaker. In this area, we were spoiled for choice. The 80's was a fertile period for Fantasy filmmaking. The video boom had resulted in the emergence of countless independent companies. Genre magazines bombarded their readers with articles on numerous titles from new companies every month. One of the most prolific of these was EMPIRE FILMS.

Empire had been churning out SF and Horror quickies for years. Much of their output was slipshod to the point of surrealism yet possessed of an inventive charm that made them anything but boring. Recently however, the company had started to boast slicker, studio-level pieces like TRANCERS and the cult-classic RE-ANIMATOR. It was clear that they were developing an eye for quality. Thanks to a stroke of luck, we'd recently acquired their address and decided to make it The Surgeon's first port of call. The way I looked at it, we were doing Empire a favour by giving them the first bite at this magnificent apple. The eponymous creatures of ALIEN, THE THING, and PREDATOR had netted millions for their respective companies, now this was Empire's chance to have an iconic beastie of its own. I saw it all: the company, upon realising it had just acquired a property of unheard of originality and value, would snap the package up in an instant, and frantic negotiations would begin. It all made sense. At least it did until Empire collapsed under a pile of debt.

Shortly afterwards the company's leading executive, Charles Band began trading under the name 'Urban Classics Video' (soon to become FULL MOON PRODUCTIONS). It was to this new company that the script was dispatched; then we waited. It was only a matter of weeks, perhaps even days before the fateful phone call came. Urban Classics Video's first production would be The Surgeon. Band's financial problems - and ours - would be washed away by this brilliant new production. We continued waiting. Weeks became months, became a year with no result, nothing. Band started working on a number of new titles, not one of them called The Surgeon. It made no sense: here was the perfect project for his new company. It was a great script - flawless, brilliantly original (so I kept telling myself), a masterpiece completely without equal. Logically it should have filmed. And yet it wasn't. I

Sad, desperate dreams

concluded that Band, in refusing to see things from my point of view, had to be insane, completely and utterly insane; totally, barking mad. No matter, his loss. There were plenty of other destinations for the property.

With the help of others who became associated with the project, the script was to find itself on many a desk as the years wore on. It would take too much space to recount the years of effort that lay ahead of us as we attempted to get this particular production off the ground. There are enough bizarre stories there to fill another book. As the 80's gave way to the 90's, I would become involved in countless rewrites of this and other projects with other collaborators, honing my skills with each story (and learning to spell into the bargain). The script would be reworked from an imagined masterpiece into a sharp little screenplay.

It came close to being filmed on one occasion. A deal between the Film Development Corporation and the Isle of Man film fund almost brought our creature into the real world. Sadly, this collapsed two weeks before pre-production started. Despite moving onto solo pieces, The Surgeon was to remain the most important of all my ongoing projects.

In those years, my moods would veer back and forth between bursts of sudden frenzied creativity and periods of crippling depression and instability depending on how any project fared at any given time. When things looked promising, I would plan my glorious future. Were the current project to fall through (as it so often did), my revenge fantasies returned and the mutilation of Whitehill became my preoccupation once again. During these periods, I would ruminate and refine my observations over the world of human injustice I saw all around me. I only realised I was becoming locked into this thinking when some of my collaborators asked me to stop talking about teachers during script discussions.

Contrary to what I had been told by my ophthalmologist, my tearfilm had returned partially (mostly in the left eye). It fluctuated over the years, sometimes thickening, other times thinning, yet never returning to normal, still staying on the side of that persistent stinging. Dry heat in particular could return me to the atrocious burning of the 80's. I no longer needed to use artificial tears and could produce small amounts of artwork but nothing a career could be based on.

Desperate for answers, I pressed specialists further and was eventually admitted to a pain clinic at Glasgow's Gartnavel Hospital. After listening to an hour's worth of ranting, the specialist explained neuropathic pain to me. This was a very real sensation generated by damaged, diseased or altered nerve fibres. According to research, such fibres - and there are a higher concentration in the eyes than anywhere else - sensitized by years of activity, could fire up spontaneously, magnifying existing sensation and generating pain where there was little physical cause. In the case of the eye, this is called, Corneal Neuralgia. In other words, despite an improvement in my tearfilm, my eyes were still sending me pain as though still severely dry (Boston ophthalmologist Perry Rosenthal is the foremost authority in this field. Much of his work can be found online). This revelation did little to lift my spirits and I carried on through 90's in a mostly grim and bitter mood, avoiding doctors thereafter.

It was during one of the never-ending and increasingly fruitless rewrites of The Surgeon that something shook me out of my rut. I remember it perfectly. It was the last months of the 90's. The millennium was almost upon us. The Halfman had gone to his grave a decade before, courtesy of some well-deserved cancer. Mum was just three months from her death by emphysema. I was in a bleak and embittered state of mind. The Surgeon, my life-saving project was dead in the water once more. The script's persistent failure had become an embarrassment and I was beginning to wish I'd never come up with the whole waste of time.

Other projects by other creators had come and gone; new careers had been established, films had been made and remade but not mine. Getting into the film business was a whole lot harder than I had anticipated. It made no sense; the logical pattern of events had not occurred. I was still a failure with no social status, having escaped neither the pain nor the misery of my old life. There were no fanfares heralding my brilliance and my stupidity had yet to be disproved. Despite my best efforts I remained the worthless nothing Whitehill had predicted I always would be. My sense of destiny had begun to stretch thin. Doubts, hatred and instability had resurfaced, and the familiar terror of being trapped forever had crept back into my thinking. The appeal of suicide crept back with it.

This particular day I'd run out of milk for tea and decided to brave a trip to the local grocer. It was there I glanced at the newspapers which sat on a rack at the end of the counter. The photographs plastered across each front page were the out-of-focus, taken-on-the-spot images that were only printed when something big or bad happened.

Something had, at an American school called COLUMBINE.

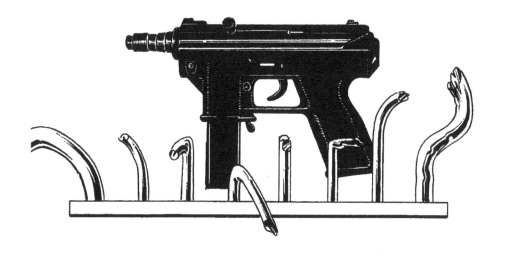

TERRORIST THINKING

CONFESSIONS OF A HATER

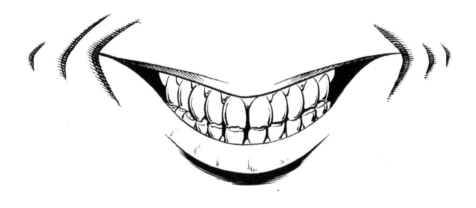

On early morning, September 12 2001 - the day following my thirty-ninth birthday - I found myself walking along an area of Glasgow called George Street, leading to the city's main square (the same stretch used to depict the streets of Philadelphia in the film WORLD WAR Z and San Francisco in CLOUD ATLAS). I had not slept for a few days as a result of threats from a local gang so, in a state of considerable agitation, I took to walking back and forth along this familiar stretch of road at a time when there would be few pedestrians to bother me.

As it turned out, I was not alone. While I studied the patterns of the pavement (and looked for money), I became aware of a young Asian backpacker walking a short distance ahead of me, muttering intently to himself. Although it did not seem to be directed at me, there was a definite undercurrent of hostility in his grumbling diatribe. Just before we reached the square, he waved his fist to no-one in particular and chuckled 'I kill you all!' As slow on the uptake as ever, it took me until evening to make a connection between his exultant cursing and the atrocity of the previous day. When I did, my immediate reaction was: 'What a creep, gloating over something as sick as that', and 'Someone ought to kick his f#%*^g head in'.

This brands me as a hypocrite or worse, considering I'd spent the last couple of years walking up and down my own street in the early hours, chortling in triumph over Columbine and the many school shootings that followed in its wake. Anyone walking behind me on such occasions would have eavesdropped on a whole slew of muttered arguments justifying these atrocities, or as I preferred to describe them: 'Military strikes against institutions of oppression and abuse.' During these strolls, I even compiled a glossary of pseudo-militaristic terms to justify these 'Punishment Executions'. In a calmer mindset I recognise these as revolting; in my darker moments, they make perfect sense. (They belong inside my head and nowhere else so I'll refrain from putting them on paper.) I never quite punched the air in triumph or called out 'I kill you all', but I followed the same path as this young man; towards a different target perhaps, but definitely singing the same song.

I've encountered other haters over the years, The Halfman being the most extreme by far. We are found in all walks of life. The less skilful of us betray themselves all too quickly, others learn to keep it out of sight, letting slip only when the pressure of containment becomes intolerable. We're a pretty ugly bunch, all things told. Our thoughts, bared fully, would be a vile sight for the 'normal' mind, though we're usually not as bad as the forces that shaped us. As you may understand by this point, no-one becomes a hater without a little help. I suspect being in hate is like being in love. It's such an all-consuming experience that you have little objectivity about it. On the odd occasion you are shocked into seeing things from another perspective - as was the case with listening to with this young Asian - it can be a jarring experience.

I'd had a similar jolt of objectivity a few years earlier upon finding what I thought was a black and white reprint of a TINTIN graphic novel. I read Tintin books in my childhood and quite enjoyed the clean, open style of drawing by the strip's creator HERGE. This piece was called TINTIN: BREAKING FREE. My first impression was that the artwork standards were slipping. (The wobbly tracings of Herge's art looked unhealthy and slightly repulsive.) After a few pages, I realised the comic was not an official publication at all; it was some kind of imitation or, more accurately, an appropriation. As it transpired this particular incarnation of the boy reporter was an anarchist parody written by one 'J. Daniels' and published by an anarchist group called 'Attack International'.

The story was a pretty vehement piece, featuring dialogue punctuated by the word 'Bastard!' and depicting acts of 'justified' violence against both authority figures and anyone not portrayed as beer-drinking working class.

Since my family had been ostracised and often persecuted by working class people for the crime of being even poorer than they were, I felt no kinship with such causes and didn't enjoy the book for that reason. The philosophy of the piece came to a head during a riot on page 90 in which the main characters sing 'P.C. Blakelock, P.C. Blakelock, he ain't on the beat no more!!' PC Keith Blakelock was an officer with the London Metropolitan Police who was hacked to death by a mob during a riot on the Broadwater Farm housing estate in north London in 1985, a fact the author considered a triumph.

Returning to the volume a few years ago, I realised what I had been reading was hatred. A different type from my own, with a different focus, but nonetheless possessing all the hallmarks of my own thinking: hostility; resentment; an all consuming sense of injustice; bursts of vehemence and a philosophy sharply directed against 'Them': an enemy class to be feared, loathed and hopefully punished. This is the thinking of the hater. From my own experiences, I know the foundations of this mindset stem from more than mere resentment, a great deal of it comes from the feeling that you are *still* on the ropes when it comes to your dealings with the world.

If you have an injured sense of self, if you have been programmed to see things in adversarial terms then you will believe that 'They' still have part of you, that 'They' will always have part of you. This perceived vulnerability means that you feel incomplete no matter what. This is where resentment comes in: you rage over the fact that 'They' have made you less than you should be as a result of their attacks. Because you will always be less, in your own eyes, this means 'They' are *still* attacking you, and *still* able to hurt you. This is the part that leads to fear. Anything that challenges you now, anything added to this inner war is another assault, no matter how slight, it is a threat that increases in danger the longer you think about it.

There is an awful gravity to these emotions. You can stay ahead of them for a while but they are never far behind. On the occasions other pressures slow you down they will always catch up and smother you. When that happens, it becomes clear that everything is evil and part of the same big, HUGE conspiracy.

It is very hard for me to grasp perspectives outside my own. What my thinking must look like to others is a subject usually beyond my reach. Seeing this ugly mindset depicted in this book, a medium I related to, actually managed to give me a rare jolt of objectivity; another anchoring point perhaps. 'Is that what I'm like?' I wondered for the first time. The sad answer to that is: yes, that's exactly what I'm like, me and all the others like me, your children amongst us; so many of us, all created so by the wonderful machine of education.

If by this point you can accept the possibility of greater depths behind these school atrocities, then you may have grounding for the rest of the book. If, like Lem and many others, you are still a slave to your programming; still consider school abuse to be 'rough and tumble', if you have no problems with the tragedy of Jack then you might as well throw this book away because you have no hope of understanding the reasons behind school shootings.

~~~

Columbine barely registered with me at first, or even for several weeks afterwards. There is always a delay during which my mind digests information at its own rate. The more profound the mouthful, the slower my brain chews. Scotland had already experienced its own school atrocity with the appalling Dunblane massacre of 1996, in which madman Thomas Hamilton slaughtered 16 primary children and one teacher (an event that shocked even me). There had been earlier American school shootings, but none of these triggered the intense preoccupation of Columbine. This assault by teenagers Eric Harris and Dylan Klebold, that left 15 people dead - killers included - was no mere act of madness. It was a meticulously planned gesture of defiance by two young haters that reached many, including me, particularly me.

I became aware of an entirely new group of feelings emerging after Columbine. These came in waves and left me feeling hollow and rage-less in their wake. Over the next few months, I watched them build in momentum and intensity. Eventually, they hit me full force, swamping me with a mixture of relief and *justice*.

I am experiencing them as I write this. There is the inevitable gloating born of hatred but it doesn't end there. Beyond the gloating is an intense, almost physical, sensation that a 'warning' has been sent out, and a battle has been won for the first time. A malevolent force that steals from me and from my kind has been made to pay for that theft and I am more complete because of this. There is a feeling that something which refuses to listen has been made to listen. I feel stronger, more empowered, better defined, recognised and no longer alone because of these attacks. For the first time in my life I feel *safe*.

With each shooting, this sense of protection and definition sharpened, leading me to stop thinking in terms of 'I' and more in terms of 'We'. This generated a novel and comforting sense of belonging, of being part of something able to protect and force recognition of itself by acts of violence. For a while, the mob in the changing room and the cartoon of the common room lost their power and shrunk away. I was not free, but I no longer felt trapped, certainly not as much as before.

The implication of the slaughter staggered me. This was my fantasies come to life, nowhere near as bloody or sadistic but altogether more exciting because it was real. The Enemy - hitherto untouchable - had been wounded by these two 'soldiers', driven back and punished, hideously. A school, a bastion of torture, had been scarred, perhaps forever. The event, seen worldwide, appeared to send a message that the damage inflicted on the underdog was finally coming back with added interest. My Whitehill emotions had gained a direction, a cause. More, they had gained champions.

Nothing I had done, nothing I had ever achieved imbued me with the sense of power I drew from the Columbine killers. The unbelievable pressures of my childhood and teenage years, every jibe, every boot, every thrown fist and burst of pain exploded towards the acts of these two young men. Theirs was true power, not like the Hulk or Superman or all the rest of that Fantasy rubbish. Old-fashioned heroes of that type quickly faded into the background to be replaced by Eric Harris, Dylan Klebold and all the others who followed; a new breed of heroes, freedom fighters sending their message out far and wide.

I know many will ask what kind of message is sent by the death of a child, but try to imagine the perspectives of minds that grow up facing the aggression of an entire society. I have never met these young victims and I know they were not the same people who attacked me, but these emotions make no distinction between individuals. To them, there are no innocents, all are guilty, all are The Enemy. Normal people had everything. By the simple virtue of being 'accepted' they were setting standards I could never live up to, and this meant they were hurting me and *attacking* me.

In the aftermath of Columbine and other shootings, a number of books appeared on the shelves for the purpose of throwing light onto these atrocities. I devoured many of these and found myself occasionally surprised by their content. Some displayed a degree of genuine insight, a few even opened my eyes to factors I had never considered (geography and culture), and at least two proposed some semi-effective methods of defusing violence before it occurred.

Despite this, not one evidenced any understanding of the unbelievable pressures found in even an ordinary school. Although I searched, I could not find a single word to accurately describe what had happened to me nor to explain the even greater cruelties I had seen inflicted on Jack. Many of the books were filled with academic appraisals of the phenomena that, despite being the work of experts, painted a sanitised picture of the school experience; one hopelessly blind to the brutality suffered by the underdog. Stock phrases like 'Warped meaning systems' and 'Distorted perspectives' were bandied about with little understanding of the forces that did the warping and distort-

Harris and Klebold. Monsters to some, heroes to others.

ing. Reading these, I wondered if the authors had the slightest grasp of what it was like to live as an outcast or had the slightest interest for that matter.

If these books are using this approach to communicate the anguish that provokes these killings then they are not making a good job of it. I consider this type of wholly detached appraisal – even from a technical standpoint – to be inappropriate as it cannot furnish a complete picture. These are not just physical situations; they are intensely charged emotional ones as well. It is easy to look upon the suffering of others from a mechanical standpoint; it is an altogether different matter to live and to be *shaped* by such forces. It is just as easy to mistake a shallow interpretation for an objective one, particularly in an area filled with facts no-one wants to hear.

Writing about such things from such a detached viewpoint is also a very effective way of avoiding seeing them in terms of blame. You need voice no moral opinion on the forces behind these killings if you insist on describing them as phenomena. I suppose it's here I find my greatest disappointment with these books: no moral stance; no need to name a terrible wrong and do anything concrete about it. Conversely, writings on racism and other prejudices are allowed to take such a stance and venture opinions based on it. Being a victim, I had hoped that literature on this subject was capable of a similar, human dimension when it came to highlighting this evil, and the evil of those who allow it.

Two books that avoided this approach were Mark Ames's superb GOING POSTAL and Brooks Brown's NO EASY ANSWERS: THE TRUTH BEHIND DEATH AT COLUMBINE (written with Rob Merritt). Both felt like a breath of fresh air for daring to suggest a larger evil behind the killings. Brown, an ex-Columbine student and friend of Eric Harris, paints a harrowing picture of a school saturated by a culture of bigotry, oppression and fear. This is in sharp contrast to Dave Cullen's COLUMBINE, a book which reads as little more than a sanitised exercise in public relations for the benefit of the school. Brown and Cullen paint entirely different pictures of the Columbine event; one blaming the school, the other the killers. The former writing from the trenches, as opposed to the latter, who was simply told about it all afterwards.

This attempt to render education blameless was a direction taken by many of the later books I devoured. The more academic of these broke down into two distinct groups of authors: the psychologists and the sociologists. The former seemed determined to prove the problem lay with the kids themselves. According to this group, school shootings were the result of schizophrenia, schitzotypical personality disorder, psychosis, sociopathy and a smattering of vague and undefined emotional problems. The possibility of blame lying with the schools didn't feature much in their theories. (Mental health problems may very well be part of this problem but the books that took this route didn't offer a convincing explanation as to why these disturbed young souls persisted in attacking their schools instead of shopping malls, churches or cinemas.) The sociologists, on the other hand, seemed more open to accepting external forces as a possible cause. Unfortunately even they tended to be somewhat vague when it came to defining the exact nature of these. I tended to favour the latter group, even if I had problems grasping much of their language.

Again this may sound like the overreaction of a hater, but when I explore this literature I became angry at its air of indifference and apparent avoidance. This seems to be another aspect of the 'conspiracy of acceptance' I sense all around me. These books do not stand with me against this evil, therefore they did not reach me, and if they are not reaching me then the minds behind them are not reaching these kids either. The problem is worse than simple lack of communication. I consider this literature to be quite damaging. It furthers a great misdirection: the rather arrogant assumption that this society is, for the most part, in the right. What if that is the wrong approach? What if the first move in getting to the heart of this problem is to entertain the possibility that we – as an entire society – are in the wrong, *horribly* in the wrong?

For my part, I have neither academic grounding nor qualifications in this or any related subject. But I have lived this life. For me, the suffering is not a concept. My speciality is fear, pain and rage. Hatred is my only qualification but since hatred is the language of these attacks, it may be the most important qualification of all. A subjective appraisal of this phenomena —based on shared feelings— is possibly the only valid one. At the very least, it might add the missing part to the other studies.

~~~

At this point, accusations of taking the killer's sides are inevitable. My answer is of course I'm taking their sides. I'm a product of the forces that shaped many, if not most of them. If I said I was capable of doing otherwise I'd be lying and you'd know it. That doesn't mean I agree with what they did. Believe it or not those are two different things. It is hard for me to grasp the tragedy of these attacks, but not impossible. I've watched interviews with tortured parents as the camera panned across images of their children's graves and felt nothing. Abstractions like these simply wash over me. This is not the case when confronted by a picture of a student killed by school shooter Kip Kinkel. There is something in this image - taken from a TV documentary - that reaches me.

For several years, my mother and I looked after a colony of inbred, feral cats. This involved feeding them and trying to home their offspring. It also meant dealing with their little bodies after their deaths. Death in the wild is far from dignified. It often twists the remains into strange, spastic con-tortions. In the image of this boy, lying twisted in a pool of blood, his shirt ridden up, I recognised this same body language of death and was reached by it. Likewise a commonly shown picture of Daniel Mauser - a fifteen-year-old murdered at Columbine - is similarly able to breach my barriers. This, obviously framed, image of the boy shows the reflection of a person and room on its glass surface (possibly the picture is sitting in a frame or an album). It is the room that reaches me. This place, possibly the living room of the boy's home is now lacking a person - he has been removed from it and from his own life.

As it was with the cats, I have precedent to help me relate to this. Many years ago, I suddenly lost a dear friend. I was one of a group helping to empty her house after her passing. Looking at her home, I was struck by its sudden emptiness. My friend was gone. She was the purpose of the place. It existed to shelter her. But she was gone. There was nothing to shelter now. The place had no purpose. It was at that moment her loss really hit me. Daniel Mauser's home is also missing an essential part: a child. Through these indirect routes, I am able to comprehend loss and pain. Looking at these images of two young people, robbed of their basic right to existence, I feel shame that I am twisted enough to grasp the reasoning behind their deaths.

I have two wildly differing sets of emotions here. The first are an entirely adversarial set of responses which rejoices in anything that hurts The Enemy. I know that these did not originate in me, I was taught them at Whitehill. The shame belongs to a second, unrelated group of feelings; I suspect these belong to the person I could have been had I not suffered the abuse of my old school. Despite the rage that churns in me, I am able to use this shame as another anchoring point; this one for my conscience.

The following chapters are a hater's view of the school experience. You'll learn what I feel towards certain mechanisms within education and what I believe these provoke in other outcasts. This is a runt's perspective on the damaging effects of institutions you consider normal and acceptable. It will make some judgments on the callous mechanics of education and the conse-quences of ignoring these. It is true there are many aspects of schooling, both British and American, I have never experienced but I know what provokes anger in me, what makes me feel worse and what makes me feel better. If it does this with me then I think it safe to assume it will do the same with many of these kids.

~~~

I was warned about putting such thoughts on paper. Revulsion on the part of many is unavoidable, but I'll risk it. Despise me if you must, but I'm sure that if cancer were able to communicate its origins and mechanisms you would benefit from listening. How subversive is it to explain —in plain, non-violent language— the cold mechanics of something that drives young minds to kill? These 'school terrorists' are not monsters who have sprung spontaneously into existence. They are your own children warped out of shape by forces you still refuse to recognise. They kill and applaud the killing because they embrace values totally opposed to your norm. What you should be asking is how they got those values and what part your 'norm' had in shaping them. This will mean facing some ugly truths about commonly held attitudes and recognising, for the first time, what they are actually teaching your kids. The process will involve attacking the popular picture of the human animal and its sacred institution of education; an approach I consider necessary, as hiding the finger of blame under a multitude of grey areas cripples other literature on this subject.

For anyone who suggests I'm glorifying this phenomena or, worse still, trying to incite further attacks, my reply is this: I will be putting nothing in the following pages that is not already known and embraced by many of your own children. If I want to see more atrocities all I need do is shut up and sit back as this particular killing machine has been running for decades, maintained perfectly by the irresponsibility and deliberate ignorance of our entire society.

WE ARE AT WAR

In addition to a wealth of literature, a number of studies on the school shooter are also available. Chief amongst these is 'The Classroom Avenger Study' by James P. McGee, Ph.D. and Caren R. DeBernardo, Psy.D. The report, described as a 'Behavioural composite' of the typical school shooter, can be found online for anyone interested in learning more about the subject. Whether or not they will is debatable.

What interests me most about this study is not so much what is in it, but what *isn't*: and that is the aforementioned finger of blame. So far as I am concerned, any study of this type needs such a thing. Unfortunately, I seem to be in a minority here. The study —like others of its kind— suffers a familiar lack of focus and moral stance. It looks at the reactions and makeup of these killers with only a passing interest in what they are actually reacting to. I suppose it's naive to expect any better. Regardless of its academic credits, this type of study is the product of minds that grew up accepted within society and, as a result, haven't the slightest hope of any objectivity about it.

Imagine an openly racist society with openly racist schools. In these schools, the abuse of racial minorities is the norm (as it is in the adult society around it). The schools do not attach any real seriousness to the abuse and only make a gesture of protection by classifying it under the rather vague term 'bullying'. This does little to stop the problem because it only focuses on the abuse and not the attitudes that lead to it. Ultimately there is no real protection for the minority kids despite persecution so extreme some of them are driven to suicide. Eventually a number of these youngsters snap and lash back viciously. The schools and the larger society around it are mystified by this retaliation since they are incapable of recognising the maltreatment of these minorities as being in any way serious. Several reports on the subject are commissioned by the racist authorities. These are researched and assembled by a wide selection of racist psychologists. The studies evaluate the physical, emotional and social backgrounds of the killers. They loosely acknowledge that the shooters belong to certain 'minorities' and vaguely imply these minorities *may* possess certain characteristics that *may* be targeted by others around them.

However, rather than making this the focus of the report, the authors skirt around the point, concentrating instead on a range of other elements unrelated to race; eventually suggesting that the killers may be inspired by a multitude of factors like their home lives, mental illness or violent entertainment. Ultimately, the reports fail because they neither recognise nor define the prejudices that shape these killers, nor the depth of pain that motivates them. They loosely analyze the shooter without giving any real suggestions on how to prevent him being brought into existence in the first place and, as a result, do not offer a concrete course of action on how to avoid future killings.

Those of you who understand the point of this book may grasp the fatal flaw in these fictitious reports: at no point does the word 'racism' feature in any of their pages. This is because it does not exist in this particular society's vocabulary. The attitude is not considered serious enough to merit a word to confront it. Furthermore, the society - at its highest 'moral' levels - is neither civilised nor responsible enough to create such a word, even in light of the suicides and killings the prejudice provokes.

In our society, a similar situation is unavoidable: how can we expect our academics to write objectively about prejudices invisible even to them? One phrase that crops up regularly in school shooter literature is 'imagined slights'. This is a reference to the school shooter's supposed tendency to react to attacks that are more imagined than real. But what if these slights aren't so much imagined as just invisible? Shooters, with few exceptions, tend to occupy the lower rungs of the school pecking order, an area seething with hostility and intolerance. For such bottom dwellers, school life consists of a daily conveyer belt of *very real* slights whose scope and subtlety are often undetectable to the socially accepted and well-adjusted.

For this reason these reports (just like the books in the previous chapters) strike me as inadequately researched and incomplete. Their focus is wrong. They start by dissecting the classroom avenger with little attention to the forces that shape him. They read like a study on the symptoms of a disease with little mention of the actual disease itself.

A classroom avenger is a double act. There is always an unseen partner: the place where the avenger was trained, the classroom itself. In my opinion, any complete study should start with an unflinching look at the, often staggering, brutality of this environment. Since such studies are clinical by nature, it would be unrealistic to expect a moral evaluation of the classroom arena (unfortunately), but I would have at least hoped for a responsible acknowledgement of the severity of the pressure generated there. Sadly, this is not the case with the Classroom Avenger Study or other reports of its type. As usual, we are left with yet another in an endless stream of sanitised studies that seem to start at chapter two instead of chapter one. I suggest adding 'Carrie White burns in hell', 'Stanford' and 'The Blindspot' to the start of any new reports. Think of them as chapter one. Now the studies are complete.

A great deal of controversy surrounds reports of this kind. Many experts and professional bodies argue that profiling school shooters is pointless as there is very little to actually link them. That is not true: they don't shoot up their shopping malls or churches; they shoot up their schools. The school is the one constant in *all* cases. The logical conclusion is to stop profiling the shooter and to start profiling the school instead.

~~~

For the underdog, school is bad enough, but some are that little bit worse. American schools in particular boast a feature which brings the entrenched viciousness of juvenile society into sharp focus like sunlight concentrated through a lens, allowing its inequalities and cruelties to become part of the school culture at an almost official level.

Flash Thompson was the first 'jock' I ever saw, although I don't know if the term was actually used to describe him in the early issues of SPIDER-MAN where he first appeared. He clearly fitted the profile: Successful, athletic, powerful, attractive to girls and remorselessly hostile to poor lonely Peter Parker. Astonishingly, despite being depicted as an uncouth specimen, Thompson was also shown to be extremely popular and respected by all, including even the teachers at his high school; a subtle commentary on injustice honestly and admirably woven into many issues of the comic.

The term 'jock' initially confused me, as the word is both a Scottish name and a slang term for any Scots person. (In my various war comics, English soldiers often called their Scottish counterparts 'Jock'.) Yet Thompson and his kind didn't seem in any way Scottish. As I devoured more and more American comics over the next couple of decades, I learned a lot about these creatures. Jocks were unique to American schools. They were robust young males associated with competitive sports, a subject that, for some insane reason, seemed to occupy a position of importance greater than actual learning. Their efforts often brought glory and even financial rewards to the schools they represented; this elevated them to an elite occupying the highest echelons of school society.

Most elites are identified by a uniform, jocks were no exception They were drawn with vaguely militaristic buzz cuts (or later, mullets) and wore sports jackets adorned with either numbers or a letter across the back. This uniform was usually topped off with a girl or two, permanently attached to each beefy arm. In almost all of their comic appearances, jocks were depicted as a malevolent force persecuting the main character or at least one of their associates (usually referred to as 'nerds', 'dweebs' or 'geeks').

I began to grasp the message my comics were sending These jocks were the personification of something larger than themselves: a culture of intolerance accepted and perhaps even endorsed by the school authorities. Reading the subtext of these stories, it became obvious that aggression and contempt for weakness were attitudes considered worthy, at some unspoken level, by those who pulled the strings in these places of learning.

Such a paranoid concept had to be a 'comic' idea of course; an exaggeration typical of the medium. No educational system could be callous and irresponsible enough to embrace such a injustice. Unfortunately, truth is stranger than fiction and often as sick. As I researched this book, I came across countless real-life examples of the astonishing favouritism heaped upon these honoured sons of the school. The most chilling of these can be found in Brooks Brown's memories of the brutal and utterly unfair regimes of Columbine High. I would advise reading his book for a more in-depth look at this problem.

Brown isn't the only one with bad memories of Columbine. British student Polly Graham had her own unnerving experience during an exchange trip to America. In her April 22 1999 article, 'I watched the tension simmer at Columbine', Graham described how she made the mistake of sitting in a 'Popular people only' area of the Columbine cafeteria (a transgression apparently comparable to a black person sitting at the front of the bus). She was hurriedly dragged out of her seat by an agitated student and shown where it was 'safe' to sit. As it transpired, the cafeteria was divided into areas allotted to different types of student One end was reserved for jocks and cheerleaders. This area was off-limits to everyone else. The section at the opposite end of the canteen was for 'geeks' and other social rejects; Graham was advised to sit in the middle. During her brief time there, she watched the popular students indulge in loud behaviour obviously intended to aggravate and provoke their less prestigious peers. Graham was appalled at the atmosphere of the place and expressed mystification that the teachers and administrators allowed such dangerous pressures to build up.

This prevalent attitude of Columbine towards its weaker own could best be summed up in the words of Evan Todd, a Columbine jock: 'Columbine is a good clean school, except for those rejects. Most kids didn't want them there.' Columbine High was once described as 'An unashamedly Rah Rah! School'. In light of such attitudes being voiced openly, 'Rah Rah!' does exude more than a faint whiff of 'Deutschland überAlles'.

There is no jock culture in British schools. Whitehill certainly had no such divisions. There was only me and the 'real' students, a separate class I knew I could never belong to. Favouritism was present as regards individuals, but it was personal and not institutionalized. (It did sting however, watching well-dressed, intelligent students being shown respect from teachers I knew had little time for a dim-witted scruff like me.) We did have one notably robust individual in the senior years. Like many larger-than-average young men aware of their physical advantages, he was fond of throwing his weight around, particularly towards the unpopular. Ultimately, however, he was an isolated specimen. There was no sports culture to make a little god out of him. I do wonder what things would have been like if he had belonged to a class of such individuals. Had he and his kind been given leeway to create a culture based on such testosterone-fuelled physical ideals; one honoured by the school itself; a culture that effectively told them they were more important than normal students. Such a culture would have its own expectations of aggression and intolerance that he, probably, would have felt pressured to live up to.

Many argue that the aggression of jock culture is situational. Knowing human nature, I think it's a bit of both with the situation giving stage to inbuilt aggression. Two psychologists specialising in collective brutality, S. Alexander Haslam of the University of Exeter and Stephen D. Reicher from the University of St Andrews, described this tendency thus: 'Group members cannot resist the pressure of the assumed situations, and brutality is the natural expression of the roles associated with groups who have unequal power.' Critics of Stanford suggested that by giving certain students roles as guards, Zimbardo put them in a position where they felt obligated to live up to that role. It doesn't take a genius to see this also applies in American schools. Looked at in this light, even jocks are not completely to blame for their excesses; the fault lies with the society that put them on their pedestals in the first place, a society that clearly values their strength and aggressiveness over the 'lesser' characteristics found in 'lesser' youngsters.

This is a particularly damaging lesson to teach young males who don't fit the profile. It tells them they are failing to live up to society's expectations of 'masculinity' (in the same way cheerleader culture must teach girls some fairly unhealthy lessons about the acceptability of certain body types). I'm glad Whitehill had no jock culture; it was an ugly, twisted place by itself. It's clear, however, that it could have been a whole lot worse.

The opinion held by many is that jocks are given preferential treatment and at least partial immunity from punishment because many school Principals and administrators were once jocks themselves and possibly embrace similarly intolerant values. A glimmer of this is evident in the aftermath of the slaughter at Westside middle school in Jonesboro, Arkansas. On March 24, 1998, thirteen-year-old Mitchell Johnson and eleven-year-old Andrew Golden killed four students and one teacher and injured ten others during a shooting there. In a related interview with Harvard researchers, one of the administrators at the school, John Marks, displayed clear pro-bullying sympathies. One statement of Marks, in particular, perfectly illustrates this repulsive attitude: 'Knowing Mitchell [Johnson], I'm not sure what *he did* to get picked on [laughs]… [Mitchell was] known as a whine-bag. I mean in football he was always whining because the other kids were bullying him... I talked to a lot of kids that get bullied, *they brought it on themselves...'*

I have personal experience of such institutionalised contempt for vulnerability within education. My PE teacher - like many others - had no problems with the abuse inflicted on me. Perhaps he considered me a 'whine-bag' who 'brought it on myself'. Maybe he believed I needed some toughening up or even a little 'character building'. I know from this and countless other incidents in my old school that the prejudices I discussed in The Blindspot are just as entrenched in the educational machine as they are in the rest of human society and perhaps more strongly focussed.

It would be naive and bigoted to suggest that aptitude in sports automatically transforms young men into bullies. Bullies come in all shapes and sizes; many are not jocks and many bullies classified as 'jocks' are not even into sports. The jock aspect of bullying culture is only part of the whole problem. Jocks are not necessarily bad but the brutality of jock culture is, not only because of what it does but what it highlights.

Whether or not you believe the official world capable of such favouritism is irrelevant. What matters is that most American school students do. In any situation in which rampant bullying and alienation are apparently tolerated - even without jock culture - resentment against 'unfair' authority is inevitable.

However, making unassailable champions out of certain types of aggressive young men can only serve to sharpen such feelings to a far keener level. (I'm not being critical of America, here, just observing that the American educational system —above all others— seems perfectly designed to suggest collaboration between authority and abusers and, as a result, perfectly designed to provoke resentment against such apparent 'corruption'.)

It's fairly obvious this particular sense of injustice is the cornerstone for most, if not all, resentment for authority found in US schools. Alienated students see authorities accepting their plight, and this final Dark Lesson teaches them that such injustice is all that awaits them once they leave school. That this belief has been allowed to flourish proves, beyond question, that those behind education lack even the slightest inkling (or perhaps, caring) of just how powerless a badly designed curriculum can make a young mind feel.

~~~

Popularity, what a truly sick and twisted idea: you only have worth if we say so. I can't imagine how anyone could be irresponsible enough to tolerate such a nightmarishly amoral system of human grading in a school, let alone promote it. Yet the American educational system exposes teenagers to the concept of 'popularity', the need not only to fit in but to be respected, even admired, by your peers via its unusually aggressive sports and social programs (proms, etc). It emphasises both the attractiveness of popularity and indeed its *normalcy*. Sadly, there is no light without shade. If you promote a culture of popularity then you also create a culture of unpopularity, one that carries this message: the school (and, by extension, the whole world) says that the popular kids are 'right' and those who do not achieve this status are 'wrong', and that's official.

This problem isn't just limited to America or to sports. One side effect of any form of Social Education (and that includes Sex Education) is to stress the normalcy of social acceptance, assuming, as it does, that all young people are capable of such a thing. In the real world, this effectively pressures the outcast to 'fit in' while refusing to confront society's almost universal habit of closing ranks on those it finds wanting. Lessons intended to help ordinary youngsters integrate into society can inflict terrible scarring on the outcast, as they only serve to remind them of the 'abnormality' of their deficient lives. Worse still, they often invest them with a sense of blame since (as pointed out in previous chapters) such underachievement is more often than not considered a contemptible failing in our culture.

Imagine what it must be like for a developing mind to feel itself found wanting in such a sensitive area and by such a gigantic entity as the educational system. It's bad enough to be young and not allowed to be young, to have all the desperate drives of youth denied at every turn; but to have that rubbed into your face at an official level with a hefty dollop of shame is a two-pronged attack that feels like wrestling a tag-team. This stigmatises kids with social problems as 'failures', a judgment that often leads to a vicious circle of inadequacy and resentment.

An equally vicious circle is generated earlier in the school experience by education's lax attitude towards bullying. School takes a young person's freedom and yet will not protect them in return. Abused youngsters are expected to show responsibility with no sign of responsibility being shown towards them. As the youngster grows older and wiser, the inevitable response is: how dare school demand this? How dare it expect of them what it refuses to give in return? How dare it order that they hold themselves accountable to a code of behaviour which has never been held accountable to them? How dare it judge them on top of all that? Outcasts look to the school for protection and, when it isn't forthcoming, we know the ultimate rage a child feels when it's parents abandon it. To us, this is not just failure but betrayal.

Don't underestimate teenage paranoia (particularly when dealing with developing brains whose pathways may have been physically modified by years of abuse). Young people are assembling their first adult picture of the world around them. Many will arrive at this one, particularly if education gives them plenty of raw material to work with.

Complicating matters is the extremist nature of the teenage mind. This applies to victims as well as bullies, *particularly* to victims. To a youngster buckling under this type of pressure, you are either with them or against them. There is seldom any in-between or any innocents. Everything and everyone is absolute. During the retarded adolescence of my twenties, anything that challenged me was not just evil but *absolutely* evil; anything which was not with me was *absolutely* against me. Show apparent favouritism to 'popular kids' or bullies and the outcast will see an enemy that stretches far into the adult world around them. I know, because when my time came I did, with a vengeance.

I didn't experience this at school; it occurred during my stay at Huntley Lodge during the middle 80's. My medication was doing me no good and I was slipping into deeper and deeper periods of despondency and rage. The blame can't be laid entirely at the feet of chemicals. This had been building since the beginnings of my twenties. The drugs had perhaps accelerated it during this period. As the weeks wore on, something strange began to happen: after each burst of fury, there was a lingering afterthought that told me the anger was justified. It was a slow resentment that smouldered even after the initial rage had abated. In the past, when my problem was simply anger, I was able to distance myself from that emotion after it faded. This new mind-set was different It would not go away. It clung to my thinking and coloured everything I tried to distract myself with.

I now know this was a result of the more complex cross-references my brain was starting to make. As a teenager, I was far too immature and narrow in my focus to link my experiences and grasp the larger injustices marring my life. Individual events occurred, generated fear, humiliation, pain and occasional bursts of anger. Once this was over, the resulting memory would burn itself into an isolated niche as my mind settled itself via the usual preoccupations. In my twenties this damage woke up, when maturity (what little I could muster) stripped away the insulation between these memories and I started to form an overall picture.

It was after leaving hospital that this picture came into focus and I finally understood Whitehill's message. The Lesson which had been gnawing at the back of my head was now gnawing at the front. It went something like this: 'FITTING IN IS NORMAL. OTHER PEOPLE FIT IN. YOU MUST FIT IN TOO. WHAT IS WRONG WITH YOU THAT YOU CANNOT FIT IN? YOU MUST BE ONE OF 'THOSE' PEOPLE, THE ONES WHO ARE DIFFERENT. YOU ARE WRONG FOR NOT BEING ABLE TO FIT IN, FOR BEING DIFFERENT. DIFFERENT IS WRONG. DIFFERENT IS BAD. YOUR KIND ARE WRONG. YOU ARE WRONG, BAD, WRONG, INFERIOR, WRONG, WORTHLESS, WRONG, WRONG, WRONG!!'

I was the bad guy again, only there was no longer any need for an external source of persecution. My Whitehill memories, far from diminishing were gathering momentum by themselves. I felt more trapped and under attack than at any other period in my life. A profound change occurred around this time. The focus of my rage shifted from the students and teachers of Whitehill to the school itself and all the intolerance it represented. The entire diseased entity of Whitehill became The Enemy. The idea of the entire school paying for its crimes became an obsession and I found myself repeatedly muttering 'Whitehill must die,' under my breath.

This sense of being judged (and found wanting) began to extend out and encompass the world around me, a world I could feel radiating robust contempt for a stupid, unmanly specimen like myself. I began to drift away from TV and films and other forms of popular media. Apart from the fact that such things were physically too painful to look at any more, I found myself sickened by anything that depicted happy, normal, young people enjoying life; the life I was convinced they had somehow denied me. I loathed them for the doors they had open to them, doors they had closed to me. I knew, behind their shallow smiles, they despised me, worse, they despised *My Kind*.

My Kind!

'Er … well … that is to say … duh!'

As I looked back over the social skills classes, remembering what it was like to sit amongst those hopeless young pariahs, I finally realised I had never been alone. I belonged to a specific group of person, a type held in very low esteem by society This lead to an expansion of perspectives, an awareness of a larger evil surrounding me. Society wasn't just attacking me, it was attacking My Kind. The entire world was operating on principles no better than racism and education was at its core.

Those young outcasts in the social skills classes had been shaped by education, and destroyed by it. Education warned us about the evils of sexism, sectarianism, racism and even homophobia but had never in any way condemned what had happened to them. Their maltreatment seemed to be some type of twisted norm. The teachers and all the others behind education knew it was happening; it was impossible for them not to have seen it on a daily basis. The only way they could have allowed this abuse was for it to be their norm as well. *This twisted lousy abuse of My Kind was their norm, all of them.* I realised that education lied about the human race, about life and everything; it was obvious that it lied to My Kind all the time. This new viewpoint came with a sense of dislocation from The Rules and all other values I'd held dear up till this point.

The Rules were not fair It hit me like a ton of bricks.

I had spent my entire life thinking I had failed them. In this new light, I realised they had failed me and worse, failed My Kind. I now saw The Rules and all other forms of educational propaganda for the lies they were. The Rules were supposed to help and protect. You respected them for that purpose. Obey, work hard, pass your exams and everything will be alright; everyone will accept you and you will live life to its full. The Rules will look after you.

But they didn't.

Despite their insistence on obedience and responsibility, they just stood there and let all that happened to me, and people like me, occur without lifting so much as a finger. They actually put My Kind into situations that caused lasting pain and damage. The Rules did not give, they took, they stole. They couldn't explain what was happening to me. They never told the truth about what happens to the outcast; if anything, they seemed to cover it up. They had not prepared me, or any of the others, for the life of isolation and mockery that waited after school. The more I looked at The Rules, the more they seemed designed for the benefit, perhaps even the pleasure of those who hurt My Kind: The Enemy. The truth was obvious now: The Rules were intended to protect The Enemy, to give them the freedom they wanted. The collusion between the two became clear the more I thought about it. The Rules *were* The Enemy.

All institutions operating on them were The Enemy also. And the standards behind those rules, expectations of normalcy we could never live up to; expectations that were rubbed into our face from day one were the sickest, most cruel attack of all. By their unfair, selective nature they were obviously intended for the sole purpose of causing pain to My Kind.

This 'Flipover' happened almost instantly. The world simply inverted, revealing a new picture of things. The machine of education was now revealed for what it had always been: a device used for the oppression and abuse of My Kind. It did not just fail us, it *betrayed* us. The school and the authority it represented became the incarnation of the corruption I saw around me, the absolute focal point of the hostility that had assaulted me all my life.

I realised that such forces, far from being random and thoughtless, were actually the manifestation of genuine malice at an official level. It didn't stop at education either. The more I thought about it, the more I saw that the entire framework of our society, its laws and institutions, was designed to protect the strong and the vicious and to torment those who were in any way different. Society's entire purpose was to support, to promote abuse, not to stop it. These were not just attacks on me; they were 'officially sanctioned' attacks on My Kind. In light of this, descriptions like 'callous' and 'irresponsible' gave way to 'evil', and 'malicious'. 'Incompetent' gave way to 'Collusion'. 'Bullying' gave way to 'War'.

War, I'd never considered such a thing. Yet this society-wide devaluation of My Kind didn't seem like a mere attack, it really did have the feel of something much larger and much more sinister: *a state of war!*

NOT RAGE, OUTRAGE

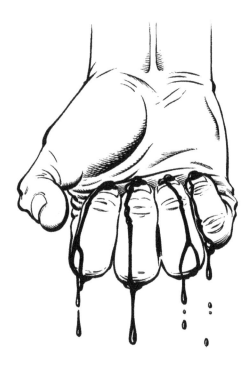

In British schools, isolated kids, awkward loners and the like occupy the lower social rungs. In American schools, with their sharply defined hierarchies, this stratification is not limited to individuals, it encompasses entire classes, or sub-classes of student.

Marginalise any section of the population and they will inevitably gain awareness of themselves as a minority, how they fit - or rather, don't - into the scheme of things. American youth culture is no different. Over the last few decades, young people have gained increasing awareness of the divisions promoted within their ranks and the educational hypocrisy and injustice behind this. In America, the outcast is not necessarily alone; they can belong to an outcast minority (or perhaps even an *outcast nation*).

Most minorities develop their sense of identity quicker when they are under attack. This is clearly the case in US schools. Unpopular youngsters perceive themselves as a minority defined by the aggression and disrespect of their more successful peers and the adult society that honours those peers. A casual browse of just about any youth-orientated website voicing opinions on school issues will illustrate this belief. To these youngsters, popular and unpopular kids are virtually members of a separate species. For many who embrace this larger picture, even the smallest act of humiliation becomes an attack not only on them but on 'Their Kind'.

I suppose my condition and lack of maturity is an advantage here. I'm locked into the trauma of my adolescent memories, constantly re-experiencing the feelings of my youth while simultaneously scrutinizing them from the perspective of a middle-aged man. To these emotions, the accepted viciousness and divisions in schools —all schools— suggests the powers-that-be are all in on this particular joke, all having a good laugh at the expense of the underdog.

As an adult, I know this is not the case. What I am looking at is simply callousness and irresponsibility, staggering callousness and irresponsibility. As a teenager, however, I'm not so sure. This acceptance really does feel like compliance. Unfortunately, when dealing with paranoia, there are only a few steps between compliance and conspiracy. (There are a number of writers open-minded enough to accept the possibility that school shooters have real reasons for attacking their schools. Some suggest it is for failing to protect them. I think this is only part of the story. During my time in Huntley Lodge, I was convinced that Whitehill had not only accepted the attacks against me, but had actually planned much of what occurred.)

I can deal with a malevolent school that is opposed to me. Certainly it enrages me, but this is just anger, something I can handle. The idea that school is opposed to My Kind is a larger issue that produces far more extreme feelings. What I experienced as I faced the cartoon in Whitehill was a mixture of brief emotions, chief amongst them, rage. What I experienced at Huntley Lodge, as I grasped this larger injustice, was something entirely new: *outrage*.

Having experienced both states, I can say they are very different in scale. Rage is an unthinking, transitory thing; it explodes then dissipates. Many of you may have experienced this, perhaps before saying something hurtful or even throwing a fist. Outrage is vastly more powerful and longer lasting than mere anger. I remember attempting to rationalise the emotion during a counselling session. It did more harm than good. Discussing the facts in an 'objective' fashion only reinforced the sense of injustice and left me worse than when I started. Outrage, as I was to discover, is a thinking state, able to sustain and justify itself. Rage can blind you for a moment, outrage for a lifetime Outrage can take hold in a mind, it can become a philosophy, and even a *cause*.

In the case of school shootings, I think that outrage is even more dangerous than the soldier mentality I described at the end of chapter six. (They certainly make a devastating combination: adversarial conditioning coupled with a growing rationalisation that the situation is actually *worse* than you suspected.) Revenge is obviously part of the school shooter's motive but it's naive to assume that's all there is to it. Had I been armed when I stood before the cartoon in the common room, I would have fired then and there because I was angry and afraid (particularly afraid). But would I have planned for weeks, months or even a year to kill, knowing at every step that I would be throwing my life away in the process? The answer to that is no; rage alone could not have made me do that. An atrocity of that scale would have required something different, something far more potent.

I suspect what is behind many of these planned assaults on American schools is not so much 'school rage' as 'school outrage'. The outrage of a minority who see themselves at war with their society's norm because that norm incorporates brutalities they cannot live with. One young shooter who came close to explaining this was sixteen-year-old Luke Woodham, a disturbed young man who, after stabbing his mother to death, proceeded to gun down nine of his classmates, killing two, in October 1997. Woodham is quoted as saying: 'I killed because people like me are mistreated every day... I did this to show society, push us and we will push back.'

That's an interesting statement. Woodham could have said '...because *I* was mistreated every day' instead he said '...*people like me* are mistreated every day...' His threat ended with '...push *us* and *we* will push back.'

Words like this strongly suggest Woodham was motivated by something larger than his own personal anguish. Even in the video diaries of Columbine killers, Eric Harris and Dylan Klebold, a similar perspective is hinted at. Dylan Klebold, presumably sending a message out to school aggressors, does not just refer to himself but instead is heard to say: '...do not mess with *that frikkin' kid*.' Eric Harris follows up the statement with: '...if you ever touch *him* again, I will kill you...' From listening to these tapes (all of which struck a note with me), I get the distinct impression what these boys are raging against is not just one bully or group of bullies but an entire culture of abuse targeted at *kids like themselves*.

It is possible this flip-over into seeing a larger perspective, far from being rare, is actually very common. When a belief system comes crashing down, it can be extreme and absolute. All it requires is a rigid mindset, something all-too common in teenagers subjected to abuse. The mechanisms that trigger this collapse are experienced by youngsters at all levels of education: the hypocrisy of lessons preaching about right and wrong and fairness and responsibility in the face of accepted brutality and obvious favouritism; the wrenching conviction that education has been lying from the start.

I was distanced from immediately processing this by my condition, only experiencing it years after leaving school. This is not the case with neurotypical kids, particularly nowadays. Today's youth culture is far more sophisticated and socially aware than ever before. I think many youngsters experience this flip-over while still attending school, and still exposed to these situations of injustice and suffering. Most dangerous of all, they are doing so while in contact with a society of peers who are reaching the same conclusion: that the world is waging war on Their Kind.

~~~

The most disturbing thing about outrage is its first victim: conscience. We comfort ourselves that we - and our children - are incapable of true evil because our conscience would not allow it. And yet with the right circumstances our conscience can be twisted to 'justify' almost anything. Some of the most appalling acts in human history - from race purges to the torture and killing of loved ones - have been the result of conscience. Even the most ordinary people can carry out exceptional or heinous acts if they believe they are acting for a greater good.

Just look at the problem we are having with terrorism. Most of these killers destroy and maim in the belief that what they are doing is intrinsically right. This has sprung from their adopting a value system they consider more important than themselves and even their loved ones. For these people, there is a larger issue at stake than their own lives or those of their victims. When something more important than you is under threat it is not just an attack, it is war.

Slap a person of faith on the face and they may turn the other cheek. Tell them their brethren are being slapped and they may mount a crusade against you. Similarly, a young person who sees the world in such antagonistic terms may still be restrained by their conscience. The same youngster, seeing an attack at this higher level, might be less impeded in their actions because their conscience is the very thing telling them retaliation is the 'right' response. Just before starting work on THE SURGEON, my murder fantasies in Huntley Lodge moved on from mere revenge for what had happened to me. In time, they focussed on injustices inflicted on My Kind. The sense of righteousness that accompanied each imagined torture and killing was incredible. In every way it felt like 'the right thing to do' as part of a larger picture of responsibility to something more important than just myself.

~~~

Enough abuse can drive anyone to suicide. Having reached such a point, a person may feel entitled to take the lives of those they believe put them in that position in the first place. Unfortunately, in this state of mind, the person may have an open-ended definition of 'legitimate target'. Another side-effect of chronic school abuse I encountered was an inability to perceive innocence. If, as a child, you are constantly targeted by your peers, you eventually stop separating their assaults. Your mind fuses them into a single attack that seems to stretch back throughout your entire history.

This is dangerous territory because, as I discovered, the process of merging does not end there. Collective assault - taken beyond a certain point - can strip you of the ability to see people as separate individuals. In time, I came to perceive everyone - even those who had neither spoken nor raised a hand in my direction - as a single aggressive entity totally opposed to me. It could be argued this only occurs under extreme circumstances but you would be surprised just how extreme a group of aggressive peers can be to an isolated mind. (Incidentally, in addition to 'perceived slights', another phrase that often crops up in related literature is 'the disproportionate response of the school shooter'. Disproportionate to what? This phrase does not take into consideration the scale of the attack these youngsters often suffer. Just because the authors of such statements are able to divide a life of brutality into individual acts doesn't mean those forced to suffer those lives can do the same.)

Outrage does not generate this perception of collective guilt but it does seize on it with a vengeance. Although it had faded slightly during my early twenties, I found this sense of all-encompassing hostility returning during my stay at Huntley Lodge. At this time, I ferociously hated certain residents for things that had been done to me in school, despite these individuals having never met me before. This started when I was confronted by a staff member for hurting another resident's feelings with an insensitive comment on the death of a loved one.

As the lady (quite rightly) challenged my thoughtlessness, I began to resent her for many of the attacks I had experienced at Whitehill. This was pretty creepy as I found myself simultaneously wrestling with two conflicting schools of thought. On the one hand, she was clearly innocent, having never even been at Whitehill. On the other hand, she was a member of the species that had abused me and, as a result, was as guilty as anyone who had laid a hand on me. Collective guilt won, and, from that moment on, a belief in universal culpability began to spread out to others. It is one of these mental states that comes and goes for me. For the most part, I'm moving away from it, but on the odd occasion it rears its ugly head, it becomes hard for me to tell people apart; everyone seems cut from the same malign cloth.

Slipping into this thinking is second nature for me. Remembering the beatings and degradations of Whitehill provokes feelings of rage, deep rage. Yet, despite this, school shootings make no sense to me. They are appalling, costing innocent lives and tearing families apart. But then I look beyond my own experiences and see the abuse of countless others like myself; child suicides; Jack and the other second-class citizens in those social skills classes. From this larger perspective these attacks really do feel like a state of war. From a war perspective, killings *do* have a horrible logic behind them. There are no innocents in war, just The Enemy. My Kind are not 'real' people to them, but that's okay, The Enemy are not 'real' to us either, simply a type of vermin. Their lives are unimportant. They have no value other than to be used as examples to prove a point, to carry a message. The one message the enemy cannot laugh at and cannot ignore: atrocity.

This viewpoint employs another form of school dehumanisation, the type taught to victims. If you are a bully you can learn to dehumanize your victim, but if you are a victim you can be forced to dehumanize the entire society you feel is attacking you. Does such a perspective make a monster?

~~~

Eric Harris was born a monster, so we are told. His problem wasn't bullying, he was just a sociopath. Dylan Klebold was schizotypical and Kip Kinkel was a schizophrenic. If we are to believe certain parties, then the pressures within education have very little to do with the shootings that take place there. Classroom avengers are driven by a variety of personal problems that are in no way connected to school. Despite being a layman, I still find explanations of this type all-too convenient. To me, they smack of an official world desperately pointing the finger of blame away from itself and towards the dead and the defamed.

With very few exceptions no-one decides to throw away their lives and that of others on a whim. Regardless of how these boys were born, they became shooters later, only after years of exposure to an environment of intolerance and open hostility. Can you imagine a place better designed to trigger dangerous reactions in a vulnerable or unstable mind? We will never know if Eric Harris really was a sociopath with the excessive ego-driven needs of such, but assuming this was the case, what happens when a sociopath is forced to attend an institution in which he is openly mocked and abused by an elite he can never belong to? An elite seemingly immune to the disciplines and punishments foisted on him because of favouritism? How would a sociopath deal with that? How would any young person with a mental health issue or personality problem for that matter?

The diagnosis of Eric Harris' sociopathy stems mostly from his writing. Supposedly this reveals a cold, sadistic, deceitful and manipulative mind, bloated with self-importance, looking down on the whole of mankind as deserving punishment for its inferiority. It would be easy to agree with this diagnosis. My problem is that I found nothing in his words that hadn't passed through my mind as well (including the use of pseudo-militaristic terms to justify mass slaughter). Violent fantasies in every way comparable and exceeding Harris' were the basis of my thinking during the mid to late 80's. There was no sentimentality in my scenarios, no regrets, just outrage, indignation and hatred. The fools of the world - my inferiors - had no time for me so I had no time for them or their banalities. Many kindred souls I've encountered have admitted to similar thoughts. The source of their hostility was not sociopathy but pain.

The ego is an unpredictable thing; assault it for long enough and it may collapse entirely, as was the case with Jack. However, the opposite is also possible: ego can compensate through anger or a false sense of superiority. In extreme cases, it can overcompensate through an abnormal level of desperate self-importance. Shortly after leaving psychiatric hospital, I found myself flickering back and forth between both extremes. One moment, I was the lowest slug, the next a visionary without equal. It's easy to see why.

In order to survive Whitehill's attacks on my sense of self, I had to compensate via imagined greatness, being an unrecognised genius fitted that bill nicely. This illusion was my most cherished possession Anything that challenged it, both insulted and *threatened* me. Had anyone suggested I was really just an embittered social failure then they would have become public enemy number one. Anything that proved such a point had to be rejected (and hopefully destroyed). I would like to point out that such a mindset —fuelled by rage at the world's refusal to recognise its superiority— usually stems from the world's refusal to recognise it as an equal.

Many of these sociopathy and 'superiority' theories also focus on Eric Harris demeaning his victims as 'nerds', despite himself hailing from the same strata in the school pecking order. Has no-one ever heard of denial? Many vehement homophobes are secretly gay. The same shame, self-loathing and self-deception can be found in other minorities. Jack disturbed me at a deep level because, ultimately, I knew he and I were trapped in the same situation, the part of me that craved superiority loathed and feared what he represented for that reason.

I think Eric Harris' hatred of 'nerds' stemmed from shame rather than sociopathy; and his hatred of his school stemmed from the belief it had allowed or perhaps even conspired to pigeonhole him as a member of this 'inferior' and 'shameful' minority. In all likelihood he targeted Columbine through these ordinary kids and not the loathed jocks for this reason. The young lives Harris snuffed out were probably only a means to an end. His mission was to permanently scar the institution and the 'corrupt' authority behind it; an authority he believed had legitimised his devaluation. While he slaughtered his victims, he was heard to cry out 'This school is dead!' As someone who spent most of the late 80's obsessed with the death of Whitehill Secondary, I found myself understanding the sentiments, if not the actions.

On the subject of his dishonesty, I would also point out that a young person who perceives the world to be attacking them may have no qualms about employing deceit as a weapon of defence. Again, shame, not personal gain, is usually the motivator for this particular tactic.

I'm not defending what Harris did. It was wrong, horribly wrong. But it is too easy to lay the blame on his arguable mental architecture and leave it at that. There is almost certainly more to his actions than we have been told. The events of his life, how the world actually *did* treat him and his kind deserves far more intense and honest scrutiny.

To me, this rush to diagnose and categorise such killers (while downplaying the possibility of external causes) smacks of the same avoidance culture that dumps outcasts into social skills classes rather than confronting the prejudices that marginalize them in the first place. It is yet another example of the blindspot in action.

~~~

Love him or loathe him, the classroom avenger has arrived and will not be leaving anytime soon. He can be found in books, comics, films and computer games. His actions have made him a cultural figure and a role model for many to idolise, and even copy, whether motivated by genuine outrage, revenge or a naive desire for immortality. The avenger's mission is their mission also. Every time he strikes, it is a 'call to arms' in their eyes. I know this is the case because I feel it also. Even as a middle-aged man, I experience a strange excitement after each shooting; a feeling that 'revolution' is in the air. I don't condone killing at all, but I cannot deny these emotions, their reality or their effect. They are a message being received far and wide.

Bandied from website to website, the shared rage of the underdog has grown into an ideology and, to some, a cause; one that has found champions. Harris and Klebold (or REB and VoDka as they are more commonly known to their followers) in particular have achieved anti-hero status, with a massive online cult expounding their virtues and that of school shootings in general.

'Meet the cult of REB and VoDka' and 'REB and VoDka fans ur not alone' are but the smallest sampling of discussion titles found with even a cursory search. These discussion groups, boasting thousands of members, are split between condemnation and open support. Pro REB and VoDka fans paint their heroes as martyrs and revolutionaries in a holy mission to cleanse schools of the hated oppressors of all unpopular kids - the popular ones. With the two sides depicted as warring factions, comments like 'It was war, just not the way war is usually thought of' and 'They did what so many of us young people wanna do' are typical of the philosophy expounded in these sites. 'Eric And Dylan Martyrs', a site run by a 'REB-N-VoDKA lover' conducted an online poll asking if the Columbine killers had followers. The reply was 83% yes with only 4% saying no.

~~~

I know what you are thinking: 'How can they be terrorists? They're just a bunch of kids, *our* kids!' It is recognised that political, racial and religious tensions are able to create terrorists. I'm astonished that our society is unable, or perhaps unwilling, to recognise that school tensions are capable of the same effect. The eventual retaliation of any abused minority is one of the oldest stories in the book, and age is no hindrance to this. In a 2004 post, Rory Schmitt, a contributor to Eric and Dylan websites summed it up in this online statement: 'Unless the way high schools work in America is totally changed... unless there is a revolution in our hallways and libraries and dining halls, there are going to more and more of us... Eric said he was only the beginning, the first revolutionary. He was right.'

The Conceit of the Adult rears its ugly head here. Genuine outrage involves a maturity we are reluctant to credit young minds with. Just as our kids are presumed incapable of suffering profound and lasting damage through school abuse, so are they presumed unable to evolve a culture of retaliation in response because of their age. Where exactly is the logic behind this assumption? In the case of high school students, you are not dealing with children but an intelligent, near-adult section of your population who, as our society has progressed, have come to learn far more about their position in it than you have.

Of all the invisible crimes committed by this society, the Dark Lessons are perhaps the most heinous. The old betray the young, dumping them into these learning cages we call schools. There we allow them to weed out, abuse and cripple their weaker own. We expose them to a culture of normalised evil, and teach them intolerance, cruelty, mistrust, shame, fear, despair, second-class citizenship, dehumanisation, mental illness, rage, hatred and even-

The inevitable

tually outrage. Out of this whole vicious, amoral warzone emerges the school shooter and still we refuse to see our hand in creating him.

We scurry around for every explanation except the right one because it is too ugly and we have the luxury of ignoring it. We insist in looking at these young killers' atrocities as though they were some kind of ghastly youth fad. We call it 'school rage'; a phrase that belittles it as a child's lethal tantrum. Our children cannot develop philosophies opposed to us. They cannot be terrorists because such a thing is too ugly to accept. Yet so many of these young people see a society that displays open contempt for characteristics they possess, one that wages war on them through its bigoted, preferential machine of education. How can we expect them to feel anything less than outrage and see their response as being anything other than a state of war in return?

NAÏVE SOLUTIONS

O n April 26, 2002 Robert Steinhauser slaughtered sixteen people at Erfurt Academy in Gutenberg, Germany. Thirteen faculty members were amongst his victims. As with Harris and Klebold, I don't approve of what this young man did, but I would still be a liar if I said I shed any tears that day.

This chapter is aimed at teachers and other employees of the educational machine. I'll try to be civil about this but it's not easy. I can see that you are just ordinary people with ordinary lives. You have families, loved ones and children. You entered teaching with a genuine desire to help the young, at least some of you did. Yet part of me hates your profession with a ferocity I cannot put into words, so I suppose this is the one area in which I can be accused of bigotry myself. I have no voluntary control over these emotions but at least I'm honest about them and, in being honest, I'll do my best to keep them in check.

Some unpleasant facts about your chosen profession: a small, but very real, percentage of the children who pass through the educational system, through your hands, will suffer long-term mental health problems as a result of damage encoded into their personalities while there. In extreme cases the damage will be permanent. There are young people sitting in front of you every day who have no chance of living normally —ever— as a result of what you are allowing to happen to them. Some, maimed by their school experiences, will grow up to face pointless lives of emptiness and suffering. Others won't grow up at all, committing suicide while in school or after leaving. A smaller number will take other lives with them… and it's your fault. You are enablers of this crime; you know full well it is happening. You have decades of proof all around and yet still you support this.

I suppose that's where my hatred stems from. It's more than just a reaction to my own experiences. As my understanding of educational betrayal has deepened, so my loathing has moved on from the youngsters who inflict this abuse to those adults who allow it, and that's you. Teachers are the thinking components of this machine, the parts in direct contact with the youngsters being abused. With few exceptions, I look upon you as cowards, criminals and betrayers, collecting your pay checks and pensions over the ruined lives of My Kind.

Perhaps your hands were tied in this area, but only because you allowed them to be. As isolated individuals, teachers have limited influence, but collectively you have always been the single greatest force within education. The machine cannot function without your compliance. Had you really wanted, you - en masse - could have forced much needed change years ago. The fact that you didn't, makes you, more than any other group, responsible for the slaughter we are seeing now. And that's the reason I have to reach you: you are the one group in a position to do something about this.

The greatest flaw of education is that its priorities are in reverse. The current system works like this: educate first, protect second. The message this carries is that school considers teaching more important than the lives of the students. Perhaps this is naive of me, but I think it should be the other way around. A human life should always be more important than any information you are trying to feed it. In my opinion, education should be restructured from the ground up so that the protection of the youngsters in its care becomes its first priority, over *everything* else. Anything less is a violation of their basic human rights and a crime.

Recently, a number of American schools have initiated their own voluntary programs to deal with school abuse. At White Pine middle school in Ely, Nevada, Principal Aaron Hansen interviews bullies to better understand their reasons for picking on other students. Another aspect of his program involves enlisting helpers called 'Defenders' from the student body. These are intended to act as 'Buddies' to look out for young people who are in danger of being picked on. Despite admiring this type of approach, I still have a few reservations.

The first problem lies in their voluntary nature. None of these programs are an official or permanent part of the curriculum. They have been brought into existence by a small number of caring professionals. Should any of these individuals leave their position, and be replaced by someone less responsible, then their creations face the possibility of vanishing; something that could leave a number of dependent youngsters in a very bad situation indeed.

The second problem lies with their ability to be enforced. To a certain extent, methods of this type require the bullies to have respect for authority. I can't help but feel all it would take to derail such programs is a head-on encounter with some of the hardened proto-criminals found in every school, the type who intimidate even the teachers. (I know this is all worst-case scenario thinking but I have found that, with matters educational, such an approach is usually a sensible one.) Although I find these methods admirable and I salute their creators, based on my own experiences, I do not consider them to be enough. By all means, employ such methods whenever possible, but should they fail, then it is time to bring on the law.

~~~

The idea of police in schools was unthinkable when I was young. Short of murder, what happened in the classroom and schoolyard was never serious enough to merit such. These days the world is very different. We have drugs, armed students and an increased number of attacks on staff members. This has finally forced the law into the classroom, at least in the US. (There is talk of policing British schools, tellingly, this is due to attacks on teachers and not students.) Is this for the better? I'm in two minds here. Protection by the law in Whitehill would have been a dream come true for the likes of me, but would protection have been the law's priority?

Stories are emerging that suggest otherwise. There seems to be a definite swing towards totalitarianism in schools who employ their own police (or School Resource Officers as they are often known). In the state of Texas, primary or pre-high schoolers can now be issued with 'Class C misdemeanour' tickets for 'Classroom Disruption', a blanket term that covers any number of heinous acts from leaving crumbs on tables, throwing paper planes, wearing inappropriate clothes, being late or simply misbehaving. These citations can lead to fines, community service and even prison time should the fine remain unpaid when the student reaches the age of seventeen.

A good example of this absurdity is the case of Sarah Bustamentes, a twelve-year-old student at Fulmore Middle school in Austin, Texas. In response to taunts that she 'smelled', Sarah, who has bipolar and attention deficit disorders, sprayed perfume on herself in class. Her teacher considered this a crime serious enough to merit the attention of the law. The law, in the shape of the Campus Police Officer, considered spraying perfume serious enough to arrest the child and issue her with a class C criminal misdemeanour citation, a criminal charge that could have remained on Sarah's record for life and seriously jeopardized any chance she had for higher education. Thankfully Sarah's mother took the case to court and, after several months of fighting prosecutors, finally had the charges dropped.

Used like this, the law probably would have destroyed me. I often experienced problems understanding both 'correct' behaviour and also what my teachers wanted from me. This confusion was usually interpreted as wilful disobedience and punished as such. Had my teachers - some of whom were openly antagonistic towards me - been able to involve the law in their punishments, I would have almost certainly ended up heavily penalized or even jailed for my 'crimes'. So far as I am aware, the function of the police is to protect the citizens. I can't say what happened to Sarah Bustamentes gives the impression of such. What it does show is that our schools are, as usual, more interested in running smoothly and protecting their own interests than the students in their care.

The presence of police in our schools is an area fraught with controversy. Many are bitterly opposed to what they see as an unnecessary intrusion into their children's development. Despite my own misgivings, I'm still in favour of it. In my opinion, there should always have been police in schools. The lack of such was a nightmarish mistake that condemned generations of youngsters to suffering and suicide. I don't see how we can expect to create a civilised society if the first thing we do is dump our offspring into artificial communities in which they are taught that the law is an absent father unable to either protect them or to *stop* them. I will agree that the current use of the law in schools seems totally inept and actually damaging. Any officer who issues criminal citations to kids for spraying perfume on themselves is not only squandering their authority but is, in fact, in total dereliction of their duty; which is the protection, not the oppression of young people.

Ideally, I would like to see these heavy-handed SROs replaced by teams of detectives tasked with investigating crimes involving harassment, intimidation or violence against students or teachers. These detectives would realistically assess incidents before deciding whether to take matters further. Should they decide that an incident does merit punishment, then they could issue bullies with on-the-spot penalties, either financial or academic. In extreme or persistent cases, they could submit evidence for the prosecution of either the bullies or their parents. Ideally, the powers of these detectives should extend outside the school and also cover areas like cyber-bullying. Bullies need to recognise their criminal status and need to be taught that they can be hunted, caught and punished.

The mental immunisation I referred to in chapter seven is probably unavoidable, so I think we should try to reverse it. There is nothing cruel about students growing up surrounded by a framework of responsibility and accountability whose priority is their protection, not the enforcement of petty disciplines. Such a thing will not break their spirit The only thing it might impair is their ability to hurt others. Indeed, if - in American schools - the isolated, unpopular students are shown that even the hated jocks are answerable to a non-preferential system of authority then this may go a considerable way to defusing the culture of resentment and 'conspiracy from above' that provokes many of these shootings.

There are several arguments as to why we should not police our schools, but not one is based on the value of a young person's life. No matter how intelligently couched, these arguments are effectively saying there is a section of our population who do not deserve of the full protection of the law. I'm sure those who espouse such beliefs mean well, but they have no idea of what the real world is like, that other world at the absolute bottom. They have never been hunted, never grown up as prey, never been shaped by blind terror, nor been driven to the point of taking their own lives. They don't speak for those kids and they insult their lives and memories by presuming they do. Their suggestions that these youngsters should be left to the nonexistent mercies of their abusers is yet another Dark Lesson, one perfectly designed to sow further resentment. The real problem with having the law in schools is the question as to whether or not it would actually stop bullying. Would it have stopped it at Columbine where the administration did not admit that it was happening? Unfortunately the law, like education itself, may be limited by our society's one-dimensional concept of what constitutes bullying and who carries it out.

Just as the word bullying does little to protect the bullied, initiatives that operate around this outdated term will share similar limitations since their focus still lies on tackling the symptoms rather then the underlying cause. To be honest, I have never liked the word 'bullying', In fact, like 'school rage', I consider it both insidious and damaging as it only focuses on closing the barn door after the horse has bolted. Terms like these divert attention away from the real problem. You cannot protect these youngsters by calling this problem bullying. They are the victims of a prejudice; the bullying is just a symptom of this.

If an individual is abused for reasons of race we're not allowed to simply call it bullying, we have to call it racism; why? Two reasons: firstly, racial minorities are powerful enough to force us to do so; secondly, because we know that the word bullying is inadequate to protect racial minorities from abuse. The word, 'racism', not only confronts and condemns racist acts it also confronts and condemns the attitudes that lead to the acts before they occur. It is pre-emptive in its confrontation, it has to be. Bearing this in mind, how can we expect the one-dimensional word 'bullying' to protect the victims of an even older prejudice? The answer is, it never has.

Obviously, it isn't just outcasts who suffer bullying (although they receive the lion's share by far), ordinary kids can become targets for this evil as well. The bullying can start for a variety of reasons. Revenge; a disagreement that gets out of hand; a friendship that comes to an end; a girl is too pretty; a boy is too fat or his hair is too red. Yet most of these so-called reasons are just an excuse. They may attract the initial attention of the bullies but they are seldom their chief motivation. Should the youngsters be strong enough to inflict suffering back on their tormentors then their stint as a victim will be brief. This is because what the bullies are really targeting is *vulnerability*.

Prejudice against vulnerability - the most primal of all prejudices - is at the core of all bullying, everywhere. Trying to protect the victim of a prejudice by focusing only on the acts it inspires is as effective as trying to stop someone being shot by catching the bullets in mid-air. It is an approach so obviously impractical that its continued use by education is irresponsible. Any real protection must, like the word 'racism', be pre-emptive. You must confront this prejudice before it becomes the act we call bullying. To do this requires something most are either incapable or simply unwilling to undertake: a realistic evaluation of the human animal and its attitudes.

~~~

I don't think discussing sex was the last taboo in our society. In my opinion, it was always evil, to be more specific, *ordinary evil*. To explain this requires looking at the prejudices highlighted in The Blindspot once again. As I pointed out in that chapter, our society is not entirely honest about itself, preferring to paint a somewhat unfocussed picture of its behaviour in certain areas. It has been suggested that being on the spectrum has given my thinking a certain linear quality. (My Art teacher once accused me of seeing everything as lines, presumably because of the line aspect of comic illustration.) Far from being a disadvantage, I think this may be helpful when trying to bring these areas into much needed focus.

What happened to Jack was not the work of racists, homophobes or any kind of recognised bigot. The suffering inflicted on this damaged, helpless young man was at the hands of ordinary people openly voicing attitudes considered acceptable —perhaps even admirable— within this society.

The first question I have to ask is, why did they do it? The obvious response is perhaps they were motivated by some kind of xenophobia (fear or hatred of strangers, foreigners or of that which is strange). This is often cited as the basis of many prejudices, but I'm not sure it applies here. Jack was certainly strange with his nonexistent social skills, but anyone who spent more than a few minutes with him could see that he presented a danger to no-one, quite the opposite: Jack was intensely and painfully vulnerable. Bearing this in mind, I suggest another reason they treated him in this fashion: I think it gave them pleasure to inflict pain on an innocent, so perhaps what really motivated these ordinary, intelligent people was not fear but *evil*.

A lot of people don't like that word. Many dismiss it as naive or simplistic. I suspect it makes them uncomfortable because its very nature incorporates its own moral stance. Many I have talked to refuse to entertain it as a concept, preferring to break it down into blameless motivations in much the way cancer can be broken down into component proteins. Obviously there are countless definitions of evil. To clarify matters, I'll submit my own. Evil: the urge to hurt the innocent for the pleasure of hurting the innocent, the urge to do what you know to be wrong for the pleasure of doing what you know to be wrong.

Ordinary evil, the capacity of everyday people to carry out acts of cheapness, cruelty and outright viciousness is by far the hardest of all ideas to communicate and to name. Suggesting that such an appalling motivation could be part of everyday behaviour, at a society-wide level, is an idea automatically rejected before it can be entertained. This leaves me in an awkward situation because, contrary to what everyone else seems to believe, decades of observation have shown me that, in certain areas, this society's norm is irresponsibility, callousness, prejudice and evil, genuine evil.

Human beings are an unforgiving breed and vulnerability is the thing they forgive least of all. Far from inspiring compassion, Jack's exceptional awkwardness and vulnerability provoked a level of viciousness that was horrible to watch. Furthermore, it was clear that even those who didn't participate in his abuse did not see - or chose not to see - his maltreatment as being in any way wrong. No-one saw the cruelties for what they were, nor the horrendous damage they were inflicting. (I suspect that their collective ability to lie to themselves was so entrenched they would have denied the wrong behind their actions, even if confronted with hard evidence.) This isn't just limited to Jack; entire sections of our population find themselves on the receiving end of such abuse as part of their everyday existence.

Again the proof is in our language, or rather lack of it. We have a wealth of unofficial terms to mock and belittle the vulnerable, the awkward and the outcast but little, if any, official language to say that such condemnation is wrong. Decades later, we still have no word to accurately describe what happened to Jack, what is happening to Jack and what will continue to happen to people like him. This intolerance is one of the constants of our society. It permeates all levels of our behaviour, underscores and defines much of our interaction. In its milder form, it inflicts suffering on the vulnerable. At its most extreme it kills them. Most of us never see this evil for what it is because we seldom feel its sting. Those, who do, usually cannot see anything else.

School is a creation of this society and as such, mirrors its values and vices. The various injustices heaped on the underdogs in school are really just intensified versions of the betrayals adults heap onto their own outcasts. Cancer rages unchecked in the body because it is not recognized and countered by the immune system; similarly this evil flourishes because it is not recognised by our society, and the teaching profession is no exception to this unspoken rule. In adult life I have encountered several teachers in social situations. I found them no different from any other type of intelligent person. Their ideas of right and wrong were largely derived from the culture around them and were not something they had actually arrived at themselves. Not one displayed any understanding of these prejudices neither in terms of their scale nor in their subtleties. A number displayed callous and prejudiced behaviour themselves and voiced opinions that could be described as openly cruel. The obvious question here is how can teachers hope to curb a prejudice in schools when even they are programmed not to recognise it in themselves?

The only solution is to start facing some home truths. The popular picture of the human species as being civilised is an ideal to live up to, not to complacently believe is actually here. The Halfman was a brutal, animalistic thug, but he did have surprising moments of insight. In between beatings, he once told me an old proverb I think has relevance here: 'Confucius say, when one knows that one does not know then wisdom begins'. We could apply this to ourselves. If we ever have the courage to admit that we are not a truly civilised society, then we might be taking the first steps towards becoming such a thing.

A good start would be incorporating a more accurate picture of the human animal into the educational system; a picture that recognises bigotry - in all its properly defined forms - as a widespread species characteristic rather than an isolated and safely contained phenomenon. (The adult society that devalues and marginalises the outcast after leaving school can only come into existence because teachers refuse to educate about it.) Second-class citizenship is taught in our schools, it's just not taught about. Currently, no

An ordinary school anywhere and everywhere

educational literature confronts just how cliquish, amoral, and cruel everyday human collectives - both juvenile and adult - tend to be.

In addition, the type of initiatives employed by schools like White Pine and others should become permanent and compulsory parts of the curriculum, everywhere. Teachers should be trained in all areas of anti-bullying. Schools should regularly condemn this abuse and subject its vile subtleties to the level of scrutiny we reserve for mathematics, physics and literature. Not only should we confront these cruelties, we should examine and condemn our desire to carry them out in the first place. (A major re-evaluation of PE is also needed. The capacity of this subject to focus hostility and create a culture of officially sanctioned emotional mutilation has never been taken seriously; it's high time it was. No educational system or institution should have the right to breach a young person's physical privacy, it's as simple as that.)

We should also start looking at the positive application of shame. I'm not suggesting we create a culture of shame in our schools. The sad truth is that it is already there and - being another human constant – won't be going away anytime soon. What I suggest is we start being practical by redirecting it back at its source. Schools should pursue an aggressive policy of shaming the cowardice behind bullying. Sustained bullying by individuals or groups is really a form of stalking. It should be classified as such, shamed as a crime and immediately and *severely* dealt with.

I would repeat here that the more advanced anti-bullying policies employed at White Pine have clearly had some effect on this problem, but these are just bespoke solutions and not official policy; furthermore they *still* do not focus on the underlying bigotry that triggers the problem in the first place.

School life might also benefit from some much-needed perspective on the cruelty of adolescent culture. The obvious way is to implement lessons that question the close-minded and limited thinking behind much of its values. Teaching those who stigmatise outcasts that their attitudes and cliquishness are as wrong as racism is a good idea. Telling young outcasts that a lack of popularity in school is no indicator of personal worth in the 'real' world is another. The transitory nature of its judgments should also be highlighted. Regularly reminding youngsters of a world that waits beyond adolescence might be the healthiest lesson you will ever teach them. On the occasions I was able to glimpse a future for myself, the idea of killing was a terrible thing. But there were moments I could not see beyond my immediate pain. During these, death became an attractive escape and killing acquired a horrible and attractive logic. After all, why should others be allowed to enjoy a future I was forever denied?

Finally, an understanding of all aspects of bigotry should be made compulsory in order for a student to achieve grades and move up into higher years. Passes should be based on a student's moral as well as academic progression. If school is supposed to teach young people to fit into a civilised society we might begin by showing them what civilised actually means.

Incidentally, if there are any teachers or school administrators who consider this excessive, I suggest they pop along to some adult social skills classes to see the appalling consequences of the methods currently employed. It might be an education for them to meet the crippled, medicated results, the second-class citizens whose creation they are party to.

~~~

One of the worst things about being an outcast is the knowledge that you belong to something the world considers legitimately contemptible; that what is happening to you is normal. This is what outcasts see when we look on your 'civilised' world: a place that is, at best, cold and unwelcoming and, at worst, enemy territory, forever poised against us.

Exposure to such a culture of intolerance, one that has the last word on your life, is the greatest attack of all. The lessons of Little Russia left their scarring but nothing like Whitehill. Those wounds have never healed. There are a multitude of terms, both clinical and popular, to stand with me against The Halfman. I have evidence from literature that he was a twisted aberration and the fault was his, not mine. I've had no such closure with my old school. There is nothing to tell me that the mutilations it inflicted on me were in any way wrong or that they were not my fault. I am still alone facing that terrible place.

As 'Oddballs', 'Geeks' and 'Nerds', Harris and Klebold knew they lived in a society that despised them. This was a lesson hammered home by its educational brutalities but, most of all, by its lack of protective language; something that denied them any chance of ever communicating their plight and their anger. In such circumstances, a closed ear can be a dangerous thing. To better illustrate this point means returning to the words of Luke Woodham: 'I am not insane, I am angry... All throughout my life, I was ridiculed, always beaten, always hated. Can you, society, truly blame me for what I do? Yes, you will. ...It was not a cry for attention, it was not a cry for help. It was a scream of sheer agony saying that if I can't do it through pacifism, if *I can't show you through the displaying of intelligence, then I will do it with a bullet.*'

Had this young man been given another way to articulate his outrage then he might not have resorted to violence. Language is the lynchpin of awareness and communication. Your lack of such a thing has always been your greatest stumbling block when it comes to grasping this problem. I have never encountered professionals, nor read any literature that seemed to think these prejudices should be named. To this day we have no language that targets this problem and, as a result, we have no real understanding of it. This deliberate ignorance hides a cycle of invisible brutality, one that seeks out those who are different or vulnerable and clings to them, twisting them out of shape, creating a culture of fear, resentment and, eventually, the culture of retaliation we are seeing now. This vicious circle needs to be broken immediately. The only place this is possible is in our schools.

I'm hoping to see some honesty and perhaps courage from the teaching profession here. Live up to your job description, break free of your own programming, recognise these prejudices both in yourselves and in the society around you. Name this evil, shame it and introduce that name and the awareness it will bring into the curriculum.

Abandoned to their own devices, these young minds have found their own voice: atrocity. You, above all others, have always been in position to give them an alternative; a tangible, verbal definition of the evil they face. If you arm them with such a thing, they may not need guns. I know what fuels the outrage in these young men because it feeds mine too. I know what could have reached me and can *still* reach them: an admission of truth; some honest language: words. These are the missing part of all these anti-bullying packages; the final, vital components.

The correct word can do many things. It can be an anchoring point for an entire world of awareness, prevention and protection. It can lift a culture of shame away from its victims and throw it back onto its perpetrators. A word can force a prejudice into the open; force a society to deal with it and defuse the pressure it creates. It can tell a despairing young mind there is recognition of their plight; and that the world is not completely against them. It can give a much-needed perspective of a life beyond immediate suffering; give hope and, in doing so, take a finger off a trigger. A word - or words - can do no end of good if we are honest enough to bring such things into being; and had there been words within the English language to confront and protect against prejudice towards vulnerability and social inarticulacy, then the students of Columbine High and indeed most of those other schools would probably be alive to this day.

HEADS MUST ROLL

If anyone reading this still believes the only way of dealing with this problem is to grab a gun and shoot up the nearest school, I would advise against it (and suicide for that matter). There are other ways of getting your own back at that vile institution that don't involve killing or throwing away your own life.

The first reason for not taking that path involves a concept almost alien to me: innocence. Looking back at Whitehill, I can see that every one of my fellow students hated me and wanted to hurt me, at least I *feel* this. But, if I am honest, I must look beyond my rage-tinted perspectives and face some truths. Although - at least in the later years - the majority still despised me, there were a limited few who did not. This group was divided into a small number of individuals who displayed indifference to me and a, yet smaller, bunch who actually treated me in a fairly reasonable fashion. That is not to say they welcomed me into their lives as a friend, they simply never used me as a target, and occasionally even listened to me as I rambled on about the subjects which obsessed me.

So why do I still harbour such negative feelings even towards them? I suppose that boils down to plain old-fashioned, monumental envy. These young people enjoyed an acceptance I knew was denied me. It wasn't their fault, they were entitled to live those lives and were under no obligation to make me part of them. Unfortunately, the pain of the outcast seldom listens to logic, and jealousy can all-too quickly become irrational and *unjustified* hatred. The point I am making here (and this is particularly hard for someone like me) is that just because someone isn't your friend, that doesn't make them your enemy either, no matter how much you feel they are or *want* them to be.

Don't get me wrong, I'm not going to feed you some naïve drivel about rising above anger or hatred. If you are a victim of school abuse, then you have every right to feel such things. You are no less deserving of protection simply because you are young, far from it. You are the point of education; you should always have been its highest priority. Anyone who is constantly abused in school is entirely justified in hating those who target them, but they should feel even worse towards the callous swine who allow this to happen in the first place. It is this group, this agency which has truly betrayed you. And that brings me to my second reason for not advocating violence: the true nature of your enemy.

To see this enemy requires you to pull back from your immediate pain and look at things from the larger perspective I mentioned in the previous chapter. Should you do this it will become obvious that neither a single person nor group of people are responsible for your suffering. It is the current educational system —and by that I mean the minds behind the whole mess— who are the real enemy of you and your kind; and it is they who truly deserve your vengeance.

My thoughts on the educational system have changed over the last decade. Instead of looking on my old nemesis as a force of pure evil, I now see it as clumsy, stupid, ill-tuned and callous. Unfortunately, this callousness often proves as destructive as evil. At this point, you have to ask just how the educational system is able to get away with all this.

To answer that, try picturing it as a huge beast that sits at the top of its food chain. The Beast has no real enemies, just some annoyances who occasionally nip its ankles in court. The appearance, at least in America, of new anti-bullying laws means that the odd school or school board may pay for its injustices but never the body of education itself, never the unreachable minds at the top. (Incidentally, the appearance of these very laws proves, beyond doubt, education's utter callousness in this area. A responsible educational system wouldn't have to be *forced* to protect you.) As a result, this particular beast makes minor improvements here and there, but has never needed to evolve at a deep structural level. To recap what I said in the last chapter, 'evolve' means education completely restructuring itself from the ground up to prioritize your protection above *all other* considerations. Yet, despite these new laws, we have still to see such a thing.

All is not lost though. A few years ago, I came across the phrase 'social exclusion' in reference to the ostracism of students in school. To the best of my knowledge this phrase did not exist in my schooldays. Far from being pleased to see this in print, I found myself deeply annoyed. 'Social exclusion': a half-hearted admission of a wrong without any mention of the motivation behind the wrong and certainly not of the long-term damage inflicted by such a thing. It has been almost four decades since I was forced to pull down those bigoted cartoons at Whitehill. In that time education has managed to join two words together to make an insulting understatement which covers this problem as effectively as a sticking plaster covers a stab wound. It has progressed less than an inch when it should have travelled a mile. Still, it does show that the idiots behind the whole mess are capable of change. Unfortunately, this is all-too slow for me and for you as well, I suspect.

The truth is, you could be properly protected at all times were it considered important enough, but it's not. Doing such a thing would involve too much hard work for the educational system and could incur a loss of face by highlighting the design flaws at its core. Lastly, it would cost money, money The Beast considers more important than you. Education will not change to protect you, but it will to protect itself. The solution is obvious. The Beast needs something to force it to change. It needs an enemy, one specifically designed to hurt it and make it feel fear. Such fear cannot be provoked by a gun. Despite my torture/mass slaughter fantasies, I can see that violence is a dead end; one that will rob you of any chance to initiate genuine progress.

The school shooter is often painted as a revolutionary figure whose efforts will bring justice to the corridors of our schools. Time to dispel a few myths on that subject. As many of you have come to realise, bullying is not a problem for education, it's simply an embarrassment to be swept under the carpet wherever possible. The awful truth is that school shootings are not a problem either, they are simply a larger embarrassment that education can, and will, sweep under the carpet so long as it is able to place the blame on the shooters. Columbine and all those other shootings had nothing to do with education; they were the fault of mad, bad kids and that's all there is to it, blah… blah… blah!

Wake up and smell the coffee: the educational beast is totally bullet-proof and completely without conscience. Its higher echelons are run by people as far away from the realities of school brutality as a general is from the battlefield, people for whom the suffering and death of a child is simply a concept, nothing more.

Any shooter who thinks that their efforts are going to hurt such an enemy is fooling themselves. Our schools have been killing kids from the very beginning. In Britain, they kill an average of sixteen every year (though the actual number is almost certainly far higher). I strongly doubt there is any way of accurately calculating the number in America. The educational beast has killed more kids than every school shooter combined and will continue to do so without the slightest concern. Education doesn't give a damn about its victims, why should it care about yours? Do you honestly think a killer of this magnitude can be hurt by something as insignificant as violence?

You can fire as many shots as you want into your school and The Beast will simply carry on. It will walk over you, your life and your pain. It will pat itself on the back for being perfect and everyone else will cheer in agreement. The Beast will live to sin against your kind again and again while you die or end up facing a life sentence in a living hell far worse than any you could ever imagine. *If you kill, you will lose.* You will lose because you will have thrown away the most important thing you have in this struggle: your own life. (You may not consider it to have any value but it has: value to others of your own kind.) You will have discarded the most devastating weapon ever to be used against The Beast: a determined, intelligent mind. You will lose and The Beast will win because nobody will ever learn the truth about what it was doing to you.

Killing will achieve no changes to the injustices of school. Neither Harris, Klebold nor any other shooter has ever managed to inflict the slightest damage on the true architects of their misery. They never even touched them. Is Columbine dead? No. Did Harris and Klebold achieve their objective by wiping the place off the face of the Earth? Not in the slightest. Columbine High still exists and, in all certainty, still inflicts the same damage it did before the massacre.

I wonder what Harris and Klebold were feeling just before they ended their own lives. Was it elation, a sense of achievement? Did they still see themselves as avengers, as champions? Or were they just two very frightened young men who realised they were more trapped at that moment than they had ever been at any point, knowing that every chance and freedom they might have had was now gone, leaving them with no option other than to die? I also wonder what they would be doing now had they not taken that path. Despite their problems, both were intelligent and articulate. It is entirely conceivable they could be holding down high-paying jobs now, doing far better in their lives than the morons who made their time hell (contrary to popular myth, not all jocks end up with multi-million-dollar sports careers) and enjoying that fact. Perhaps either of them could have written a book similar to this and made a better job of it.

Atrocity will get you nowhere. Education will never be touched by anger so long as it is voiced in that fashion. In fact, the system has always remained safe because youngsters squander their energies in acts of violence, energies that could be better used, better directed. It is true that education needs an enemy but is must be one that can *stay alive* to hurt it with more than mere force of arms.

~~~

In 2011, New Jersey began implementing the toughest anti-bullying laws in America. Under these, each school was required to report every incident of bullying and implement an effective plan for dealing with the problem. Schools would be graded on their bullying standards, policies, and incidents. All administrators and teachers in each school were expected to deal with any incidents reported to, or witnessed by them. Far from facing lenient punishment, bullies now risked suspensions or expulsions should they be convicted of any type of bullying from minor teasing to physical violence. It's about time someone employed such measures, but why not employ them in every state and equip schools with teams of fully trained detectives as well?

Some of the more thoughtful books on the classroom avenger have suggested changes to be made in schools. Many of these sound pretty sensible but whether the powers-that-be within education care enough to employ fully them or do so quickly is another matter. Keeping this in mind, it might be better if something were to take the choice out of the educational system's hands. Something that could achieve what the school shooter cannot.

In recent years, a number of groups have sprung into existence to highlight the plight of the bullied student and press for improvement in their protection. A basic search online will yield a range of bodies from the Anti Bullying Alliance in Britain to Bully Police USA in America. Bully Police is an exceptional organisation founded by Brenda High who lost her thirteen-year-old son, Jared, to bullycide. Bully Police functions as a watchdog organisation that advocates for bullied children and reports on state anti-bullying legislation. The organisation's achievements have been remarkable: since its inception Bully Police has been influential in the passing of anti-bullying laws in Washington, Oklahoma, Arizona, Vermont and Idaho (where 'Jared's Law' was named after her son).

It strikes me that there is room for another organisation or social movement in this arena. This one should differ from everything that has gone before in that its purpose is not to protect but to attack, an 'avenger' organisation rather than a protector. This group could include adults who have survived bullying in school (or lost children to it), who have seen what is really happening within its corridors and are prepared to do something about it. Its aims should be to gain legal and eventually political power to make things very uncomfortable for the educational beast. This could be accomplished by exposing individuals or groups of individuals working within the educational system, teachers and administrators or higher, whose incompetence and laxity results in the ruination of young people's lives. Once identified, these dangerous fools with their child-murdering policies could be made the target of a barrage of lawsuits designed to destroy their careers. There is proof that such an approach works: in the US, the church of Scientology forced the IRS to recognise its status as a religion via a sustained war of litigation against the agency (that's not to say I approve of the Scientologists, they seem a pretty sinister bunch, but they did prove such an approach to be a viable one).

In my opinion, true change cannot occur if education is punished as a faceless body. To really effect such a thing, you have to hurt the people within it, teach them real fear and real pain. Why not? Child abusers and killers are the vilest creatures in our society. No-one who inflicts misery and damage of this magnitude on the young should be beyond punishment, no matter who employs them or how high on the pecking order they may be. These criminals must be named and shamed, examples must be made of them, and heads must roll.

~~~

To anyone considering a violent response to their school abuse, I ask this: why throw your life away when, instead, you can direct your rage towards creating such an organization? It may sound far-fetched, but it is actually well within your abilities. Think about it: in a few years you will be adults with determination, numbers and adult rights. This is all that is needed to bring such a thing into existence. There is a movement waiting to be born here, a striking force to be reckoned with and you can be part of it. In your worst moments, picture the educational beast driven to its knees by the new and terrible enemy you will become.

In a more immediate sense, it can't hurt to drag your school's name through the dirt as well. Bully Police USA grades different states for their effectiveness at dealing with bullying, why shouldn't this be done for individual schools? Abused students could start websites that name and shame their schools should they be lax when it comes to protection. Such sites could feature a list of young people harmed or killed by The Beast, with facts and figures updated constantly. These could link up with others online to form

Education needs an enemy

an educational 'Hall of Shame'. The truth about what is happening in school is too important to be swept under the carpet any longer. The educational system has always been very flexible in its interpretation of facts, particularly when it comes to the plight of certain students. It employs the same flexibility when divulging information on how it deals with their protection. You now have the enormous power of the internet to challenge its lies. What have you got to lose? What can they do to you that would be worse than the death you were planning?

While we are on the subject, it would be a healthy thing to start a whole new language to communicate accurately what is happening to you. (I touched on this idea in Chapter Eight.) Proper communication is always the first thing an abuser society denies its victims; this must be reversed. The creation of more specific terms would be a step towards addressing this problem. A perfect example of this is BULLYCIDE. This, relatively recent, word quickly and honestly communicates the idea of a person driven to take their own life as a result of abuse by their peers. We need many more like this, so here's a couple to add to the list I started earlier. Personally, I think they're a bit formal and probably lacking in imagination but I'm sure anyone out there who wants to use them can improve on them immensely.

EDUCATIONAL ABUSE: The process by which the educational system violates the rights of young people.

EDUCATIONAL BETRAYAL: The process by which the educational system ignores its obligations as regards the safety of young people in its care.

Terms like these and many others really deserve to be immortalised on T-shirts, badges and posters far and wide. While on the subject, it would be nice to see slogans like: EDUCATION LIES; EDUCATION KILLS AND CRIPPLES; EDUCATION: THE MURDER MACHINE; BULLIES ARE STALKERS and PUNISH THE BEAST committed to print or fabric also. Our culture - at a popular level - must be made to recognise that the current educational system is very often a force of death. There is no chance that education, left to its own devices, will ever admit to this, so it's up to you to get the truth out to as many as possible. A massive, well organised anti-education backlash is long overdue. The Beast has been a sacred cow for too long. It's time for you to knock it off that pedestal and smear some dirt over it.

Of course, you have to live to do this, so it's important you survive everything school throws at you. I'm not suggesting you forgive and forget your torment. Store it up for when you leave school, keep it all alive and make a cause out of it, then get together with others of your own kind. You are far from alone. Think about it: just how many bullied youngsters leave school each year? The numbers you will be joining are like an army. A single person cannot punish the scum of education, no matter how dedicated. Your enemies must be ganged up on; it's time for you to enjoy that little pleasure. The world has changed since my day (not quickly enough, but again that's up to you); there are so many other possibilities for acceptance and justice in this computer age.

I know that many reading this are in atrocious pain and desperate to lash out right now. More than anyone, I understand this. For your own sake don't give in to despair. Look beyond this moment to a future you can shape by staying alive. There can be life beyond school and payback too. I know you think killing is your only option, but I can tell you what I did not know back then: there is *always* another way. A lone killer who self-destructs early on is no threat to The Beast. It can ignore any one of you by yourselves but not all of you working together. For this reason, it doesn't want you organised. Your voice joined with others of your kind can hurt it more than anything else on this planet. Save your pain for that.

The world can be made a better place but only through the honesty and efforts of the adults you will become. Your experiences are nothing to be ashamed of, they are more valuable than you can imagine. They are the building material of a better world because they do not contain the lies of this one. Your lives have armed you with one fantastic gift: you know the truth about the human animal, and when it comes to making real changes, this particular truth, not the gun, is the better weapon by far. It's the only one The Beast fears.

STILL TRYING TO ESCAPE

T he Halfman looked good in a coffin. The undertaker had glued
his evil mouth shut so —after a quarter-century— he stopped
accusing me of madness and crimes against the state. Some
people leave this world with laughter lines etched on their faces;
The Halfman had rage lines, a distinctive spray of wrinkles that form when
a face crunches up in fury all of its waking moments. A layer of makeup had
been used to cover these with little success. His face remained in death what
it had been in life: the mask of a hater. By the perversity of fate, I have been
driven down a path almost identical to his, and in doing so, have come to
understand him that little bit better. He was a dreamer who survived the horrendous brutality of his youth through the goal of a better life. He worked for
that too, studying to be a draughtsman during the Great Depression. The loss
of his arm and his abuse-crippled mind crushed any chance of escape, locking
him into the hell of his own past.

But it wasn't our fault. We were just innocent children, his children. None of what happened to him had the slightest thing to do with us. He thought otherwise, deciding he had the right to make us pay for what the world had done to him. That's when he went from being damaged to evil, from being a disabled person to a halfman.

I had my final and only confrontation with him shortly before his death. Highly unstable as a result of medication, I faced the creature on his doorstep. Peter Campbell senior, my father, sadist, maniac, abuser, diseased subhuman coward, destroyer of my family and would-be murderer of my mother. I was larger than him by that point. The cancer had taken its toll. He was frail and shrunken, The Arm shrivelled to a stick. His voice, formerly a roar, was now a whisper. He hadn't been diagnosed so I attributed his deterioration to some form of rapid old age. Summoning up every drop of drug-fuelled courage, I told him why I was there.

'I've come to kill you.'

I wasn't really going to kill him, it just sounded good. I had no idea what I was going to do. Perhaps I was hoping he would start a fight so I would have an excuse to beat him. Unfortunately, his hearing had worsened over the years. He just stared in confusion and cupped his ear.

'Eh?'

This really deflated my big moment. My confidence at confronting the monster almost collapsed on the spot. I repeated the threat, louder this time.

'I said, I've come to kill you!'

'Eh?' Leaning closer and repeating the gesture.

I wanted to run by this point but knew that doing so would mean never being able to live with myself afterwards. I shouted in his ear and pointed at his stump.

'I said I've come to kill you, *halfman!*'

When he understood, his eyes widened with fear and disbelief. Evidently a full-grown man was a less appealing target than a helpless woman or small child because he quickly backed away into his house not realizing I was as scared as he was.

'I'll get the police to you, Tommy,' he said, slamming the door in my face. It was almost funny. He'd spent years threatening to kill me, the moment I returned the sentiment he started squealing about the police, gutless to the absolute end. I didn't feel particularly courageous at that point either. My last reserves of synthetic bravado had completely evaporated. I scuttled away to hide under a nearby bridge. There I sat, chewed some paper and contemplated my hollow victory. Many men cherish the moment they stood next to their father as an equal. For me this was when I told him I was going to kill him.

Just my luck the bastard was too deaf to hear me at the time.

His funeral was a sparse affair. No drinking buddies or dedicated communists turned up to bid their comrade farewell. A few years later the Berlin wall came down and his precious Soviet Union collapsed. It was a fitting epitaph for a truly worthless life.

Yet I am still haunted by him, by what he became and how he became it. That face in the coffin could be a vision of the future, a prediction for me. We were the result of his second marriage. (He'd destroyed his first one —and his first family— years before.) I was conceived in his fifties - the age I am now. As I grow older and the flesh sags against my skull, I am witnessing the emergence of a familiar set of wrinkles. I wonder if genetics or something more sinister shapes this resemblance. Am I using the same set of facial muscles as him? Is it my destiny to end up a hate-ravaged old man lying in my coffin also? I suppose, and hope, the difference lies in my ability to recognise my feelings for what they are and to manage them as well as possible. The Halfman gave me a good example of what happens when you don't.

~~~

In 2006 I was given a late diagnosis of Aspergers syndrome. With this, the last piece of the puzzle behind my behaviour and uneven thinking dropped into place. I have always been strange, even in the company of oddballs and outcasts. To discover this was the result of a recognised disorder at long last lifted the stigma of being 'weird'. The shame of not being able to live up to 'normal' behaviour no longer cuts as deeply as before. The pain is still there, particularly around Whitehill, but I have a shield of sorts now; it helps, at least sometimes.

And I'm not alone in my world, either. Despite being an especially bleak period in my life, the 80's did introduce me to my lifelong friends Jim Campbell and Lesley Affrossman. Since meeting them in the early days of my illness, they have gone from being friends to husband and wife before divorcing and returning to friends again.

Initially, their behaviour confused me. Both kept in contact with me, despite my inability to produce artwork, and both treated me with respect. In fact, they were completely supportive to me across decades of illness. Looking back now, I am ashamed to say I did not recognise their gesture for what it was: the hand of friendship, offered without terms.

The support of a decent person is one of the best teachers you can have. This couple taught me more about fitting into this society than any number of social skills classes. Their support went further than even that. Both gave a patient ear as I voiced the ideas that led to this book. It was Jim who advised

'I've come to kill you … Halfman!'

me to write it and Lesley who edited it. Incidentally, I do have a better social standing these days than at any other point in my life. True, I cannot really function in groups unless I am in comic or Fantasy orientated company but that's okay. I know when to keep my mouth shut now, and when not to, which brings me up to the present.

~~~

For a while, The Surgeon's apparent failure caused me no end of bitterness. The film —had it been made— could have saved me. It could have opened the door to a better life had someone just given it the chance. But no-one did. All that work, all those years of desperation and effort in the face of pain, all of them for nothing... all wasted.

And yet they weren't. Only recently I realised The Surgeon actually did succeed, it *did* save me. The project has carried me across this last half of my life. The hope behind it has kept me sane and alive where medication and therapy have failed. Even unrealised, this hope became a stable platform on which to build other dreams. I still use these as a way of getting through the day in much the same way others use drugs or drink. There is a lesson to be learned from this. Many I have known from my past have collapsed under their own pressures or taken their own lives. Where I differ from them was having a goal. I cannot think of a more effective means of protecting yourself from whatever demons life throws at you.

In 1999, shortly after Mum's death and the events at Columbine, The Surgeon was published as a modest two-part, black and white comic by Scottish-based Rough Cut Comics. It was a taut little adaptation that jettisoned the subplot on the psychic side-effects of time travel in favour of a leaner, faster-paced action story. The comic was released to several good reviews, the best of which came from no less than British Horror legend, Ramsey Campbell (no relation) who wrote the introduction to a softback compilation of issues one and two. Campbell lamented that the film had not yet been made, commenting on the project's 'infinite potential' and ending his intro with: 'Who knows? Perhaps the delay in getting this feature film made will allow visual effects to catch up with these gruesome fantasies and then, The Surgeon will truly cut his way into all our hearts.'

Rough Cut has produced a quite a few comics since then. You might want to check them out at www.roughcut-comics.com. Incidentally, I don't consider the saga of The Surgeon over. The property is a still viable. If there are any film makers out there, looking for a versatile and lucrative new franchise, then they should consider our time-travelling serial killer. His full cinematic potential still deserves realisation.

~~~

Whitehill has never left me. It attacks from all sides with sticks, stones, bottles, bricks, lit matches, boots, punches, and an ocean of spittle, urine and snot. It stamps on my ribs, drags my face across the ground, drowns me, rubs ink and faeces into my face, mobs me, beats me, leaves me bleeding, terrified and humiliated. It says I am deplorable, stupid, talentless and worthless, and, in my worst moments, I still believe it. Whitehill is the ultimate judge in my life. Like a parasite eating away at my thinking, it finds me wanting at every level, every day. All I have ever felt is the need to escape it, a need that obscures everything else. Everything that I have worked on, every decision I have made as an adult is based on this desperation.

I've often come under criticism for this. Many have assumed it was a voluntary process and suggested I 'put it all behind me' or 'come to terms with it'. Well, that's what I am trying to do with this book. I've learned a lot while writing it; I hope anyone who reads it learns something too.

The key to stopping school shootings doesn't lie in changing our schools, it lies in changing the society that creates them and that involves looking at ourselves, rather than just these atrocities, from another angle. I would like to see an end to these killings but, just as importantly, I'd like to see an end to the evil that provokes them in the first place. The brutal truth we must face is that even if we stop these shootings tomorrow our schools will continue to kill young people.

To any expert thinking of writing something new on the subject, first get off your high horse and see *your* part in all this. Look objectively at the standards and attitudes that even you take for granted; the world you helped create, whose true nature you ignored. Ask yourself why someone as civilised and responsible as you never saw a need for real language to confront this. More importantly, will you bring such language into being after you put this book down or will you dismiss the points raised here?

We will never progress until we confront this ordinary evil, this last stronghold of bigotry at the core of our interaction. Doing so would be the ultimate test of just how civilised we really are as, to the best of my knowledge, no prejudice has ever been confronted without an empowered minority to force the process along. In the long run we must, as it is within the Blindspot that the outrage behind these killings festers. Keeping this area unfocussed was always a short-term measure whose detriments we are seeing now.

I mentioned briefly in Chapter Sixteen that hate crimes against the disabled are on the increase. In Scotland there has been a twelve per cent rise in the number reported. One Scottish newspaper recently covered the story of a wheelchair-bound man who had been the victim of two violent assaults. The same paper featured a column by Glasgow's Lord Advocate, Frank Mulholland, in which he voiced his intention to tackle the problem. The article and Mulholland's comments left me despairing. At no point was there a mention of the motivating prejudice behind the attacks. I'm sure Mr Mulholland's heart is in the right place but his methods won't work because their focus is all wrong. He is still closing the barn door after the horse has bolted. Currently *everyone* is closing the barn door afterwards. Is it too much to suggest they try closing it before the horse takes flight?

It is the opinion of many that, no matter how much we train him, man will always remain a non-PC animal for whom the expression of such 'little cruelties' is second nature. That might be true, but then retribution is also human nature. In a world where advancing technology places ever more lethal mechanisms into the hands of the persecuted, the blasé acceptance of this natural order is becoming a dangerous indulgence. In the past, these prejudices only produced people who died, now they are producing people who kill. The balance has shifted forever; the runt is now capable of inflicting terrible retribution on the pack. It is time for the pack to change its ways.

~~~

I want to write comics now. They're my first love and all I'm really good at (although I might be prepared to attempt a book or two as well). I'm pretty incompetent with normal jobs. I cannot work with groups as the presence of others agitates me, but I'm fine in isolation. Comics are really the perfect medium for me. Despite being visual, they do not rely on my eyes anywhere near as much as art; and comic scripting is slightly easier for me than prose as it uses images rather than words to convey a story. For me, writing, particularly comic writing, is the most satisfying creative experience of all, even more so than stippling. My mind runs free when I write.

And there's no shame in being in comics now. The days of the medium being solely for children and 'retards' are long gone. Comics and graphic novels are afforded a greater level of respect than at any point in past. True, they had to fight tooth and nail for it and it was given grudgingly, but given it was.

I suppose I could carve a niche by writing stories based on my experiences of 'real life'; of poverty, illness, misfortune, and the desperation that walks hand in hand with them; how it scars and yet inspires. I've seen, both in myself and in others, just how mutilated the human soul can become through tragedy and frustration. Perhaps I should use my ASD perspectives to put these observations into the panels of my next piece? Comic geniuses like WILL EISNER have made this type of realism very fashionable. (As a matter of fact, I did participate in a script called PRIESTS, which is loosely based on

The Halfman's experiences in the Catholic boys' home during the 1920s. It is an idealised black comedy that takes a more optimistic path than his real-life experiences.) So, perhaps I should take this 'respectable' route and milk the field for some recognition of my own.

To tell the truth though, I'm only really interested in Fantasy. Real-life depth has little appeal to me. I want to work with giant robots, vampires, aliens, sea monsters and superheroes. I want escapism and all the lovely, shallow emotions that go with it, the kind we're told aren't good for us but, in reality, are wonderful. I want to write for big comic companies... *And* have my stories made into multi-million dollar feature films... *And* make huge sums of money that will allow me to live like a king. *And... And...And...* (It's great to dream.)

Knowing that the contents of your mind have a place in a better, cleaner world is the greatest feeling of all. I experienced this briefly when it looked as though I was going to be a film designer. There was a sense of contentment, an end to worthlessness and something I'd never felt before and have never felt again. I think it was peace. I want to reclaim that feeling. If life cannot really be like the Bangles' 'Manic Monday' video and the 'Miami Vice' titles, then I want it to be as close as possible.

Thanks to the help of others, I've recently had the chance to write for the two biggest comic companies in America and, in both cases, I blew it. This time, the fault was mine and no-one else's. Comics giant Grant Morrison did me a huge favour by suggesting me to DC Comics; I'm ashamed to say I didn't live up to his recommendations. On both occasions, I had problems understanding editors. I had no idea how to keep in contact with the one at DC. I had been advised by Grant to keep pestering him but found this difficult as I suspected it may have irritated him. I gave up on that first opportunity to write this book, deciding it was the more important of the two courses. I stand by this decision as I believe, more than anything in my life, what I have put to paper here.

The second time, Marvel Comics, wasn't so noble. I totally misread what the editor wanted of me. I had problems grasping a couple of the criticisms he made of my submission - they seemed too vague - and found myself too embarrassed to communicate this. Looking back, I realise he was *telling* me to make changes when, at the time, I interpreted his words only as *suggestions*. (This type of professional politeness is the norm in the industry; saying 'I don't think this works' as opposed to 'I don't like it. Take it out'.)

And this was the problem: I assumed that, had the editor really wanted changes, he would have flatly ordered them. Creative minds tend to follow certain, very specific paths when engaged on a project; this is doubly true of autistics. Suggesting something to me when I am locked into such a path is a waste of time, as suggestions, like opinions, aren't a defined course of action like an order. Ordering me, in straightforward terms, to make changes would have saved an enormous amount of time as I respond to orders instantly.

That submission went around in circles before going nowhere. From its failure, I deduced he wasn't interested in my work and ceased submitting. Shortly afterwards, I discovered this was a mistake on my part, but by that time it was too late. All I can say is that I thought I was wasting his time and took what seemed the most sensible and polite course of action. That's the curse of Aspergers: the autistic mind can be uniquely creative yet lack the means to properly externalise this. In my case, the difficulty doesn't lie in writing the comics; it lies with my not being able to grasp what the publisher means, at least not quickly enough. Bah!

This is typical of my track record. I've almost succeeded at several points in my life so I must be doing something right, just not right enough. Do I resent all the time and effort lost on the various projects I have worked on? Do I think I was lying to myself about success and resent things that little bit more? Not in the slightest. If you don't do something with the pain in your life then the pain will do something with you. All that energy had to go somewhere; synthetic hope seemed a sensible direction. If you have to manufacture the myth of a better future in order to survive the present then do so because in the middle of that lie you may discover the real thing. I've been trying to escape my demons for the last forty years. I don't know if I ever will, but there's no sense in giving up. Walking towards an imaginary light might still be a fool's errand but it will always beat standing still.

Final Word

Special thanks to:
Alan Moore
Clive Barker
Frank Quitely
Grant Morrison
Curt Sibling
Patricia Affrossman
and
Duncan Lunan

If you enjoyed this book, please consider leaving a review at
the online bookseller of choice.
Thankyou
or
Check out other Sparsile titles at www.sparsilebooks.com

Further reading

Sparsile Fiction

The Promise
When promises can mean lives

L. M. Affrossman

Eight-year-old Daniel Gallagher is dying. His mother refuses to believe it, and Daniel is too afraid to make her listen. Then, by chance, he meets Sadie Gordon, an eighty-one-year-old survivor of Stalinist Russia, and everything changes.

It isn't long before he has captured her heart and she can't imagine life without him. Only then does the secret that has made Daniel old beyond his years come tumbling out.

And, in a moment of confusion, he exacts from her a promise to accompany him to heaven when he dies. Sadie is left with a terrible choice. Should she compromise the moral beliefs of a lifetime or betray the trust of a dying child?

Sparsile Fiction

Simon's Wife
A secret history

L. M. Affrossman

Three decades have passed since the death of Jesus of Nazareth on a Roman cross, and Judea is teetering on the brink of apocalypse. Caught up in the horror that will inspire the Book of Revelation, a young woman is fighting for survival.

In the dark days that follow the Roman devastation of Jerusalem in AD 70, nineteen-year-old Shelamzion bat Judah finds herself captured and awaiting both her own execution and that of her husband, former rebel-leader Simon bar Gioras. Alone and forgotten, there seems little reason to go on living, yet a strange friendship begins to grow between Shelamzion and her austere, old Roman jailor, Fabius Cornelius Grammaticus.

With his pretensions to be recognized as an historian in the style of Livy, it is to her he turns to record the true version of events behind the insurrection in Judea that led to the destruction of her country. Time is running out, however, and unknowingly history is being rewritten by a traitor's hand.

Science for Heretics
Why so much of science is wrong

Barrie Condon

SCIENCE IS BROKEN.

Throughout history, philosophers and scientists have warned about the fundamental flaws lying at the heart of all aspects of science.

The possible extinction level risks that mankind runs by ignoring these warnings have generally been forgotten.

This book, written by an established scientist, looks at the hollow foundations on which our maths, physics, biology and medicine are built and describes better ways to navigate the hidden dangers of the universe. It aims to be accessible to the general reader who lacks a scientific background.